MICRONESIA:
TRUST BETRAYED

Altruism vs Self Interest in American Foreign Policy

DONALD F. McHENRY

CE Carnegie Endowment For International Peace
NEW YORK   WASHINGTON

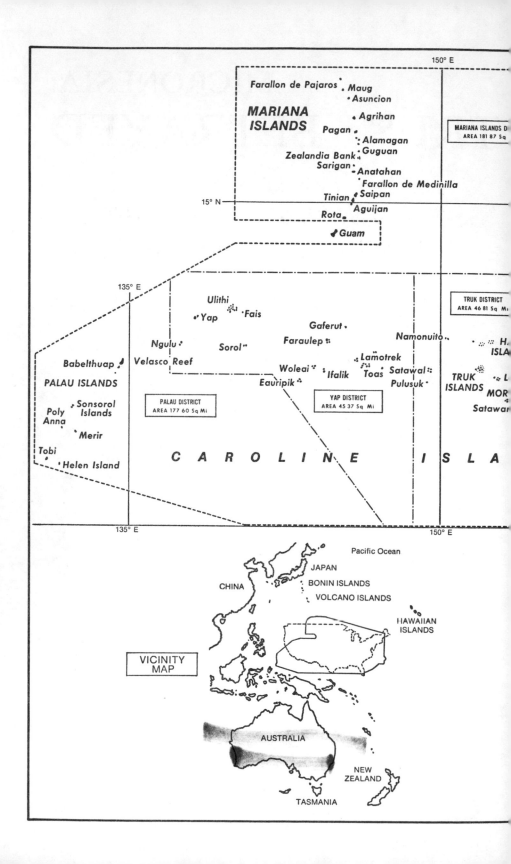

150° E

Farallon de Pajaros • Maug
• Asuncion

**MARIANA
ISLANDS**
• Agrihan

Pagan •

MARIANA ISLANDS D
AREA 181 87 Sq

•: Alamagan
Zealandia Bank •: •• Guguan
Sarigan •— Anatahan
• Farallon de Medinilla

Tinian • • Saipan

15° N ——————

Aguijan

Rota •

• Guam

135° E

Ulithi
• Yap •• • Fais

Gaferut •

TRUK DISTRICT
AREA 46 81 Sq Mi

Namonuito ••

•• H.
ISLA

Ngulu •
Velasco Reef

Sorol ••

Faraulep ••

Lamotrek
•• •
Woleai •• • Ifalik Toas • Satawal ••

TRUK
ISLANDS

• L

Babelthuap •

PALAU ISLANDS

Eauripik ••

Pulusuk •

MOR

Satawa

Poly
Anna •

Sonsorol
Islands

PALAU DISTRICT
AREA 177 60 Sq Mi

YAP DISTRICT
AREA 45 37 Sq Mi

• Merir

Tobi •
•• Helen Island

C A R O L I N E   I S L A

135° E   150° E

Pacific Ocean

JAPAN

CHINA   BONIN ISLANDS

VOLCANO ISLANDS

HAWAIIAN
ISLANDS

VICINITY
MAP

AUSTRALIA

NEW
ZEALAND

TASMANIA

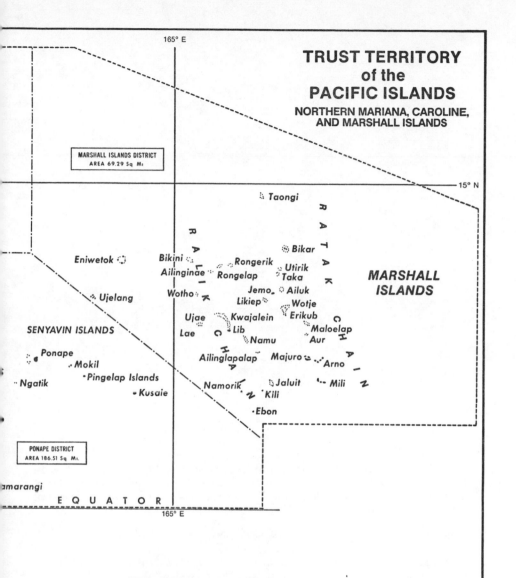

TRUST TERRITORY
of the
PACIFIC ISLANDS
NORTHERN MARIANA, CAROLINE, AND MARSHALL ISLANDS

MARSHALL ISLANDS DISTRICT
AREA 69.29 Sq Mi

15° N

Taongi

RALIK

RATAK

Bikar

Eniwetok

Bikini
Ailinginae
Rongerik
Rongelap
Utirik
Taka

Ujelang
Wotho
Jemo
Likiep
Ailuk
Wotje
Erikub

MARSHALL ISLANDS

Ujae
Lae
Kwajalein
Lib
Namu
Maloelap
Aur

CHAIN

SENYAVIN ISLANDS

Ponape
Mokil
Ailinglapalap
Majuro
Arno

Ngatik
Pingelap Islands
Kusaie
Namorik
Kili
Jaluit
Mili

Ebon

PONAPE DISTRICT
AREA 186.51 Sq Mi

amarangi

E Q U A T O R

165° E

165° E

OCEAN AREA APPROXIMATELY 3,000,000 Sq. Miles
LAND AREA APPROXIMATELY 700 Sq. Miles
2,141 ISLANDS

0 25 50 100 200 300
MILES

NOTE: Broken lines indicate territorial area and districts of
jurisdiction and are not to be interpreted as boundaries.

I.S.B.N.: Cloth 0-87003-000-0; Paperback 0-87003-001-9
Library of Congress Catalog Card Number: 75-42570
Dust jacket photograph of the reef and Arekalong Peninsula, Babelthuap, Palau Islands, by Douglas Faulkner.

The title for this book was suggested by the title of a November 18, 1967, article in the *Economist* ("Trust Betrayed") and is used with permission of the *Economist* (London).

Selections from *The Office of Territorial Affairs* by Ruth G. Van Cleve, © 1974 Praeger Publishers, Inc., New York, are reprinted by permission of the publisher.

Selections from the book *Who Owns America* by Walter J. Hickel, © 1971 by Walter J. Hickel, are reprinted by permission of the publisher, Prentice-Hall, Inc., Englewood Cliffs, New Jersey.

Printed in the United States of America

Contents

Foreword

Trust Betrayed is the first full length book to come from the Carnegie Endowment's Humanitarian Policy Studies Program. The book probes the domestic and international implications of United States policy toward Micronesia, a territory placed under United States trust by the United Nations in 1947.

The United States had taken the islands in some of the most fearsome battles of the Second World War, and afterwards it was inconceivable to many that we would do anything but hang onto them. Not only were they "ours," but it was said that they would always have great strategic importance. At odds with such views was the otherwise strong stand of the United States in favor of self-determination for colonies and dependent areas around the world. Establishment of a so-called "strategic" trust attempted to reconcile these conflicting views of our purpose in Micronesia by clouding them over with ambiguity. Following the 1975 independence of Papua-New Guinea, the United States alone now administers a trust; of the eleven trust territories established after World War II, only Micronesia remains. It is proving increasingly difficult to reconcile development towards self-government and maintenance by the United States of unrestricted authority in Micronesia.

The humanitarian aspects of the Micronesian issue have come clearly into focus since the negotiations began toward a new status for Micronesia. Micronesia is a huge scattering of sparsely populated, tiny islands. Will the United States honor the rights of the Micronesian people if those rights seriously impinge upon United States interests? And once a new status for Micronesia is created, what will be the implications for areas such as the Commonwealth of Puerto Rico and the territories of Guam, the Virgin Islands and American Samoa? This study should provide perspective and facts for discussions of these issues as well.

Calling attention to such problems is the purpose of the Humanitarian Policy Studies Program. While the opinions expressed here are those of the author, by supporting this and other Humanitarian Policy Studies projects, the Endowment affirms a belief in the importance of examining the tension between the human dimension and narrower manifestations of the national interest.

Donald F. McHenry, the project director, was with the Department of State from 1963 to 1973 where he served as Officer in Charge of Dependent Area Affairs and Special Assistant to the Counselor of the Department of State. He served as an adviser on numerous United States delegations to the United Nations. In 1966, Mr. McHenry received the Department's Superior Service Award. From 1971 to 1973, while on leave from the Department of State, Mr. McHenry was guest scholar with the Brookings Institution and an International Affairs Fellow of the Council on Foreign Relations.

Mr. McHenry has been with the Humanitarian Policy Studies Program since 1973. As he points out in his introduction, many students worked with him on the report. The experience and insight into the workings of government that these students gained are separate and considerable achievements of the project too. Comments or inquiries on this and other projects in the program are welcome and may be addressed to the offices of the Carnegie Endowment for International Peace, 11 Dupont Circle N.W., Washington, D.C., 20036, or 345 East 46th Street, New York, N.Y., 10017.

Thomas L. Hughes
President
Carnegie Endowment for
International Peace

Preface

This study was undertaken as part of the Humanitarian Policy Studies Program of the Carnegie Endowment for International Peace. The Humanitarian Policy Studies Program conducts research into problems of humanitarian dimensions of United States foreign policy and international relations. The program offers research opportunities in Washington to young people interested in public affairs.

Micronesia was selected for study not simply because it was a current issue. The right of the people of Micronesia to decide their own form of government and to govern themselves is also a uniquely humanitarian issue which, however, has been and regrettably continues to be subordinated to the political and strategic interests of other countries. Very few of those who have the power to influence, indeed to determine, Micronesia's political status have taken the time to reach an informed conclusion. "Who cares?", is too often a candid but revealing observation.

Fortunately, during the course of this study, which included a six-week visit to Micronesia, we discovered a number of people who do care. The group includes Micronesians, of course, but it also includes many persons in and out of government. They did not all agree on the wisdom of United States policy. Many would disagree sharply with the observations of this study. Many others were concerned but, given the paucity of information available, were uninformed. But they cared. We hope that this study will increase the number of people who are informed *and* concerned.

* * * *

One of the most interesting and stimulating aspects of the Humanitarian Policy Studies Program is the involvement of young people, mostly graduate students, for brief periods in research and writing on foreign policy issues. The Micronesia study included:

Ernest C. Downs, Williams College

Mary Grace, University of Louisiana at New Orleans

Khristine Hall, University of Kansas Law School

Cindy Harmer, Colorado College

Susan Hillis, University of Oregon

Paul Kaplan, Boston University

Robert Lacks, Columbia University

Mark Lefcowitz, University of Pittsburgh

Gail Storm, University of Southern California

Cheryl Yamamoto, University of Chicago

Cy Mugunbey, a Micronesian student from Yap, studying at the State University of New York at Brockport

In a group research project, the research and writing contributions of some are greater than those of others; acknowledgement of that fact is indicated by special listings in the table of contents. Even that listing does not fully reflect the contributions of Chuck Downs, who remained for most of the project, or of Carol Ritter, who served in the dual capacity of secretary and researcher-writer.

An important element of the study was a review panel, jointly sponsored by the Carnegie Endowment for International Peace and the American Society of International Law. The fifteen members of the panel, many of whom had experience in government, met four times for extended discussions of the research. The panel consisted of recognized experts on domestic and international law, territorial affairs, military strategy and international organizations, as well as on Micronesia and the negotiations. We are grateful for the time, care, and candor with which panel members read and discussed the report. Their assistance, as well as that of Robert Stein and John Lawrence Hargrove of the Society's staff, was most valuable. Neither the panel members nor the Society bears any responsibility for the contents of the report.

Inevitably, there are a large number of people who contribute to a study of this kind, not all of whom can be specifically mentioned. We are especially grateful to those who consented to be interviewed, some on several occasions. In every instance where requested, we have respected their desire to remain anonymous.

Almost all of the Endowment's Washington secretarial staff at one time or other helped with the typing. At a crucial moment, Diane Bendahmane joined the Endowment's staff and took over the demanding task of editing the manuscript. Only those who have had the experience can fully appreciate the contribution of a skillful, interested and, above all, patient editor.

I myself was involved at one point in Micronesian questions as a member of the United States government. That experience was the beginning of my interest in Micronesia. However, most of the material included in the study is based on developments which took place since 1968 when I no longer had a connection with the subject in any official capacity.

Finally, I am indebted to the Carnegie Endowment for International Peace and to its President, Thomas L. Hughes, for supporting the research.

Donald F. McHenry
Project Director

Micronesia: Trust Betrayed

The concept of strategic trusteeship appeared to be de facto annexation, papered over with the thinnest of disguises. On the other hand, trusteeship implied a measure of international accountability, and as such was initially resisted by American advocates of outright annexation.

—Stanley de Smith

I

The Micronesian Dilemma: Altruism Versus Self-Interest

When the United States captured Micronesia from Japan in World War II, the territory presented America with a dilemma: how to reconcile traditional American views in favor of self-government and self-determination with the belief that American control of Micronesia was required in order to defend the United States and to maintain international peace and security.

The problem was not resolved in 1947 when the United States and the United Nations Security Council reached an agreement under which the islands were placed under the United Nations trusteeship system. Unlike other trust territories, Micronesia was designated a *strategic* trust which allowed the United States to maintain almost absolute control while Micronesia worked toward self-determination. Stanley de Smith, in his book *Microstates and Micronesia*, suggested that the concept of strategic trusteeship appeared to be de facto annexation "papered over with the thinnest of disguises."[1] Indeed, American control and administration of Micronesia went unquestioned in the late forties and throughout the fifties.

However, it was inevitable that the conflict between United States strategic interests and Micronesian self-determination would have to be resolved eventually. The United States could not fulfill its obligation under the Trusteeship Agreement to promote the economic, social, educational, and political development of Micronesia without ultimately having to reconcile the dilemma. First, given advances in communication, transportation, and improved education, the Micronesian dilemma would have come to a head even if the United States had done nothing to develop the area politically. The United States could hardly teach the principles of American democracy at increasingly higher levels of education and yet escape the eventual question of why the same democratic principles were not applied to Micronesia.

Second, Micronesia no longer exists, if it ever did, in isolation from other world-wide political developments. The world of 1947, when Micronesia became a United Nations Trust Territory, had changed drastically by 1960. Instead of 50 nations in the United Nations, there were 99—and now there are 138 member nations. The new nations see a duty and obligation to help the remaining dependent peoples achieve self-determination. Colonialism, even in the form of trusteeship, is an outmoded concept.

Finally, since 1945, defense requirements in the Pacific, as elsewhere, have also changed. Of the major countries in the Pacific, Japan was an ally in World War I, but by World War II, Japan had become the enemy. In the post-war era, she is again an ally. China was a friend in World War II and was considered an enemy in the fifties and sixties. Now the trend is toward détente and the establishment of working relations between the two countries. A similar situation

---

[1] Stanley de Smith, *Microstates and Micronesia, Problems of America's Pacific Islands and Other Minute Territories* (New York: New York University Press, 1970), p. 128.

exists with the Soviet Union. The United States and the Soviet Union fought on the same side during World War II, but became antagonists after the war. With the Soviets, too, there is now a move toward détente.

The concept of strategic trusteeship developed in its embryonic form in the period of conventional warfare. But the atomic bomb, ironically first perfected and dispatched from Micronesia, introduced a new era. Conventional warfare was by no means eliminated and certainly remains preferable to using weapons of mass destruction. However, conventional warfare in the global sense of World War II is less likely. The probability that a Micronesia in unfriendly hands might be used for World War II-type warfare has been reduced greatly.

Today, although island bases are often useful, the primary means of defense is not via isolated island locations, but by submarine and land-launched missiles equipped with atomic warheads and by supersonic, long-range aircraft capable of delivering weapons of mass destruction. Even the logistics of conventional warfare have changed drastically. Islands remain useful for weapons and storage, but they are not essential. Aircraft can now transport huge quantities of men and material wherever they are needed in extremely short periods of time.

Thus, at the same time that dependent status is no longer acceptable to either the international community or to the Micronesian people, the military justification for keeping Micronesia a strategic trust is also questionable. However, this is by no means a universal conclusion. For thirty years United States control of Micronesia has been aimed at denying the area to other powers. The United States has had a network of bases throughout East Asia—in Korea, Taiwan, Okinawa, Japan, the Philippines, and Thailand. However, as United States military strategists have seen the need for less restrictive, more politically secure, and less costly bases away from the Asian mainland, military objectives in Micronesia have changed from denial to active use. The military has advanced many of the old reasons and some new ones for continued American control of Micronesia. Even the military, however, has recognized that there has to be a new legal basis for continued United States control. In hearings on the 1976 defense appropriations bill, Secretary of Defense James R. Schlesinger made the point concisely when he said that the United States sought "only to change the form of the [trusteeship] arrangement while retaining the basic objectives and responsibilities we have had for 30 years." In Schlesinger's view the reasons for the change were "largely international and political."

THE ISSUES

This is the story of America's second effort to reconcile conflicting American and Micronesian interests. Unlike the first attempt in 1947, this more recent effort is far more complex. Illustrative of the range of questions involved are the following:

- What is the role of Micronesia in the United States defense posture in the Far East?
- Will a permanent United States military and political presence in Micronesia affect United States-Soviet and United States-China relations?
- What is the role of the United Nations in determining Micronesia's future? Is there a continuing United Nations responsibility and, if so, what is it?
- If parts of Micronesia split off and establish a permanent relationship with the United States, what are the implications for
  1) the economic, military, and political status of the remainder of Micronesia?
  2) the attitude of United Nations members, particularly "third world" members, toward fragmentation/secession?
  3) the concept of "self-determination"?
- What are the economic, political and strategic implications of a rejection by Micronesia of any permanent association with the United States?
- What will be the nature of a permanent relationship between the United States and Micronesia? What are the implications of a new status for other United States territories (Guam, the Virgin Islands, American Samoa) and the Commonwealth of Puerto Rico?
- What are the implications of a new relationship for traditional United States policy in support of self-determination? Is Micronesia America's Namibia (South West Africa)?
- What problems face the Micronesians as a new American minority and how can their rights be protected?
- What are the respective roles, of the Congress, the executive (and within it the Departments of State, Interior, Defense, and Justice) in determining United States policy?

Some of these same questions, of course, also arose when Micronesia was placed under United Nations Trusteeship. However, today, in addition to the changed factors already mentioned, there is a new and even more basic factor. There is a new party participating in the decision-making process—the Micronesians. Since 1967, Micronesian representatives have been studying the future political status alternatives open to the territory. Since 1969, the United States and the Micronesians have engaged in formal negotiations on the territory's future political status. In 1947 decisions were made by the United States without consulting the Micronesians; until even fairly recently, it was thought that the Micronesians would go along with whatever the United States wanted to do. But the Micronesians have not been willing to go along so easily. They came to the negotiations full of hope and confident that the United States had their best interests at heart, but today, the Micronesians consider that hope naive—even those from the Marianas who have negotiated an agreement with the United States.

MICRONESIA'S FOUR FOREIGN RULERS

Participation in decisions regarding their own status is a new experience for Micronesians. They have known four foreign rulers: Spain, Germany, Japan, and the United States, the latter two under the general supervision of the League of Nations and the United Nations, respectively.

Spain maintained nominal control over Micronesia from the late 1600's. The period was marked by numerous disputes with Germany and England over trade. Spain was also faced with native resistance to efforts to impose Christianity. According to one account, Spain was responsible for reducing one population group, the Chamorros of the Mariana Islands, from 50,000 in the 17th century to 4,000 by the early 18th century.

Germany seized the Marshalls from Spain in 1885. Later, the United States acquired the Philippines and one island in the Marianas chain (Guam) in 1898, following the Spanish-American War. In 1899, Germany purchased Spain's remaining holdings in Micronesia. The German holdings made up Micronesia as it is presently known.

Japan took the islands from Germany at the outbreak of World War I, and after the war administered the islands under a League of Nations Mandate. It was Micronesia's first experience with an external ruler who did not claim sovereignty and who was to some measure accountable to the international community for the way the islands were administered. It was, however, minimal accountability. It was not thought that Micronesia would ever be able to stand alone, and Japan was allowed to administer the islands as if they were an integral part of Japan.

Japan developed the territory extensively, particularly in the production of agricultural and fishery products. Large and flourishing Japanese communities were built, complete with the necessary roads and other public works facilities. By 1938, almost 58 per cent of Micronesia's population was composed of Japanese settlers, the primary beneficiaries of Japanese development programs. It was from Micronesia that Japan launched its attack on Pearl Harbor.

The United States captured the islands from Japan after bitter fighting in World War II. Since 1947, the United States has administered Micronesia, excluding Guam, under the United Nations Trusteeship system. Of the eleven original trust territories, only Micronesia remains. Micronesia is the only territory designated a "strategic" trust. The designation has allowed the United States to exercise virtually complete control over the territory. Unlike other trust territories, Micronesia is the responsibility of the United Nations Security Council but the Security Council delegated to the Trusteeship Council the responsibility for supervising United States administration.

In the United Nations Trusteeship Agreement, the United States obligated itself to promote Micronesia's economic, social, educational and political development. However, during the first thirteen years of United States trusteeship, little progress was made except for limited advancement in local political participation. Critics in the sixties were to accuse the American administrators of the late forties and the fifties of maintaining an anthropological zoo. Micronesia was all but forgotten except for quaint stories about the removal of the people from their islands so that atomic weapons could be tested.

One thing the Navy and early Interior administrators did accomplish was progress in political development. The plan apparently was to develop Micronesian government at the community level and later at a central or territory-wide level. Accordingly, the establishment of local government units was followed by the establishment of a territory-wide advisory council and then a legislature with limited authority. But even here, American administrators have been sharply criticised. The proliferation of governmental units for such a small population, one observer remarked, makes Micronesians easily one of the most overgoverned peoples in the world. More important, the emphasis on *local* government units encouraged the continuation of isolated, expensive but entirely dependent population groupings.

* * *

The terms "Micronesia"[2] and "Trust Territory of the Pacific Islands" are used interchangeably. Technically Guam and the Gilbert Islands are part of Micronesia, but the United States had already acquired Guam, and the United Kingdom the Gilberts by the time the United Nations Mandate was established.

Micronesia consists of three island chains in the western Pacific, just above the equator: the Carolines, the Marshalls, and the Marianas. The territory has more than 2,000 islands, fewer than 100 of which are inhabited. They are scattered across an ocean area roughly the size of the continental United States; yet the total land area (roughly 700 square miles) is only about half the size of Rhode Island. The total population is less than 120,000.

---

[2] Micronesia means "tiny islands." The term is not to be confused with Polynesia, which means "many islands" or Melanesia, which means "black islands."

Although there are obvious indications of Spanish and Japanese influence, most of the present population knows only the period of Trusteeship and American administration. Fifty-three per cent of the total population is school-aged (under nineteen years of age), and, even more astonishing, 64 per cent are under twenty-five. Also Micronesia has a growing population. The average annual growth rate from 1968 to 1972 was 4.5 per cent, more than double the world average for the same period. The growth rate decreased to approximately 3.5 per cent in 1973.

Although migration from district to district is limited, the high population of the district centers shows great movement from the outlying islands. Census records show a disproportionate distribution between the district centers and the outer islands. In the Marianas, 10,745 people live on Saipan, which is more than 80 per cent of the total population of that district. A major portion of the remaining percentage can be found mainly on Rota and Tinian and a few sparsely populated outer islands. The inhabitants of the Marshalls are even more widely dispersed.

Most of the people of Micronesia have in common such things as chiefly hierarchies, collective land tenure, extended families and village organization; in addition, they are all islanders. However, there are substantial differences among the districts. The Marianas, for example, have adopted many of the practices of their alien administrators and have neither chiefly hierarchies nor collective land tenure.

Nine major languages are spoken in the territory, with many dialectal variations from island to island: Palauan, Yapese, Chamorro, Ulithi-Woleai, Trukese, Ponapean, Kusaien, Marshallese, and Kapingamarangi-Nukuoro. Many of the older people speak Japanese. English has rapidly become the common language throughout the island as a result of a 1963 decision making English the language of instruction in schools.

Micronesia's limited land area, widespread location, limited population, and lack of capital have been major obstacles to economic development. Economies of scale are virtually impossible; therefore, the costs of administration are substantial. For example, a single high school might be sufficient to service a community the size of Micronesia. However, fifteen public high schools are presently operated in Micronesia. In addition, there are twelve private high schools.

There seems to be general agreement that the United States has failed dismally to develop Micronesia economically. Micronesia's known natural resources are a limiting factor. Until recently, scrap metal from World War II was the second major export, following behind an ever-fluctuating trade in copra. Government-subsidized economic enterprises in agriculture and fisheries were highly developed by Japan but have not been tried under American administration, primarily because of the shortage of trained labor and because Micronesians dislike deep-sea fishing. (Micronesians now eat fish caught off their own shores, frozen, shipped to the United States or Japan, canned, and shipped back to Micronesia for sale.) Most economic studies look to tourism and Micronesia's potential for bases as its major immediate assets. These studies also cite fishing as a major asset, but see little prospect that the Micronesians themselves will be able to exploit those resources. Now, there is a growing belief that changes resulting from the Law of the Sea Conference will give Micronesia commercial and legal control of the large quantities of tuna and other fish which are regularly taken in the waters surrounding Micronesia. In addition, Palau may benefit from the construction of a multimillion dollar oil storage facility which Japanese interests are now considering.

The question of Micronesia's economic development cannot be overemphasized. Its economy, even on many of the outer islands, is a long way from subsistence. Micronesia imported goods totaling $26 million in fiscal 1973. At the same time, Micronesia itself generated only $6 million of its budget and that largely from taxes on the salaries of United States military operations in Kwajalein and the United States funded Trust Territory government. Another $59.4 million was from funds appropriated by the United States. Representative Raymond Setik described the islands' dilemma starkly in a statement at the United Nations Trusteeship Council in 1975.

> My colleagues and I from Micronesia would not feel so strongly about the lack of men, money, and materials at this critical time if it were not for the young people of Micronesia. We are advised that 47 per cent of 52,000 Micronesians are under the age of 15 years old. They are now being educated, for better or worse, in a western context of education which tacitly implies that if they do not stay in school to study and receive a diploma they will not be able to find satisfying and gainful employment. But the question which must be asked is where will these graduates find employment? The Government today employs approximately 7,500 Micronesians. It is predicted that by 1992 Micronesia's population will have doubled. Will the Government then employ 15,000 Micronesians? Who will pay the taxes to meet the Government payroll by 1992, a date in time only 18 years distant when we now have difficulty meeting our current payroll. Will the new Government of Micronesia continue to expect to receive large grants in aid from the United States and other foreign Governments to meet the cost of their Government?

THE AMERICAN ADMINISTRATION OF MICRONESIA

For administrative purposes, Micronesia is divided into six districts: Palau, Ponape, Truk, and Yap in the Carolines; the Marshalls; and the Marianas. The current administrative arrangement has not always been used. Originally, Japan divided the territory into as few as three districts. In 1977 Kusaie, now a part of the Ponape District, will become a separate district. The most heavily populated district is Truk, with a population of 32,732 (28 per cent of the total). Yap is the smallest area in terms of population with 7,536 (6 per cent). Palau and the Marianas Districts are about the same size, with populations of 13,025 and 13,381 respectively (approximately 11 per cent each.) The Marshalls and Ponape also have similar figures of 24,248 and 23,723, respectively.

The Department of the Interior is primarily responsible for the administration of Micronesia. Through its Office of Territorial Affairs, Interior also administers Guam, the Virgin Islands, and American Samoa—all territories over which the United States claims sovereignty. Prior to its becoming a commonwealth, Puerto Rico was also administered by Interior.

A high commissioner, appointed by the President and confirmed by the Senate, is the principal United States government official in Micronesia. The high commissioner presides over a government which resembles the government of the United States. That is, there are three branches: a bicameral legislature called the Congress of Micronesia; a judiciary, whose members are appointed by and may be removed by the Secretary of the Interior; and the executive branch, which consists of the high commissioner, a cabinet, and an administrator for each district.

However, the analogy between the organization of the United States government and the Micronesian government is misleading. The high commissioner is an extension of, and takes instructions from, the Department of the Interior, which created the Congress of Micronesia and the judiciary. Unlike the United States where the branches are coequal, the executive branch in Micronesia has final authority. The Congress of Micronesia may repass vetoed legislation, but the legislation nevertheless does not become law if the high commissioner's veto is upheld by the Secretary of the Interior. Similarly, the Congress of Micronesia controls those funds raised in Micronesia, but has only recommendatory powers regarding the funds appropriated by the United States for Micronesia. This is not to say that the Congress of Micronesia is without power. It approves appointments of the high commissioner and its views on appropriations cannot be lightly dismissed.

Since Micronesia is a strategic trust, the United States is allowed certain prerogatives to use the area for defense purposes. Within the Department of Defense, the service most interested in Micronesia is the Navy, which at one time administered Micronesia, Guam, and American Samoa. Navy still retains a major influence over developments in nearby Guam. In addition, Army is interested in Micronesia and is responsible for the Pacific Missile Range facility on Kwajalein in the Marshall Islands. The Coast Guard has a number of stations in Micronesia. Plans call for a joint Navy-Air Force base on the island of Tinian in the Marianas, and the Marines have expressed an interest in training facilities in Palau.

The Department of State represents the United States in all contacts with the United Nations. Within the Department of State, the offices primarily responsible are the Bureaus of East Asian Affairs, International Organizations, the Legal Adviser, and the United States Mission to the United Nations. The United States is represented on the United Nations Trusteeship Council, which oversees trusteeship affairs. The Department of State annually submits to the United Nations reports on Micronesia, based on material furnished by the Department of the Interior.

In brief, American administration of far-flung Micronesia can be divided into four periods:[3] 1) Following capture of the islands from Japan and continuing until signature of the Trusteeship Agreement of 1947, the United States Navy was responsible for administration of the islands; 2) From signature of the Trusteeship Agreement until 1951 when the islands (except for most of the Marianas which were shortly returned to the Navy and remained under Naval administration until 1961) were placed under the civilian administration of the Department of the Interior; 3) From 1961 to 1969 when the Kennedy and Johnson administrations began an accelerated education program; established the Council and later the Congress of Micronesia; improved transportation; and began planning for the territory's future political status; and 4) From 1969 to the present when the Nixon and Ford administrations continued improvements in Micronesia and initiated negotiations with Micronesian representatives on the island's future political status.

In the first two periods, the United States successfully postponed the dilemma inherent in the concept of a strategic trust. In the third and fourth periods, the Kennedy, Johnson, Nixon and Ford administrations sought to put American military presence in Micronesia on a more permanent footing under United States sovereignty. It is on the last two periods that this study concentrates.

---

[3] For a detailed history of naval administration, see Dorothy Richard's three-volume work, *United States Naval Administration of the Trust Territory of the Pacific Islands* (Washington, D.C.: Office of the Chief of Naval Operations, 1957). E. J. Kahn's *A Reporter in Micronesia* (New York: W. W. Norton, 1966) is useful, especially for the period to 1965. Other works are referred to in the text.

Their search was simple—just find what's right
To insure a favorable plebiscite,
And see that the long-shelved Micro-nation
Would be American-owned by affiliation.

—Joe Murphy

II

The United States
Position

United States policy on Micronesia has for the most part been hidden from the public eye and has usually differed from the policy statements of United States officials. For example, stated policy has been in keeping with American anticolonialism and support for self-determination. But what has actually motivated the United States in Micronesia has been instead an assumption that Micronesia was "ours" and would always be "ours"—though its status might suffer a nominal change. Similarly, the United States has always seemed to support United Nations resolutions against separatist movements and the fragmentation of territories. But United States policy seemed, on the contrary, to support the concept of separatism for the Marianas. Separate administration, location of the capital on Saipan, financial discrimination—all served (especially in the absence of any program to promote unity in Micronesia) to encourage the Marianas to think of themselves as set off from the rest of Micronesia. And it is a fact that the United States was quick to accept the Marianas break with the rest of Micronesia when it happened.

In addition to being hidden from view, United States policy on Micronesia has also been confused and inconsistent, arising as it has from interminable bureaucratic squabbles and suffering usually from a lack of attention of administrations distracted by "larger" issues.

Thus, United States policy on Micronesia has been emerging in two ways: the hidden policy has been forced out of hiding by events, and the inconsistencies and confusions have been resolved over the years as Micronesia has pressed for a change in status.

KENNEDY AND JOHNSON ADMINISTRATIONS

Initially, Micronesia did not benefit very much from United Nations Trusteeship Council supervision of American administration. Most United Nations attention was devoted to the larger, more populous territories in Africa and Asia. Visits by United Nations Missions were brief formalities. In 1960, however, colonialism, even that internationally sanctioned under the trusteeship system, came under sharp criticism. Newly independent countries used the United Nations forum to press for an end to government by foreign countries. At the 1960 United Nations session, where Soviet Premier Khrushchev banged his shoe and Fidel Castro plucked chickens at a New York hotel, the General Assembly declared:

> Immediate steps shall be taken in trust and non-self-governing territories or all other territories which have not yet attained independence, to transfer all powers to the peoples of those territories, without any conditions or reservations, in accordance with their freely expressed will and desire, without any distinction as to race, creed or colour, in order to enable them to enjoy complete freedom and independence.

Shortly after this Colonialism Declaration, the United Nations Trusteeship Council, which by then had only Micronesia and four other territories under its jurisdiction, devoted detailed attention to Micronesia for the first time. A United Nations Mission visited Micronesia in 1961, and since that time similar missions have visited the territory at three-year intervals.

The 1961 Visiting Mission to Micronesia was sharply critical of American administration in almost every area: poor transportation; failure to settle war damage claims; failure to adequately compensate for land taken for military purposes; poor living conditions at the American missile range in the Marshalls; inadequate economic development; inadequate education programs; and almost nonexistent medical care.

The Mission was particularly critical of the "political consequences" of the continuing division of the administration of the territory between Navy and Interior. The Visiting Mission said that Saipan, under Navy administration, was benefiting from "financial discrimination" at the expense of the remainder of Micronesia. In addition, the Visiting Mission felt that the economic advantages available to Saipan as a result of larger expenditures by the military encouraged separatism. The Visiting Mission called on the United States to "take the heat out" of the Marianas separatist movement, and included in its report material which indicated that United States naval administrators had encouraged the Saipanese to break away from the rest of Micronesia and "reintegrate" with Guam.

Later, when the Trusteeship Council considered the Visiting Mission report, U Thant, then the delegate of Burma and later Secretary General of the United Nations, sharply criticized separate administration and the promotion of separatism. The argument of the United States that strategic considerations required separate administration might be valid, said Thant, "in so far as it does not adversely affect or retard the Territory's progress towards its prescribed goal of self-determination or independence under the International Trusteeship System." Thant was particularly critical of a September 29, 1960, address to the Saipan Legislature by the naval administration. The naval administrator's statement, said Thant, spoke of the future of Saipan "as a separate entity apart and in isolation from the rest of the Trust Territory"; talked of developing Saipan into a self-governing or independent entity; confused the people about the final goals of trusteeship; and would have the effect of "intensifying separatist tendencies rather than promoting a sense of unity and territorial consciousness."

Sharp criticism of separatism in the Marianas was consistent with prevailing political sentiment in the United Nations against what is called "fragmentation." In its 1960 Declaration on Colonialism, the United Nations General Assembly had staunchly declared that "any attempt aimed at the partial or total disruption of the national unity and the territorial integrity of a country is incompatible with the purposes and principles of the Charter of the United Nations."

During the sixties, other criticism of United States administration of Micronesia appeared in such journals as the *New Yorker,* the *Saturday Evening Post*, and the Honolulu *Star Bulletin.* Some articles were inspired by United States officials who thought publicity would result in improvements. Micronesia, which Robert Trumbull had called *Paradise in Trust*, was also referred to (in various titles) as *America's Paradise Lost*, "Our Bungled Trust," the "Rust Territory" (the term could have referred to either the corrugated steel buildings which were used for schools, homes, and public buildings or to the rusting relics of World War II), *Buritis in Paradise*, "The Forgotten Islands," "Showcase of Neglect," and "Trust Betrayed."

According to one former Assistant Secretary of State, the report of the 1961 Visiting Mission and attendant publicity stunned the new Kennedy administration—all the more so because neither the Visiting Mission nor the Trusteeship Council, which endorsed the mission report, was dominated by anti-American countries or by the newly independent countries. Kennedy also realized that colonialism, even as sanctioned in the form of international trusteeship, was rapidly coming to a close. The time would soon come when pressures would build up in Micronesia and in the United Nations for self-determination. In his address to the General Assembly on September 25, 1961, President Kennedy expressed the position of the United States on Colonialism.

> Within the limits of our responsibility in such matters, my country intends to be a participant and not merely an observer, in the peaceful, expeditious movement of nations from the status of colonies to the partnership of equals. That continuing tide of self-determination, which runs so strong, has our sympathy and our support.
>
> But colonialism, in its harshest form, is not only the exploitation of new nations by old, of dark skins by light, or the subjugation of the poor by the rich. My nation was once a colony, and we know what colonialism means: the exploitation and subjugation of the weak by the powerful, of the many by the few, of the governed who have given no consent to be governed, whatever their continent, their class, or their color. . . .
>
> . . Let us debate colonialism in full—and apply the principle of free choice and the practice of free plebiscites in every corner of the globe.

Kennedy's statement to the General Assembly sealed the United States position in all subsequent debate on colonialism.

As a result of the criticism and of new sensitivity about colonialism, a series of new programs was begun in Micronesia. The programs took on increased importance when Kennedy himself became incensed over the number of people crippled by the rapid spread of polio in the Marshall Islands at a time when vaccines were readily available. The administration of the territory was moved from Guam, and, for the first time, to the Trust Territory itself. The territory was united under a single civilian administration when Saipan, Tinian and Pagan were returned to the jurisdiction of the Interior Department. An accelerated education program was begun; English became the language of instruction; and large numbers of American teachers were employed. The administration set state-side standards for health. United States appropriations for Micronesia, which had averaged $1 million annually between 1947 and 1952 and $5 million between 1947 and 1963, were raised to $15 million in 1963.

When the 1964 Visiting Mission made its report, the entire tone was different from the critical report of 1961. The mission noted "a great change" in United States policy. There was still extensive criticism, particularly of the absence of economic development and of the failure to settle war damage claims against the United States and Japan. However, the mission said it had observed the "first fruits" of a new policy—marked improvements in education, medical care, transportation, and political development—which would transform Micronesia in ways which could not be fully foreseen.

As in 1961, the Mission spoke out firmly against fragmentation. So did the Assistant Secretary of the Interior who met with the Mission. "We do not," he said, "favor fragmentation of the Trust Territory." The mission noted the firm United States statement in favor of territorial unity and saw a reflection of that policy in Micronesia. There were, the Mission found, encouraging signs that "a nation of Micronesia—a Micronesian 'self', as distinct from a collection of island communities—is emerging from what has been in reality no more than a haphazard grouping of islands and peoples which an accident of history brought under the administration of a single Power as trustee." The Mission expressed its belief that the creation of a Micronesian self was essential if self-determination was to be meaningful. The alternative, it said, would be fragmentation—the "self-determination of a multitude of separate islands or districts."

The 1964 Visiting Mission found that United States officials were vague about the future political status of Micronesia but affirmed that the United States did not "itself contemplate integration or having Micronesia come under American sovereignty." All that could be said at the present stage, the Mission recalled being informed by United States officials, "was that the range of options would start with independence and cover all other possibilities—possibilities which were changing as the territory developed." Actually, American officials were not being candid with the Visiting Mission. The full range of options might theoretically have been available, but American policy was secretly aimed at a single option—some kind of permanent association with the United States. The only thing left unclear was how that objective would be achieved.

The policy had been set forth by National Security Action Memorandum (NSAM) 145, issued by President Kennedy on April 18, 1962, almost two years before the 1964 Visiting Mission. NSAM 145 established an interagency task force consisting of representatives of the Departments of Interior, Defense, State, and Health, Education and Welfare, to oversee policy development and implementation for Micronesia. John A. Carver, Assistant Secretary of the Interior for Public Land Management (1961 to 1964) and later Undersecretary of the Interior (1964 to 1966), chaired the group. Harlan Cleveland, Assistant Secretary of State for International Organization Affairs, represented the Department of State.

NSAM 243 of May 9, 1963, established a survey mission headed by Harvard Economics Professor and later Assistant Secretary of State for Economic Affairs Anthony N. Solomon to visit Micronesia and report on economic, social, educational and political developments. The group was to "make recommendations leading to the formulation of programs and policies for an accelerated rate of development so that the people may make an informed and free choice as to their future, in accordance with U.S. responsibilities under the Trusteeship Agreement." The Solomon group visited Micronesia in the summer of 1963. Its three-volume report was submitted late that summer. At first those parts of the report which discussed social, educational and economic developments were unclassified (Volumes II and III), but the entire contents were promptly classified at the insistence of the Department of State. State officials ostensibly did not wish criticism contained in the report to be used against the United States at the United Nations. More important, they did not wish to make public the secret political policy objectives which were referred to throughout Volumes II and III.

The economic and social volumes of the Solomon Report have since been declassified after the excision of controversial political information by the Department of State. However, the NSAM's and Volume I on political development remain classified.

It is possible, however, to get an indication of the content of still classified Volume I, for the entire introduction and summary of the Solomon Report were printed in the *Young Micronesian*, a newsletter published by Micronesian students at the University of Hawaii, and subsequently reprinted in the July 10, 1971, *Micronitor* (see Appendix I). The *Young Micronesian* thus revealed for the first time the official rationale and description of United States policy objectives in Micronesia:

> For a variety of reasons, in the almost twenty years of US control, physical facilities have further deteriorated in many areas, the economy has remained relatively dormant and in many ways retrogressed while progress toward social development has been slow. The people remain largely illiterate and inadequately prepared to participate in political, commercial and other activities of more than a rudimentary character. The great majority depend largely upon subsistence agriculture—fruit and nutgathering—and fishing. As a result, criticism of the trusteeship has been growing in the UN and the US press—and in certain ways, among Micronesians.
>
> Despite a lack of serious concern for the area until quite recently, Micronesia is said to be essential to the U.S. for security reasons. We

cannot give the area up, yet time is running out for the US in the sense that we will soon be the only nation left administering a trust territory. The time could come, and shortly, when the pressures in the UN for a settlement of the status of Micronesia could become more than embarrassing.

In recognition of the problem, the President, on April 18, 1962, approved NSAM No. 145 which set forth as US policy the movement of Micronesia into a permanent relationship with the US within our political framework. In keeping with that goal, the memorandum called for accelerated development of the area to bring its political, economic, and social standards into line with an eventual permanent association.

In order to implement this policy, Solomon thought three key steps were necessary: preparation and timing of a "favorable" plebiscite; development of the type and cost of capital improvement and operating programs needed to "insure" a favorable vote; and improved coordination, especially between Washington and the Trust Territory government to insure that the necessary political strategy and development program could be implemented "with reasonable efficiency and effectiveness."

The report recommended an "integrated master plan for action" which by fiscal year 1968 would achieve three objectives:

a. Winning the plebiscite and making Micronesia a United States territory under circumstances which will: (1) satisfy somewhat conflicting interests of the Micronesians, the UN, and the US along lines satisfactory to the Congress; (2) be appropriate to the present political and other capabilities of the Micronesians; and (3) provide sufficient flexibility in government structure to accomodate to whatever measure of local self-government the Congress might grant to Micronesia in later years.
b. Achieving rapidly the minimum but satisfactory social standards in education, public health, etc.
c. Raising cash incomes through the development of the current, largely crop-gathering subsistence economy.

There were, said the report, "unique elements" in the delicate problem of Micronesia and the attainment of United States objectives that urgently required the agreement of the President and the Congress as to the guidelines for United States action: 1) The United States was "moving counter to the anticolonial movement" and was "breaching its own policy since World War I of not acquiring new territorial possessions"; 2) Of all eleven United Nations trust territories, Micronesia would be the only trusteeship which did not terminate in independence or merger with a contiguous country but affiliated with the administering power; 3) If termination as the United States proposed was vetoed, it "might have to decide to proceed with a series of actions that would make the trusteeship a dead issue, at least from the Micronesian viewpoint"[1]; 4) Micronesia

---

[1] The implication, opposed by the Department of State, was that the United States could end the Trusteeship Agreement without United Nations approval.

would, for the foreseeable future, have to be subsidized; 5) While a subsidy could be justified as a "strategic rental," it would amount to $300 annually per Micronesian and could be reduced only with long-range planning; and 6) None of the objectives could be realized without "a modern and more efficient concept of overseas territorial administration than [was] evident in the prevailing approach of the quasi-colonial bureaucracy in the present Trust Territory Government."

Among other things, the report recommended that a plebiscite present a *choice* between independence and "permanent affiliation" with the United States. The report thought an independence option was safe since it detected "little desire" for independence, and, in any event, its recommended programs, if successful, would dispose Micronesians toward the United States.

Few details are given in the summary of the nature of a post-plebiscite government, although it is said to be discussed in detail in Volume I of the report. It is clear, however, that the nature of "self-government" troubled the Solomon group. The report speaks of the "many-pronged dilemma" of satisfying United Nations demands and the expectations of increasingly sophisticated Micronesians for "self-government or independence." "On the other hand," the report states, "consideration must be given to the need for continued adequate control by the U.S. and the traditional attitudes of the Congress toward the organization of territorial government," as well as the clear limitations on the ability of Micronesians to govern themselves.

In the final analysis, the report recommended the "appearance" of self-government through an elected legislature and Micronesian chief executive. The United States would retain "adequate control" through continuation of an appointed United States high commissioner (similar to the then United States administration in Okinawa). The powers of the high commissioner could range from

(a) The minimum of being able to withhold all or any part of the US funds going to the Micronesian government and the authority to declare martial law and assume all legislative and executive powers when the security of the U.S. so requires; to
(b) The maximum additional power of vetoing all laws, confirming the Chief Executive's appointments of key department directors and dismissing the Chief Executive and dissolving the legislature at any time.

Though classified, the Solomon Report was immediately controversial within the government. Interior officials looked upon many of the recommendations as "mischievous" and maintain that all the "appropriate and feasible" recommendations were implemented. Although the report spoke of the importance of satisfying Congress, there was little effort to bring Congress in on the report. It was never formally given to Congress, but was apparently passed to House Interior Committee staffers surreptitiously.

On the whole, the Solomon recommendations represented an effort to reconcile altruism and United States self-interest. Implementation of the Solomon recommendations would have resulted in an immediate increase in all aspects of Micronesia's development, an actual fulfillment of long neglected obligations under the Trusteeship Agreement. That this was being done also in the interest of the United States was no less cynical than the concept of strategic trusteeship.

However, in the aftermath of the turbulent sixties, only the self-interest aspects of the Solomon Report stand out. The *Young Micronesian* described the recommendations as "a ruthless five-year plan to systematically Americanize Micronesia into a permanent association in clear and conscious defiance of its trusteeship obligations." The Palau newspaper *Tia Belau* and the American organization, Friends of Micronesia (started by returned Peace Corps volunteers), described the Solomon Report as "America's ruthless blueprint for the assimilation of Micronesia."

In 1971, the *Micronitor* (now called the *Micronesia Independent*), a weekly newspaper published in the Marshall Islands, carried the following poem by editor Joe Murphy, a former Peace Corps volunteer.

A POEM

Dedicated to the Wonderful and Inspiring Men
Who Comprised the Solomon Mission
July-August 1963

On the 18th of April in '62
With a fresh wind blowing, and skies of blue
The Pres approved memo one-forty-five
And the Solomon Committee sprang alive.
Eight summers ago—in '63
Nine men came out from the Land of the Free
To the sunny trust isles, facts to find—
As well as assess the islanders' mind.

Their search was simple—just find what's right
To insure a favorable plebiscite,
And see that the long-shelved Micro-nation
Would be American-owned by affiliation.

Yes, out they came, these nine great guys
To serve as the President's personal eyes
And determine which way the natives would go
When the status winds began to blow.

The objectives were stated as a, b, and c
And were geared to do everything rapidly.
Their outline proclaimed that the Trust Islands' fate
Could be sealed and delivered by late '68.

In motif their work was 'American Colonial'
But knowing this bothered them not one i-on-ial.
For these were old men who remembered the WAR
And knew that the islands had long been a whore
To Spaniards and Germans and Nippons and such
—'Protectors' who screwed without paying much.

Their final plan was really quite simple,
And resembled the act of picking a pimple.
After starting a TT-wide Congress as head
They fill it with loads of Commonwealth bread,
And when it gets soft and ready to flow
They pump in some plebiscite fever and blow.

The name of the game was 'Follow the Leader'
And the Solomon crew swore nothing was neater.
They also suggested that leaders be caught
By leadership grants and to Washington brought.

And even commented that kids in school
Could be curriculated toward American rule,
Adding that scholarships in gay profusion
Could win the voters through confusion.

To top this off, they said PCV's
Will Teach "The West" for chicken feed
And a dash of Social Security, please
(To replace the function of coconut trees)
Will guarantee, without a doubt,
That Micronesians won't get out.

The Solomon Report was submitted to the President on October 9, 1963, and was followed by NSAM 268, which apparently directed that the interagency group proceed with the implementation of the report's recommendations. One official recalls that in a covering memorandum attached to NSAM 268, a White House official passed along President Kennedy's request that he be notified by November 30, 1963, of the date for a plebiscite in Micronesia.

Kennedy died on November 22, 1963, and it is idle to speculate what policy he would have followed with regard to Micronesia's future status. One former State Department official recalls asking an Interior official about the plebiscite date shortly after Kennedy's death and being told that there was a new President! In any event, the interagency group disappeared (along with any real focus on Micronesia), although there were numerous efforts to revive or re-establish an interagency body on Micronesian questions. Pressure from the White House decreased notably as New Frontier activists left government and as Vietnam vied for and quickly won the attention of White House staffers.

The Department of the Interior once again had almost sole responsibility for the islands. But none of the big issues had been resolved. Interior and Defense on the one side, and State and the United States Mission to the United Nations on the other side, spent the next five years arguing essentially three questions:

1) Must independence be included on a plebiscite? State said yes, for political and legal reasons, and staunchly maintained that it was responsible for interpreting the legal requirements of the Trusteeship Agreement. Interior said no, arguing that *either* self-government *or* independence had to be offered, not both. Interior argued that self-government was the only status consistent with Article 6 of the Trusteeship Agreement, which states that the new status should be "appropriate to the particular circumstances of the territory and its peoples and the freely expressed wishes of the peoples concerned." Defense straddled the fence but essentially agreed with Interior on the grounds that inclusion of independence risked loss of a strategically important territory. The issue remained basically unresolved even in the Nixon administration.

2) Must the territory be *fully* self-governing? Again, State said yes and Interior disagreed. State argued that self-government meant just that and cited United Nations guidelines on when a territory was no longer non-self-governing. Interior, on the other hand, argued that Micronesia was not ready for *complete* self-government and that Congress was not willing to grant Micronesia a larger measure of autonomy than currently being enjoyed by the more advanced United States territories of Guam and the Virgin Islands. As one former Interior official put it, for State, Puerto Rico's status was a minimum condition; for Interior, American Samoa's status and maybe Guam's were the maximum to be offered Micronesia.

3) Must a self-governing Micronesia be allowed to *unilaterally* end a status of association with the United States? State said yes. Interior and Defense disagreed. State cited United Nations resolutions which provided that a territory which opted for a status short of independence or for full integration with another state, must have the right to unilaterally alter its status if it later wished to do so. In State's view, a properly developed United States-Micronesian relationship based on friendship and interdependence ran little risk of an abrupt or unilateral change. On the other hand, both Interior and Defense argued that an opt-out provision was unacceptable for strategic reasons and for the precedent it would provide for other United States territories. Congress, it was argued, had not even given such a privilege to Puerto Rico.

Ruth Van Cleve, Director of Interior's Office of Territories from 1964 to 1969 and before that for ten years Interior's Assistant Solicitor for Territories, acknowledges sharp differences within the executive branch in her book, *The Office of Territorial Affairs.* She writes:

> In connection with this question of the Trust Territory's future, the interested departments of the executive branch—principally State, Defense, and Interior—had (and have) particular and primary concerns that necessarily

differ: the posture of the United States vis-a-vis the rest of the world, and particularly the United Nations; the security interests of the United States; and good government for and the well-being of the Micronesian people. In the 1960s these concerns proved impossible to reconcile within the executive branch itself, even though during this period there was substantial evidence that the Micronesians would then have welcomed close and permanent political association with the United States. . . . Territorial status, similar to that of Guam, seemed to be what the Micronesians then wanted. But while close and permanent association between the United States and the Trust Territory was regarded as acceptable to the U.S. Congress, that status would almost surely have encountered extreme hostility at the United Nations. Any political status for the Trust Territory that would be easily acceptable at the United Nations would, on the other hand, then have encountered extreme hostility in the U.S. Congress.[2]

Van Cleve obscures and over-simplifies the differences between the three agencies, particularly when she implies that only Interior was interested in "good government for and the well-being of the Micronesian people."[3] It would be more accurate to state that on territorial affairs, Interior was concerned with its posture vis-a-vis Congress just as State was concerned with world opinion and United States legal obligations. Interior, correctly, thought Congress, as then organized, would reject any status which might meet the prevailing United Nations criteria for self-government.

In the circumstances, the administration had two alternatives. One alternative was to reach a single executive branch policy decision and press for congressional approval. However, Micronesia competed poorly with Vietnam and even most other Interior programs. There was not enough sustained, high-level attention available to raise complicated status issues to the presidential level for resolution.

It was Interior which proposed the time-tested second alternative, a device for resolving—or shelving—a sticky problem: a presidential commission. Interior's idea was to create a commission by act of Congress. The commission would involve representatives from Micronesia, the Congress, and interested government agencies. The participation of congressmen would involve and partially obligate Congress in the implementation of the commission's recommendations. At the same time, the Congress of Micronesia was petitioning President Johnson to establish a commission which would consult with the Micronesian people, so that Micronesians could freely express their views and political alternatives could be determined.

However, even these status commission proposals ran into bureaucratic difficulties and delays. It was difficult to reach agreement on legislative proposals

---

[2] Ruth G. Van Cleve, *The Office of Territorial Affairs* (New York: Praeger, 1974), p. 142.

[3] Van Cleve is not alone in making this characterization. Similar views were expressed in interviews with other Interior officials and with some members of Congress.

because each agency sought to advance its position on Micronesia's future status by including that position in the commission's terms of reference. A bill was finally sent to Congress in 1967 after what Ruth Van Cleve describes as "a legislative clearance process that involved more Cabinet-level visitations and importunings than any piece of legislation in the Office of Territories' history."[4]

But in the final analysis, the draft legislation used the exact but unclear language of the Trusteeship Agreement ("self-government or independence") and left to the proposed commission the determination of the meaning of "self-government" and of whether both "self-government" *and* "independence" must appear on a plebiscite. In other words, the basic differences within the executive were not resolved. Even Undersecretary of State Nicholas Katzenbach's explanation to the Senate Subcommittee on Interior and Insular Affairs used the inexact language of the Trusteeship Agreement. Left to executive sessions and informal lobbying was the continuation of the State-Interior disagreement on the amount of autonomy which had to be offered in order to fulfill United States trusteeship obligations in Micronesia.

Katzenbach did not address the basic differences in the definition of "self government", but he was clear and precise about the problems he thought would arise if there were mistakes in the timing of events in Micronesia. He saw considerable damage in not holding a plebiscite in Micronesia by June 30, 1972. That timing, he said, avoided two dangers: delay could create serious disappointments and cause grave difficulties at a later time; on the other hand, a premature plebiscite would not allow time to permit the education necessary if Micronesians were to make a meaningful choice, nor allow time to prepare for implementation of the alternative chosen.

Katzenbach's testimony was particularly prophetic. The accelerated education program (including the university training of Micronesians in political science and sociology[5]), the addition of large numbers of Peace Corps volunteers, and the creation of the Congress of Micronesia had set in motion a process which could not be reversed but would underscore the need to resolve Micronesia's status.

While the bureaucracy delayed and argued, the Micronesians, despairing of ever seeing a United States status commission, took matters into their own hands and created their own status commission. In the final analysis, delay jeopardized the attainment of American policy objectives. Status commission legislation never got through Congress; the Micronesians, having taken the initiative, then

---

[4] Van Cleve, *Territorial Affairs*, p. 142.

[5] One former Trust Territory education official suggests that the Micronesians should have been studying agriculture, marine biology, nursing and medicine—subjects which are development related.

more or less outgrew the status that the United States had, with such confident assurance, reserved for them.

But all the delay had its impact on the Micronesians too, for the longer they waited, the more dependent they became on United States money and the more difficult it was for them to consider going it alone as an independent country.

THE NIXON ADMINISTRATION

The Nixon administration was almost immediately seized with the Micronesia question when Nixon took office in 1969. Administration officials gave the impression that nothing had been done before then to resolve Micronesia's status. Secretary of the Interior Hickel recalls in *Who Owns America?* that within less than a month, his staff called to his attention information that the United States was likely to be sharply criticized during the next session of the United Nations General Assembly for "mishandling" Micronesia.[6] Another version of the Nixon administration's initial interest in Micronesia's future status has the question arising in the context of the so-called Nixon Doctrine, first enunciated on Guam.[7]

However, it is clear from the Solomon Report, among others, that the effort to resolve Micronesia's status predates the Nixon administration. And, as will be seen in a discussion of the strategic importance of Micronesia, general plans for military facilities in Micronesia grew out of perceived contingency needs which also predate the Nixon administration. Specific military base plans grew out of the necessity to specify military land requirements if progress was to be made in negotiations with the Micronesians.

There is evidence, however, that the Nixon administration's attention *was* drawn to Micronesia as an outgrowth of the already existing bureaucratic struggles between the Department of State and the Department of the Interior.

The Nixon administration had re-established and centralized the role of the National Security Council (NSC) in determining and coordinating foreign policy questions. Richard Sneider, a foreign service officer who had been involved in the Micronesian questions as a result of having handled Micronesian war damage claims discussions with the Japanese, joined the NSC staff to handle East Asian questions. State Department officials drafted and informally sent to Sneider the suggestion and language for a directive which would once again formally place

---

[6]Walter Hickel, *Who Owns America?* (Englewood Cliffs, New Jersey: Prentice-Hall, Inc., 1971), p. 204.

[7]The "Nixon Doctrine" was repeatedly cited in interviews by military strategists. See also James H. Webb, Jr., *Micronesia and U.S. Pacific Strategy: A Blueprint for the 1980's* (New York: Praeger, 1974).

Micronesia under interagency scrutiny. The appropriate directive was issued by the Assistant to the President for National Security Affairs, Henry A. Kissinger, at the direction of the President. The directive called for a new study of the Micronesian question by an interagency group headed by Interior, but reporting not to the NSC Review Group chaired by Kissinger, as State had suggested, but to the new NSC Undersecretaries Committee, chaired first by Undersecretary of State Elliot Richardson and later by Undersecretary of State John N. Irwin. The Undersecretaries Committee included the head of the Joint Chiefs, the Deputy Secretary of Defense, a representative of the CIA, the Assistant to the President for National Security Affairs (who almost never attended), and, for purposes of the Micronesia study, the Undersecretary of the Interior. Thus, State succeeded again in one of its long-held aims, which was to focus interagency attention on Micronesia, albeit at a lower level. Ironically, State would subsequently lose on most of the policy issues.

The Undersecretaries Committee was one way of getting priority for Micronesian programs. Appropriations increased from $39 million in 1969 to $59.8 million in 1971. Defense provided civic action teams for badly needed road and sanitary construction projects. Greater responsibility was given to the Congress of Micronesia. Micronesians were rapidly moved into governmental positions, and by 1973 Micronesians served as administrators of all areas except Yap. (That position was held by an American from Guam.) The Trust Territory government also decentralized many of its activities.

However, as carried out, "Micronesianization" and decentralization of the government had distinct disadvantages for Micronesian unity. The new Micronesian government officials were largely placed in their home districts on the substantially justifiable grounds that Palauans should govern Palau, and Yapese should govern Yap. Among other things, home assignments resulted in substantial savings in travel and housing allowances. Similarly, decentralization of government is normally a desirable objective. In Micronesia, however, home assignments and decentralization tended to reinforce parochialism and factors of disunity. Micronesia needed more interdistrict activities, such as a territory-wide junior college and a vocational school, which it got, and regular rotation of Micronesian officials throughout the districts, which it did not get. For political and economic reasons, Micronesia needs a deliberate scattering of specialized functions among the districts. (For example, in the age of jet transportation, there is no reason why some of the relatively sophisticated laboratory facilities at the Truk Hospital need to be duplicated in other districts.) Failure to promote district interdependence worked directly against the administration's announced policy of a unified Micronesia.

The Undersecretaries Committee also took definite policy decisions on the issues which, between 1963 and 1969, had been contended between the Departments of Interior, State, and Defense. Ruth Van Cleve writes that the new movement seemed to indicate that the "inter-departmental warfare" had ceased. "The Foreign Service," she said, "has swept the State Department officers to new posts, and their key Interior adversaries are also elsewhere. Harmony has returned."[8]

Van Cleve's view is only partially correct. It implies that bureaucratic differences between the agencies were largely personal rather than substantive, a conclusion which the facts do not support. The new administration did use new personnel, many of whom were entirely unfamiliar with Micronesia and with the fundamental questions at issue. More important, as will be seen from a discussion of initial proposals to the Micronesians, the Nixon administration restored "harmony" largely by adopting the Interior and Defense Department positions. "Harmony" resulted from overruling the long-held State Department view on such issues as fragmentation, the inclusion of independence on a plebiscite, and the definition of "self-government." This was to prove a costly error. Not until the administration was willing to entertain Micronesian proposals along the lines of those advocated by the Department of State was there to be progress in its negotiations.

BUREAUCRATIC INFIGHTING

Bureaucratic fighting among State, Interior, and Defense (particularly the Navy) was not limited to the question of Micronesia's future status but has characterized the United States administration of Micronesia from the beginning. And on the whole, this dissension has worked to the detriment of both Micronesian and United States interests. Events concerning Micronesia—from the establishment of a strategic trust to the onset of United States-Micronesia negotiations—have always taken place against a backdrop of bureaucratic infighting.

An insight into Interior-State Department bickering is found in the Van Cleve book. At one point Van Cleve writes that State and Interior territorial personnel "got along swimmingly" through the years. However, the whole of Van Cleve's discussion of Interior-State relations seems to imply—and she later states—what most officials candidly admit: relations between State and Interior on Micronesia were poor throughout most of the sixties. Van Cleve writes:

> Faced with U.N. criticism of the United States' territorial and Trust Territory administration during the mid-1960's, the State Department not surprisingly decided that it could do Interior's job better than Interior was doing it. And Interior, although accustomed to receiving advice from a wide variety of sources, found itself growing testier and testier with each

---

[8]Van Cleve, *Territorial Affairs*, p. 179.

new State Department incursion into its area of responsibility. So as criticism from U.N. sources of U.S. administration increased, so did disharmony between key State and Interior personnel.

Viewed from the Office of Territories standpoint, it appeared that State Department employees were bouncing all over the executive branch inspiring agencies to do things to make U.S. territorial administration look better, but always leaving the message that Interior must be the last to know. The amount of energy and imagination employed by some of State's people was phenomenal, as was their lack of candor. Inevitably the State-inspired plans, generally in the form of another agency's project to do something "for" a territory or the Trust Territory, would surface. Sometimes they would surface through the good offices of a friend in the other agency, who would ring up to tell Interior what was going on; sometimes they surfaced because the other agency, having not quite got the word, would telephone the Office of Territories for information that agency needed to plan its helpful project. Whenever the project did emerge, Interior needed to run fast to catch up. The most sensational effort was one conducted for several months during 1966, when a highly placed State Department official sought "unofficially" to cause the transfer of administration of all of the Trust Territory from Interior to State—with never a word to Interior. He failed, as befits one employing improper means.[9]

Van Cleve accurately cites the different functions and interests of the two agencies but also implies that State was nosy, indecisive, cunning, and acted with an air of superiority. On the other hand, State Department officials found Interior provincial, staid, bureaucratic, and most of all afraid of Congress to the point of being unwilling to recommend policies Interior thought correct but knew were strongly opposed in the Congress. Secretary of the Interior Udall, said one former high official of the Department of State, was progressive and in the spirit of the "new frontier" on most matters, but not on Micronesia. The official speculated that Udall simply never got deeply involved in Micronesia or had concluded that it was not worth spending his capital in the Congress.

* * *

The Peace Corps, which began operations in Micronesia in 1966, also jumped into the interagency crossfire. Originally, it had been concluded that Micronesia

---

[9]*Ibid.*, pp. 178-9. Note: We can find no verification of such an effort. There were State Department efforts to make an individual in the White House responsible for policy and an effort to have the high commissioner replaced by a Peace Corps official. Van Cleve is correct, however, about the bad blood which, apparently, does not disappear with time. John A. Carver, Jr., who as Assistant Secretary (1961-64) and later Undersecretary of the Interior (1964-66) was the highest official at Interior usually dealing with Micronesia, devoted one of his three paragraphs in the introduction of the Van Cleve book to bureaucratic hassles: "Other participants may not agree with her. One cannot imagine the Department of State people or the Peace Corps 'Establishment' concurring in her assessment of their activities, in certain respects. Some key figures over several national administrations will look in vain for their names, and some will not have the perception to be grateful."

was not sufficiently foreign for inclusion in Peace Corps programs. However, Ross Pritchard, an energetic Peace Corps official, encouraged by State Department officials, particularly Ambassador Arthur Goldberg and the United States representative on the United Nations Trusteeship Council, Ambassador Eugenie Anderson, and by Micronesians, pushed hard for a Peace Corps program not only in Micronesia but in other Pacific islands as well. The Micronesia Peace Corps program was massive—for the Peace Corps and for Micronesia. At one point there was almost one Peace Corps volunteer for every one hundred Micronesians. They worked as teachers, in community development and as business and legal advisers. They were young, idealistic, and enthusiastic. They spoke the language and lived closer to the people than any foreigners had done previously. Many of them became critical of American officials in Micronesia and of the Interior Department.

The most serious problem occurred not with the Interior (although it welcomed the result) but with the Defense Department over Peace Corps lawyers. Peace Corps lawyers began to teach Micronesians about their rights and encouraged challenges to previously unchallenged land practices. The Pentagon saw such challenges as dangerous political agitation which might adversely affect the political status desired by the United States. More immediately, the Micronesians were discovering ways to protect their land. The result was a decision by the Nixon administration to phase out the Peace Corps legal program. The problem was to arise again, however, when lawyers from the Office of Economic Opportunity also challenged administration practices. This time the high commissioner was overruled in his disapproval of a legal program.

Differences between agencies in Washington were matched by differences between Washington and American officials in Micronesia. Some of the latter were conscientious and probably made the most of the niggardly resources with which they worked. However, most American officials in Micronesia came under sharp criticism, especially in the Solomon Report, as incompetent. Many were holdovers from Navy or former Interior Department officials who had been forced to leave the Alaska and Hawaii administration when those territories became states. Some were rejects from the Bureau of Indian Affairs. In "exile" in Micronesia they were away from and insensitive to new international political pressures. Protected by their civil service status, they were vulnerable to the charge of perpetuating their positions rather than fulfilling developmental obligations which would have resulted in their replacement by Micronesians. In any event, long before Micronesians had assumed posts of district administrators, a number of Micronesians were more capable than the American officials.

Friction between Washington and the high commissioner has taken some bizarre turns. At one point, low level White House officials in the Kennedy administration decided to fire High Commissioner M. W. Goding, whose tenure gave rise to the affectionate slogan "In Goding we trust." Word reached Goding, who had his Senate patron ask President Kennedy about his status. With no knowledge of Goding, Kennedy responded favorably and Goding's position was thus secure—at least for a while. Told later what he had done, Kennedy reprimanded his staffers, "That'll teach you s.o.b's to let me know what is going on."

History repeated itself in the second term of the Nixon administration. Interior officials had decided to replace High Commissioner Edward Johnston. Two reasons were advanced. First, Johnston, who was looked upon favorably by the Micronesians, had served six years in an isolated area and had "developed problems" which made it difficult for him to handle some situations wisely and without bias. Second, Johnston was a political appointee and could not be expected to have some of the professional sensitivity necessary during status negotiations. The idea was to appoint a senior foreign service officer who would be more sensitive to the views of Washington and would carry out instructions with fewer questions. A list was prepared of several foreign service officers of ambassadorial rank and at least one was interviewed.

As in the Goding case, Johnston became aware of his planned ouster and through the office of Senator Fong had the plan killed.

* * *

It is with the above background of poor administration and bureaucratic infighting at all levels that the United States and Micronesians began negotiations of future status. Later we shall discuss the negotiations in detail. First, however, it is necessary to examine the international legal and political factors involved in changing Micronesia's status and the strategic rationale on which the United States policy is based.

*The United States feels that it must record
its opposition, not to the principle of
independence, to which no people could be
more consecrated than the people of the
United States, but to the thought that it could
possibly be achieved within any foreseeable
future in this case.*

—Warren Austin

III

Self-Determination
For Micronesia:
Some International, Legal,
And Political Factors

Following American occupation of the islands and before the final defeat of Japan, a debate took place within the United States government as to what the United States relationship with Micronesia should be after the war. It was clear from the Cairo Declaration of 1943 between Churchill, Roosevelt, and Chiang Kai-shek that Japan would lose the islands; but it was unclear who would inherit them. Convinced by the lessons of the war that American control of the area was essential to national security, military officials argued that in light of the substantial losses in terms of American lives and material in securing the islands, the United States was entitled to exercise territorial rights over Micronesia.

On the other hand, cognizant of statements in the Atlantic Charter that the Allies sought "no aggrandizement, territorial or otherwise," and in the Cairo Declaration that the Allies "covet no gain for themselves and have no thought of territorial expansion," the Department of State opposed annexation. State Department officials were also concerned that annexation might provide a precedent to support the Soviet Union's allegations of its national security "needs." State, instead, favored putting the islands under a trusteeship with international supervision. International trusteeship arrangements, however, were unacceptable to the military, even after provisions limiting the United Nations supervision to nonsecurity interests were added to an early draft outlining the trusteeship system.

The resulting compromise was a proposal to set up two categories of trusteeships: one category to incorporate what had been the original plan for trusteeship and a second category, "strategic trusts," to comply with the United States military demands. Micronesia was placed in this second category.

THE TRUSTEESHIP AGREEMENT

The Trusteeship Agreement was approved by the United Nations Security Council on April 2, 1947, and by President Truman on July 18, 1947. Prior to Truman's action, each house of the United States Congress approved the agreement without significant debate after military officials expressed their satisfaction that it had sufficient safeguards to maintain United States control, and thus to protect United States strategic interests.

Micronesia as a whole is a strategic area (Article 1) and the United States is given full powers of administration, legislation, and jurisdiction as well as the authority to apply United States laws to the territory (Article 3). A provision that the territory could be administered "as an integral part of the United States" was deleted at Soviet suggestion, but the deletion did not lessen United States authority.

In accordance with the United Nations Charter provisions that trust territories should play their part in maintaining international peace, the Trusteeship Agreement explicitly allows the United States to establish military bases, erect fortifications and station and employ armed forces in the territory; the United States can make use of volunteer forces, facilities and assistance from the trust territory in carrying out obligations to the Security Council, and for local defense and internal order (Article 5).

While the Trusteeship Agreement gives the United States broad authority, exercise of that authority must be consistent with specific obligations (Article 6) assumed by the United States

> ... to foster the development of such political institutions as are suited to the trust territory and shall promote the development of the inhabitants of the trust territory toward self-government or independence, as may be appropriate to the particular circumstances of the trust territory and its peoples and the freely expressed wishes of the peoples concerned ... to promote the social advancement of the inhabitants, and ... to promote the educational advancement of the inhabitants.

A "most favored nations" clause stated that the United States would accord to nationals of each United Nations member, and to their companies and associations, treatment in Micronesia "no less favorable" than that given nationals and companies of any other United Nations member except the United States (Article 8). Until 1974 the United States used this provision to limit investment in Micronesia to United States investors, mostly to prevent Japanese economic control before the future political status of Micronesia could be determined. However, there is ample evidence that considerable Japanese commercial activities took place behind Micronesian "fronts."

According to the agreement, Micronesia could be joined into a customs, fiscal, or administrative union or federation with one or more United States-owned territories (e.g., Guam), or could use common services with such territories so long as these were not inconsistent with the basic objectives of the trusteeship system, or with the agreement (Article 9). Despite this provision and the proximity of Guam, Micronesia has always been administered separately.

The agreement obligated the United States to provide information to the United Nations on political, economic, social, and educational developments in Micronesia and to receive periodic visiting missions, but the United States could determine when these obligations could not be met because part or all of the territory had been closed for security reasons (Article 13).

There are several significant distinctions between strategic and ordinary trusteeship arrangements. First, strategic trust territories are supervised by the United Nations Security Council instead of the Trusteeship Council, although the Security Council could call upon the Trusteeship Council for assistance in supervision. This, of course, enables the United States to retain a large degree of control over the islands, since it can exercise its veto in the Security Council on any matters it deems not in the interest of national security or international peace. Over Soviet objections, in 1949 the Security Council decided to delegate responsibility for United Nations supervision, except for security matters, to the Trusteeship Council. The Security Council itself has considered Micronesia only once since approval of the Trusteeship Agreement—regarding use of the islands by the United States for nuclear testing—and reports of the Trusteeship Council to the Security Council have been perfunctory.

Second, under the strategic trust concept, the United States as administering authority has the right, for security reasons, to close any or all of the Trust Territory to United Nations inspection or supervision. Thus, for example, the United States closed much of the Territory for security reasons prior to 1960. Even today, the American military maintains control over movements into and out of Kwajalein where the United States has test facilities for its Pacific Missile Range. Again for security reasons, the United States enjoys preferential treatment for economic development of the territory. Micronesia is the only territory that has ever been placed in the strategic trust category.

The system of trusts, including strategic trusts, was never meant to be permanent. A basic objective of the system, as set out in the United Nations Charter and in the Trusteeship Agreement for Micronesia, is to promote the progressive development of the territory towards "self-government or independence." This is in sharp contrast with the League of Nations Mandate system where Micronesia, as a "C" mandate, was not expected to attain either self-government or independence.

Of the eleven original trust territories, nine are no longer trust territories. The tenth territory, New Guinea, under Australian administration, obtained independence in union with Papua in 1975, leaving the United States as the last administrator under the trusteeship system. It was in response to this situation, to continuing anticolonial pressure in the United Nations and to demands for a new status from the Micronesians themselves, that the United States and Micronesia started negotiations in 1969 towards termination of the Trusteeship Agreement by an act of self-determination on the part of the Micronesians. These negotiations, however, involve more than merely determining the wishes of the Micronesians as to their future status. Inevitably, they involve reconciling those wishes with United States security interests in the territory.

Many complex domestic and international legal and political questions have been raised in the course of the United States-Micronesian negotiations on Micronesia's future political status. Primary among these are

1) What is "self-determination," whether a right or principle, as it applies to Micronesia? That is, what is the proper meaning of the clause in Article 6,

paragraph 1 of the Trusteeship Agreement that the United States is obligated to promote development "toward self-government or independence, as may be appropriate to the particular circumstances of the trust territory and its peoples and the freely expressed wishes of the peoples concerned?"

2) Who or what in Micronesia has a legitimate claim to exercise the right to self-determination?

3) What procedures and processes must the United States follow in terminating the Trusteeship Agreement and insuring that a proper act of self-determination has taken place? In this process, what are the rights and obligations of the United States, the United Nations, the elected representatives of Micronesia and the peoples of Micronesia?

ALTERNATIVE CHOICES

Two principal documents govern determination of future political status for the Trust territories: The United Nations Charter and the Trusteeship Agreement. In the Charter, self-determination is referred to explicitly in Articles 1 and 55 and implicitly in Article 76, which speaks in terms of "self-government or independence." The Trusteeship Agreement, Article 6, paragraph 1, provides, in part, that, in accordance with its obligations under Article 76 (b) of the Charter, the administering authority "shall promote the development of the inhabitants of the trust territory toward self-government or independence as may be appropriate to the particular circumstances of the trust territory and its peoples and the freely expressed wishes of the peoples concerned."

Nowhere in the Charter or in the Trusteeship Agreement is there a definition of "self-determination," or of "self-government or independence." Secondary materials such as preliminary drafts of the Charter, the Trusteeship Agreement, debates at the United Nations Conference on International Organization and in the Security Council, and General Assembly resolutions provide some basis for interpretation of these terms and therefore for standards by which the negotiations on Micronesia's future status can be measured.

In the earliest drafts, the trusteeship system was considerably broader in scope than the system which finally materialized. American planners intended that all dependent areas would be placed under the trusteeship system with the "status of full independence" as the goal. This plan was scrapped because Great Britain objected strongly both to putting all its empire under international supervision and to the goal of independence. Two separate systems were set up within the Charter to deal with dependent areas, one for dependent areas not placed under trusteeship, so-called non-self-governing territories, and the other, with more detailed requirements, for trust territories. Independence was not explicitly included in the list of objectives for non-self-governing territories, despite efforts on the part of China and the Soviet Union to have it included. The objective with respect to non-self-governing territories is simply to "develop self-government," though the United States argued at the San Francisco Conference that the concept of self-government included independence as one of its forms. The administrator of a non-self-governing territory had fulfilled its obligations under the United Nations Charter once self-government was attained. That limited obligation was, of course, consistent with the French view of political prospects for French colonies and with Churchill's view that he did not become His Majesty's Prime Minister to preside over the liquidation of the British Empire.

On the other hand, the objectives for trust territories include "independence." This was the compromise reached within the committee working on the drafts at the San Francisco Conference: independence could be left out of the draft on non-self-governing territories, but must be included as a goal for trust territories. Thus, the inclusion of independence as a stated goal for trust territories but not for non-self-governing territories means that the obligations of administrators of trust territories do not cease when self government is attained, but continue until independence if that is appropriate to the circumstances of the particular territory and if the people so desire.

Whatever may have been the view in 1945 about the ultimate political status of dependent peoples, subsequent practice has shown a very definite trend toward independence not just for trust territories but for non-self-governing territories as well. With the exception of Southern Rhodesia and Namibia in southern Africa where race is a deterrent factor, no territory of significant size will remain dependent after 1975. This reflects, in large part, strong pressure for independence from a majority of United Nations members, most of whom were not members of the United Nations when the major Western countries were delineating fine differences between trust and non-self-governing territories.

UNITED NATIONS RESOLUTIONS

It soon became clear that the United Nations had to develop criteria for deciding when a territory was no longer non-self-governing or when and how to terminate trusteeship status. Three resolutions of the United Nations General Assembly contain recommendations regarding the ultimate status of dependent peoples. These are Resolutions 742, 1541, and 1514.

General Assembly Resolution 742 (passed November 27, 1953). Addressed to non-self-governing territories, the resolution reasserts the need to make decisions on the basis of particular circumstances and the wishes of the people concerned. The resolution held that the manner in which a territory could become fully self-governing was "primarily" through the attainment of independence, although it stated that self-government could also be achieved by association or integration with another state or group of states if done freely and on the basis of absolute equality. Resolution 742 was passed, it should be noted, *prior* to the surge of African independence and the admission of African states to the United Nations.

General Assembly Resolution 1541 (passed December 21, 1960). Resolution 1541 is a more precise restatement of Resolution 742 and specifically states principles which should be used in determining when states should cease submitting information because a territory is no longer non-self-governing. A territory is described as having reached "a full measure of self-government" by:

1) *Emergence as a sovereign independent state* (Principle VI).

2) *Free association with an independent state.* Here free association is defined as "the result of a free and voluntary choice ... through informed and democratic processes." The association should respect the individuality and the cultural characteristics of the territory and its peoples and retain for the people of the associated state "the freedom to modify the status of that territory through the expression of their will by democratic means and through constitutional processes." Finally, the people have the right to determine their internal constitution without outside interference (Principle VII).

3) *Integration with an independent state* is to take place on the basis of "complete equality between the peoples of an erstwhile non-self-governing territory and those of the independent country with which it is integrated. The peoples of both territories should have equal status and rights of citizenship and equal guarantees of fundamental rights and freedoms without any distinction or discrimination; both should have equal rights and opportunities for representation and effective participation at all levels in the executive, legislative, and judicial organs of government" (Principle VIII).

In addition, the integrating territory should have attained "an advanced stage of self-government with free political institutions, so that its peoples would have the capacity to make a responsible choice through informed and democratic process." The resolution states that the United Nations could, "when it deems necessary," supervise a plebiscite on integration. The addition of this provision and the provision that people have the right to change their minds if free association were selected would seem to indicate considerable effort by the United Nations to insure that a decision to opt for a status short of independence must be carefully scrutinized by the international community.

The three categories of Resolution 742 and 1541 are frequently illustrated by reference to territories now or once under United States control. The Philippines attained independence; Hawaii and Alaska attained integration as states; and Puerto Rico is frequently cited as an example of free association. In fact, the

United Nations General Assembly specifically exempted the United States from further reporting on Puerto Rico on the grounds of the new "free association." This was, however, prior to either of the resolutions discussed above which define free association and at a time of American dominance in the United Nations.[1] It is unclear what position the United Nations would take today if it decided to reconsider Puerto Rico's status. United States law does not explicitly acknowledge a Puerto Rican right to unilaterally alter its status, i.e., to "opt out," and the United States Congress unilaterally extends United States laws to Puerto Rico. Some United States laws, for example, specifically state that Puerto Rico is a "territory of the United States." These provisions make Puerto Rico fall short of the "free association" status defined in United Nations resolutions.

At one point, in 1953, President Eisenhower, partially to help gain United Nations recognition of Puerto Rico's new status, authorized the United States Representative to the United Nations Henry Cabot Lodge to inform the United Nations that Eisenhower would recommend that Congress grant Puerto Rico independence if the people wished. Eisenhower's pledge, of course, is not binding on his successors any more than on Congress, which under the United States Constitution is solely responsible for United States territories. However, in the final analysis, neither United States laws nor United Nations resolutions but practicality will determine Puerto Rico's status. Puerto Rico is likely to remain associated with the United States so long as Puerto Ricans and Americans are able to maintain a status sufficiently flexible that it meets with the approval of the overwhelming majority of Puerto Rico's population.

While the attitude of today's United Nations toward the United States-Puerto Rico relationship is in doubt, no doubt exists about the United Nations attitude towards the association between the Cook Islands and New Zealand. The Cooks delegated to New Zealand broad responsibility for defense and foreign affairs but exercise complete control over their internal affairs. Moreover, the Cooks have the right to unilaterally declare their independence. This relationship was specifically endorsed by the General Assembly, which added, however, that the United Nations was still available to the Cooks should they wish assistance in changing their status.

A similar relationship exists between the United Kingdom and the West Indies Associated States (WIAS). However, the United Nations refused to endorse the new status of the WIAS and continues to carry the WIAS on the list of non-self-governing territories (United Nations General Assembly Resolution 2357, XXII). This would seem to indicate that the majority of United Nations members have had second thoughts about the status of "free association."

---

[1] Even in 1953, the United Nations vote was far from overwhelming: twenty-six for with sixteen against and eighteen absentions.

General Assembly Resolution 1514 (passed December 14, 1960). Clearly reflecting the influence of newly independent, particularly African, states, Resolution 1514 is specifically made applicable to *all* dependent territories, that is, to trust as well as to non-self-governing territories. The emphasis is on "the right to complete independence" as the ultimate political status. There is no mention of either integration or free association. In its most quoted paragraph the resolution declares:

> Immediate steps shall be taken, in Trust and Non-Self-Governing Territories or all other territories which have not yet attained independence, to transfer all powers to the peoples of those territories, without any conditions or reservations, in accordance with their freely expressed will and desire, without any distinctions as to race, creed or colour, in order to enable them to enjoy complete independence and freedom.

While the equation of self-determination with independence was implicit in Resolution 1514, later United Nations resolutions seem to make the equation explicit, frequently speaking of the right to "self-determination *and* independence." (Emphasis added.)

None of the resolutions discussed above is mandatory since the General Assembly can only recommend. And as noted, two of the resolutions did not address trust territories. However, the United States (which for various reasons abstained on Resolutions 1541 and 1514) has recognized the essential applicability of the resolutions to Micronesia. In fact, American representatives in the Trusteeship Council have repeatedly insisted on keeping open a full range of options on Micronesia's future. Thus, in Trusteeship Council recommendations, the United States has always insisted on reference to Resolution 1541 as offering a full range of choice. Similarly, the United States has consistently opposed reference to Resolution 1514 on the grounds that it would appear to restrict Micronesian choice to independence.

Actually, the United States reluctance to think of Micronesia in terms of independence or under the control of a country other than the United States has been an important element of United States policy since World War II. When the United States submitted the first draft of the Trusteeship Agreement for Micronesia to the Security Council on February 26, 1947, the objectives listed included only the obligation to promote development "toward self-government"; they did not include "independence." The exclusion of "independence" was a glaring omission, especially in light of the decision almost two years earlier to include independence among the objectives for trust territories. Therefore, the Soviet Union moved to add to the agreement the phrase, "self-government or independence as may be appropriate to the particular circumstances of the trust territory and its people and the fully expressed wishes of the peoples concerned," language patterned on Article 76 of the Charter. The United States accepted the addition of "independence," but in a statement remarkably similar to the League of Nations philosophy that inhabitants of some mandated territories could not expect independence, the United States Representative, Ambassador Warren Austin, stated: "The United States feels that it must record its opposition, not to the principle of independence, to which no people could be more consecrated than the people of the United States, but to the thought that it could possibly be achieved within any foreseeable future in this case."

The question of independence as a possible future status for Micronesia was to arise several times in the United States-Micronesian negotiations. One question which arose was whether United States strategic interests per se limited the theoretical alternatives available to Micronesia. In 1973, when the Micronesians suggested discussion of independence, the United States in effect refused to discuss it, pretending ignorance of the meaning of the term. Micronesia could not be independent because of its strategic nature. The United States representative stated: "I should say again, however, that the circumstances which led to the Trust Territory's designation as a strategic trust will continue to exist whatever your future status might be. I cannot imagine, for instance, that my Government would agree to termination of the trusteeship on terms which would in any way threaten the stability in the area and which in the opinion of the United States endanger international peace and security."

The 1973 United Nations Visiting Mission reacted sharply to the refusal of the United States to discuss independence except under prior conditions and to the implication that whatever Micronesia's status the United States had a legitimate security interest by virtue of the original designation of Micronesia as a strategic trust. The following excerpts from the 1973 Visiting Mission Report are relevant:

> In our opinion, it is implicit in the Charter and in the Trusteeship System that the goal is eventual independence unless agreement is reached on some other status acceptable to the people of the Territories concerned through an act of self-determination. Micronesia is no exception to this rule. That being so, if one of the parties concerned wishes to discuss the question of independence as one possible option, the other should be prepared to join in such a discussion. What either party sees as the conditions which should or might apply in an independence situation would naturally emerge from these discussions. There should be no insistence by one on getting an explanation of how the other party sees those conditions, before agreeing in principle to discuss the option.

> Whatever solution is finally adopted, it is important that the basic issues, including the question of which lands, if any, will be retained by the United States as military retention lands, should be settled before the Trusteeship Agreement comes to an end. It may be legitimate to say, as the United States representative did . . . that "the circumstances which led to the Trust Territory's designation as a strategic trust will continue to exist whatever its future status might be." But this is so only in the sense that, because of its geographical location, Micronesia may continue to be of substantial interest to the United States and other Powers. Naturally,

when the Trusteeship Agreement comes to an end, the idea of a strategic zone in the sense used in the Charter vanishes at the same time. The fact that Micronesia was designated a strategic zone under the Trusteeship Agreement does not, in our view, in any sense derogate from the basic objectives of the Trusteeship System.

From the above discussion, it is possible to conclude that, although the world community has indicated a preference for independence, it has not held that independence is the sole legitimate expression of self-determination by a dependent territory. Such a conclusion would seem especially warranted with respect to Micronesia.

In the Micronesian negotiations, the United States accepted a definition of self-determination as "the process by which a people determine their own sovereign status." According to this definition, *either* self-government *or* independence would be possible results of self-determination. The choice selected would seem to depend on the wishes of the people concerned, i.e., the peoples of Micronesia. If this analysis is correct, it would appear the United States was not justified in refusing to discuss independence with the Micronesian negotiators. Actually, the United States has taken both sides of the issue: on the one hand, it says that the Micronesians have a free choice; on the other, it implies and acts as if free choice does not include independence because of strategic factors or because of a belief that Micronesians are not capable of assuming the responsibilities of independence. The latter position clashes sharply with Resolution 1514 which states that "inadequacy of political, economic, social, or educational preparedness should never serve as pretext for delaying independence."

Notwithstanding Resolution 1514, there is a case to be made against independence for Micronesia. One must keep in mind the environment and surrounding circumstances. The islands are widely dispersed; inter-island transportation is extremely difficult; and, indeed in a very real sense, Micronesia is not yet a country, only what one Micronesian has called "a potential country." The lack of a common language, culture, or history for all of Micronesia makes development, and even more basically, communications, very difficult. Finally, except for its strategic location, Micronesia is without known and reliable economic resources.

It is therefore highly possible that upon termination of the Trusteeship Agreement in Micronesia, self-government as opposed to independence will be preferable. Despite a clear preference for independence, United Nations members, even some of the most avid proponents of independence, have suggested that a status short of independence is best for Micronesia, particularly if that is their free choice. There has seemed to be an emphasis, however, on *complete* self-government and on the right of Micronesians to decide—a right even to make the "wrong" choice.

Self-government was not defined in either the drafting of the Charter or the Trusteeship Agreement. However, up to now some standards have been set forth in General Assembly resolutions, specifically Resolution 1541 and, by incorporation, Resolution 742, which state that alternatives to independence are free association or integration with an independent state.

THE PROBLEM OF FRAGMENTATION

In addition to determining the substantive content of self-determination as it applies to Micronesia, there is the question of what "people" in Micronesia may have a legitimate claim to exercise self-determination. This issue arises in the Micronesian context because the United States engaged in two separate sets of negotiations: one set of negotiations with representatives of the Northern Mariana Islands and the other with representatives of the Congress of Micronesia who, however, still included representatives of the Mariana Islands. For reasons discussed in a later chapter, the Mariana Islands sought not only a separate status, but a *different* status: the Marianas prefer to come "permanently" under American sovereignty as a United States territory, as opposed to inclusion with other Micronesians in a "free associated state" which has the right to unilaterally end the association with the United States.

Critics argue that separate negotiations are contrary to the accepted world community definition of the "peoples" entitled to exercise the right to self-determination and are a violation of United Nations principles in support of "territorial integrity." The goal of the United Nations has been to preserve whenever possible the boundaries of states or territories, even when they have been arbitrarily drawn by colonial powers and cut across tribal and ethnic lines. In its *Declaration on Colonialism* (Resolution 1514), the United Nations General Assembly specifically stated: "Any attempt aimed at the partial or total disruption of the national unity and the territorial integrity of a country is incompatible with the purposes and principles of the Charter of the United Nations."

Reactions to separatist movements in Namibia, Kenya, Ethiopia, and Nigeria are evidence that the majority of United Nations member states define "peoples" in a strict sense—limiting the definition to the inhabitants of an already existing state or territory. In fact, much to the discomfort of the United States, the 1973 United Nations Visiting Mission specifically referred to Namibia:

> The United Nations has consistently opposed in principle the fragmentation of dependent Territories on tribal or regional lines. This is exemplified by the case of Namibia. On all other Trust Territories it has recommended that the Administering Authority should emphasize the unity of the country to overcome racial or regional cleavages. In the two instances when Trust Territories were divided, this was done only after a territorial referendum had taken place.

Rosalyn Higgins, in her work, *The Development of International Law Through the Political Organs of the United Nations*, argues that "self-determination refers to the right of the majority within a generally accepted political unit to the exercise of power."[2] Rupert Emerson, in *Self-Determination Revisited in the Era of Decolonization*, argues that "since there are no rational and objective criteria by which a 'people' in the large and abstract can be identified, it [self-determination] introduces an incalculably explosive and disruptive element which is incompatible with the maintenance of a stable and organized society."[3] Thus the principle against fragmentation, as evidenced by the narrow definition of "peoples," provides, said Emerson, "a fixed principle for the orderly succession from colonialism to a system of independent states."[4]

On the other hand, this definition of "peoples" is not universally accepted, and some would define the term in a sociological sense as applicable to a tribe or group of people ethnically bound together. They note that the term "peoples" is nowhere defined in the United Nations Charter and contend that the sociological definition is more compatible with basic human rights concepts. Not surprisingly, this latter definition is favored by the negotiators from the Mariana Islands and now by the United States. Both argue that, if the United Nations were to reject separate negotiations between the United States and the Mariana Islands, it would violate the right of the people of the Marianas to self-determination.

To support their case, the Marianas cite the termination of the Trusteeship Agreement for the British Cameroons. The British Cameroons was divided into two parts for purposes of administration. The Northern Cameroon was administered as an integral part of Nigeria, then a non-self-governing territory. The Southern Cameroon, although also administered as a part of Nigeria, enjoyed greater autonomy as a region with its own political organs. Upon termination of the trust, the two parts were permanently separated, based on a finding of a 1961 United Nations Visiting Mission that there was "a profound difference between them both in the administrative systems and political loyalties which were partly due to a distinct ethnical and historical development." The northern sector became part of Nigeria, and the South achieved independence and became Cameroon.

However, the precedent of the Cameroons is not entirely apposite for the Marianas. First, the division of the Cameroons was made pursuant to the recommendations of a United Nations Visiting Mission report. No such recommendations exist in the case of the Marianas and Micronesia. In fact, United Nations Visiting Missions to Micronesia have spoken strongly against separation in every

---

[2] Rosalyn Higgins, *The Development of International Law Through the Political Organs of the United Nations* (New York: Oxford University Press, 1963), p. 104.

[3] Rupert Emerson, *Self-Determination Revisited in the Era of Decolonization* (Cambridge: Harvard University Press, 1964), p. 63.

[4] *Ibid.*, p. 30.

report since 1961. The 1973 Visiting Mission noted that separate negotiations were in an advanced stage and perhaps the clock could not be turned back. However, as already noted, there is no doubt that the 1973 Visiting Mission did not accept separate negotiations with enthusiasm. Second, in the case of the Cameroons, the part which split off, the Northern Cameroon, united with an adjoining territory to form a newly independent country and indeed had been administered as an integral part of that territory prior to unification. This is not the case with the Mariana Islands. The Marianas have not been administered by the United States as an integral part of Guam, for example; nor are they presently seeking unification with Guam upon termination of the Trusteeship Agreement. Third, the two sections of the British Cameroons were never administered as one entity. On the other hand, except for a brief period, the Marianas have been administered as an integral part of Micronesia.

Moreover, separate negotiations between the Marianas and the United States may have ramifications which transcend the borders of Micronesia. Specifically, they could serve as precedent for other attempts at fragmentation. For instance, Australia's sharp criticism of the separate negotiations in the 1973 sessions of the Trusteeship Council's consideration of Micronesia was attributed by American officials to Australia's concern that the Marianas might serve as precedent for an attempt by Bougainville to separate from Papua-New Guinea (or by Papua to separate from New Guinea). At least one motivating factor is similar: Bougainville, like the Mariana Islands, is the more economically developed and has the greatest foreseeable economic potential. American officials say that Australian opposition was based on the personal views of the Australian representative and did not represent the official views of the Australian government. Australia ceased its open opposition to separate negotiations only after the United States made informal representations (called "informal discussions" by the United States) to the Australian embassy in Washington and the embassy in turn suggested a changed position to Canberra.

South Africa has for some time used arguments similar to those used by the Marianas and the United States to support its policies of fragmentation in Namibia. Ironically, South Africa's primary interest in Namibia may also be for defense purposes. Namibia serves as an important buffer against hostile black countries to the north. Americans resent the comparison to South Africa and argue that South Africa is forcing this arrangement upon the Namibians, while the people of the Marianas have voluntarily expressed their desire for separate negotiations. But there too the American response is not unlike the South African position. Few accept South Africa's case, but that country also argues that separate "nations" are being established in Namibia at the freely expressed request of tribal groups.

The fact is that the American justification for fragmentation in Micronesia is no different from that offered on other fragmentation questions. A case can always be made by some group for separation and the issue becomes whether fragmentation is politically feasible and sometimes militarily desirable. The State Department, concerned with the effect of the separate negotiations and ultimately the separate status as precedent for South Africa, is particularly sensitive to the issue and reacted sharply and indignantly to the United Nations Visiting Mission's comparison with Namibia.

For the Micronesians, the ramifications of separate negotiations are well understood. There is the obvious question of the effect on the remainder of the territory if the area most developed and thought to have the greatest economic potential were allowed to separate. As in Katanga or Biafra or Bougainville, can the interests of one group be allowed to jeopardize the interests of the whole? The United States Representative, Eleanor Roosevelt, addressed the question before the United Nations General Assembly on November 18, 1952.

> Does self-determination mean the right of secession? Does self-determination constitute a right of fragmentation or a justification of fragmentation of nations? Does self-determination mean the right of people to sever association with another power regardless of the economic effect upon both parties, regardless of the effect upon the internal stability and their external security, regardless of the effect upon their neighbors or the international community? Obviously not.

The United States, while rejecting further requests for separate negotiations, has had substantial difficulty justifying separate negotiations with one district but not with others. In 1973, the principal Micronesian negotiator, Lazarus Salii, accurately predicted that other districts would seek separate negotiations with the United States. Proliferation of fragmentation was also the concern of the 1973 Visiting Mission: "No purely ethnic argument can be seriously advanced in support of separation. Of course, the Chamorros are not identical with the inhabitants of the Marshall Islands; nor are the latter the same as the residents of Yap or Ponape. Acceptance of the Mariana Islands argument would mean acceptance of the fragmentation of the territory."

TERMINATION OF THE TRUSTEESHIP AGREEMENT

A significant aspect of the United Nations Trusteeship System is the paucity, one might even say the absence, of provisions regarding the timing of or procedures for termination of trusteeship. At the San Francisco Conference, none of the proposals submitted by the organizing countries contained provisions on termination, although earlier American Charter drafts had specified that the full United Nations membership would in each case "determine the terms and conditions under which the trusteeship shall be altered or terminated." The Egyptian delegate urged the addition of an article on termination of trusteeships, which would have given the General Assembly the power to terminate a trusteeship and "declare the territory to be fit for independence." This provision was not adopted, however, in the face of arguments that termination by decree of the Assembly, without the consent of the administering authorities, would be contrary to the voluntary basis of the trusteeship system.

In place of the Egyptian proposal, one finds in the Charter only the vaguest of references to termination of trusteeships. Article 78 provides that trusteeship cannot apply to territories which have become members of the United Nations, and Article 79 states that the terms of trusteeship, "including any alteration or amendment," shall be agreed upon by the states directly concerned and approved by either the General Assembly or the Security Council. Similarly, under Article 83, the Security Council exercises the functions of the United Nations with respect to strategic areas, "including the approval of the terms of the trusteeship agreements and of their alteration or amendment," and Article 85 provides that the General Assembly, with the assistance of the Trusteeship Council, shall have the same functions concerning nonstrategic areas. Nowhere in the Charter, however, does one find a specific provision for termination of any trusteeship.

A primary reason advanced at San Francisco for not including a specific termination provision in the Charter was that such provisions could be written into the individual trusteeship agreements. In practice only the Trusteeship Agreement for Somaliland and the Trusteeship Agreement for Micronesia contained provisions with direct references to termination. And only Article 24 of the Trusteeship Agreement for Somaliland, which provided that the agreement would cease to be in force ten years after its approval by the General Assembly, specified the process and the timing of termination. In contrast, Article 15 of the Trusteeship Agreement for Micronesia provides simply that the terms shall not be "altered, amended or terminated" without the consent of the United States. There was no provision pertaining to the processes or timing of termination.

At the same time, under Article 76 (b) of the Charter and Article 6 of the Trusteeship Agreement, the United States is required (in the words of Article 6 of the Agreement) to "promote the development of the inhabitants of the trust territory toward self-government or independence, as may be appropriate to the particular circumstances of the trust territory and its peoples and the freely expressed wishes of the peoples concerned." Accordingly, perhaps the first question which should be considered is what procedures should be followed in order to best determine the "wishes of the peoples concerned." Most of the trust territories have achieved independence after the people expressed their wishes in a plebiscite conducted under United Nations auspices.

There is no legal requirement for a plebiscite or for the conduct of a plebiscite under United Nations auspices or observation. However, a plebiscite under

United Nations supervision or observation is usually considered the most acceptable method of politically determining the wishes of the people. In Resolution 1541, the United Nations General Assembly suggested that, in those cases where inhabitants of non-self-governing territories were selecting integration with another state, "the United Nations could, when it deems necessary, supervise these processes." But Resolution 1541 was not addressed to trust territories and is, in any case, recommendatory only; the inclusion of the supervision clause was one of the reasons given for the United States abstention on Resolution 1541.

The United States planned to hold plebiscites in both Micronesia and the Marianas Islands. The question is whether the people will be given a meaningful choice. That is, will the plebiscites be valid as an expression of the wishes of the people if they contain only the alternatives of accepting or rejecting the package presented them by the negotiators? Must independence be included as an alternative choice in either or both plebiscites? Must Micronesia as a whole be given the opportunity of approving or disapproving the separate status of the Marianas?

A choice of simply rejecting a negotiated package or retaining the status quo would seem to be against the interests of both the United States and the Micronesians. United States interests would not be served by retention of the now politically outmoded trusteeship status. United States officials have already seen that delays in settling Micronesia's status have only resulted in an increased political and economic price tag. That price can only be expected to grow with increased Micronesian political sophistication. Moreover, to exclude a choice of options would be inconsistent with numerous United States statements about the right of people to make a free and informed choice. It is also inconsistent with United States support for the essential provisions of the United Nations Resolutions 1541 and 742. The latter states that one factor by which self-government is measured is the "freedom of choosing on the basis of the right of self-determination of peoples between several possibilities, including independence."

A more crucial issue is whether the whole of Micronesia need approve a separate status for the Marianas. Negotiations with the Marianas were opposed by the Congress of Micronesia. In the spring of 1973, the Congress of Micronesia announced that its Joint Committee on Future Status was the sole official negotiating body. The issue arises whether the United States is entitled to continue negotiations affecting part of the territory in the face of the express disapproval of representatives of the majority of the people of the territory and as to whether an option for a wholly united Micronesia (including the Mariana Islands) must be included in either or both plebiscites, or even whether two separate plebiscites should be held.

In the final analysis, the issue is political rather than legal. Despite international sentiment against fragmentation and the opposition of the Congress of Micronesia, the United States has not wavered from its decision to negotiate with the Marianas. At one point, the United States was even prepared to take the drastic step of rewriting the Interior Secretarial Order creating the Micronesian legislature to exclude the Marianas and thus eliminate the legal basis for objections by the Micronesian Congress. Such an action, however, would undoubtedly have resulted in a storm of protest, albeit of little effect, from Micronesia.

An important procedural issue is the role, if any, of the United Nations in terminating the Trusteeship Agreement. Specifically, should the United Nations be involved in the negotiations? Should the plebiscite be supervised by the United Nations? Most important, must the United States get the approval of the Security Council in terminating the Trusteeship Agreement?

There are no requirements in the Charter, the Trusteeship Agreement or general customary international law that the United Nations participate in negotiations on termination of trusteeship. In practice, however, the United Nations has participated in the termination of other trusteeships, directly or indirectly, through visiting missions, consultations, and the supervision of plebiscites. Some United Nations members have suggested that the United States has not given sufficient attention to United Nations suggestions with respect to Micronesia, thus downgrading United Nations participation.

Although not legally required, United Nations supervision of plebiscites in trust territories seems highly advisable from a political point of view where, as here, the results of the plebiscites are likely to be unpopular with many members of the United Nations.

Perhaps the most important procedural question facing the United States is whether approval of the Security Council is necessary in order to terminate the Trusteeship Agreement. There is ample evidence to indicate that Security Council approval is desirable for political purposes. The counsel for the Joint Committee on Future Status of the Congress of Micronesia has suggested that the United States is not legally required to seek Security Council approval of termination. A measure of support for this view may be found in the terms of the Charter and of the Trusteeship Agreement and in the negotiating history of the agreement. Article 83 (1) of the Charter, in referring to the functions of the Security Council concerning strategic areas, specifies only that Security Council approval is required for the alteration or amendment of the Trusteeship Agreement. No reference is made to the necessity of Security Council approval for termination of the agreement, Article 15 of the Trusteeship Agreement requires the consent of the United States, as administering authority, to any alteration, amendment, or termination of the agreement, but makes no reference to the

Security Council. Moreover, in the Security Council debates on this provision the United States absolutely refused to consider a proposed Soviet amendment making the alteration, amendment, or discontinuation of the agreement's terms subject to the decision of the Security Council, rather than the administering authority, and even threatened to withdraw the proposed agreement if such an amendment were adopted.

However, a close reading of the drafting history of Article 15 leads one to question the correctness of the view that Security Council approval is not required for termination. Although it rejected the Soviet amendment, in response the United States submitted a text which would have provided that the terms of the agreement "shall not be altered, amended, or terminated except by agreement of the administering authority and the Security Council." This was unacceptable to the Soviet Union, and it was accordingly withdrawn. Nonetheless, it reflected an understanding on the part of the United States that the approval of the Security Council would be required for termination of the Trusteeship Agreement. Moreover, at the same meeting of the Council, the United States Representative Warren Austin said, "The United States wishes to record its view that the draft trusteeship agreement is in the nature of a bilateral contract between the United States on the one hand and the Security Council on the other." As a bilateral contract, he added, the Trusteeship Agreement could not be amended or terminated without the approval of the Security Council.

A further argument which may be advanced in support of a United States obligation to obtain Security Council approval for termination is that the terms "alteration and amendment," found in both Article 83 and Article 85 of the Charter, are expansive enough to encompass termination of a trusteeship agreement as well. In United Nations practice, all nine administering authorities of territories formerly under trusteeship sought and received United Nations approval of termination of the Trusteeship Agreement. While Article 85 related only to nonstrategic trusts, its language on alteration or amendment of trusteeship agreements is identical to that found in Article 83 with respect to strategic trusts.

On balance, then, the language of the Charter, procedures followed in the termination of other trusteeships, and explicit recognition by the United States of a United Nations role in the termination process support a conclusion that the United States has a legal duty to obtain Security Council approval for termination of the Trusteeship Agreement. The position of American officials on the matter, however, seems to be that the extent of the United States obligation is only to *submit* the question of termination to the Security Council and does *not* include any requirement to secure the Council's approval of termination of the trusteeship. According to this view, even if the Security Council should fail to approve a United States proposal, the United States, having discharged its obligation by submission of the proposal to the Council, would be free to carry out termination despite the Council's lack of approval.

It has been suggested that, if it appears that the Security Council might reject the United States proposal for termination, the United States might attempt to avoid a confrontation in the Security Council, either by gaining the approval of the Trusteeship Council[5] and forwarding that result to the Security Council, or by merely informing the Security Council of the results of an act of self-determination and stating that accordingly the United States considers the agreement terminated. The United States could then veto any resolution which affirmed continuation of the Trusteeship Agreement. This procedure would presumably avoid a situation where a veto would block any affirmative action by the Security Council approving termination. But it is doubtful that the procedure is politically feasible or legally correct.

The need for Security Council approval for alteration or termination of the Trusteeship Agreement would also seem to indicate that, whatever decisions are made on separate acts of self-determination, the present Trusteeship Agreement will apply to the whole of Micronesia until the agreement is terminated for all of Micronesia. Even though the Mariana Islands, for example, have opted for a separate relationship with the United States, the Trusteeship Agreement would continue to apply to the Mariana Islands as well as to those portions of Micronesia which have not reached a decision. The United States can administer the Mariana Islands separately, and plans to do so, but still under trusteeship. Any effort to exclude the Mariana Islands from provisions under the Trusteeship Agreement would require an alteration of the Trusteeship Agreement and Security Council approval. In recognition of this and because to do otherwise would be of questionable political wisdom, the United States at this juncture has decided not to seek Security Council approval of any action until *all* of Micronesia has made a decision on status.

At any rate, the United States expects to avoid such problems by gaining the approval of the Security Council of any plan it may submit for termination. To this end, United States officials are relying on the spirit of détente with the Soviet Union. That spirit was clearly noticeable in the sharply reduced Soviet criticism of United States administration of Micronesia just before and since Nixon's visit to Moscow. United States officials are also relying on a continuation of the relatively mild temperament so far displayed by the People's Repub-

---

[5]There is no veto in the six-member Trusteeship Council and the votes of the United States, France, the United Kingdom, and Australia would assure majority approval even if the other two members, China and the Soviet Union, opposed. The opposition is more likely to be limited to the Soviets since the People's Republic of China does not participate in Trusteeship Council meetings, ostensibly because of a shortage of personnel but probably because the moderate Trusteeship Council does not fit into China's anticolonial image.

lic of China in the United Nations. Some officials calculate that the severe tensions between the People's Republic of China and the Soviet Union will lead those powers to conclude that it is more in their interest to have the United States occupy this strategic area rather than either of them or Japan.

The possible reaction and role of the United Nations has turned out to be secondary in negotiations on terminating Micronesia's trusteeship status. The United States, of course, has continued to report annually to the United Nations Trusteeship Council and, periodically, to submit documents on the negotiations. But these reports have been just that—*reports*, not a means of seeking or accepting United Nations advice. The State Department itself has downgraded United Nations interests in Micronesian affairs. The Bureau of International Organization Affairs (IO), which had been primarily responsible for State's policy on Micronesia, was relieved of its task and the Bureau of East Asian Affairs made responsible. The reason given was that Micronesia was a regional matter and that the move would take advantage of the experience of John Dorrance, the State Department officer who had been assigned to Micronesia to work on status questions and who was later assigned to the East Asian Bureau. However, that was only a cover, especially since Dorrance had once been in IO and State Department officers are routinely assigned to the bureau which needs their expertise. The real reason for the shift was a sharp personality clash between the Chief United States Negotiator and a Deputy Assistant Secretary in IO. Personnel in IO learned of the move when told by the Undersecretary of State that it had been ordered.

Whatever the explanation, the result was to decrease emphasis in State on the United Nations aspects of Micronesia's status and to treat the question as a bilateral political matter. The trend was increased once negotiations began with the Marianas. After the first two rounds, State Department personnel were dropped from the United States team negotiating with the Marianas on the grounds that the Marianas were negotiating a domestic relationship. State again became involved in the Marianas question to work out provisions for United Nations observation of the plebiscite. Even then, State Department involvement was late, for the Marianas Covenant was signed in mid-February, 1975, and the United Nations Trusteeship Council, which did not normally meet until May, was asked to observe a plebiscite in mid-June. There was little opportunity to assess again the place of the Marianas in the self-determination of Micronesia as a whole—even if the Trusteeship Council was so inclined, which it was not. In fact, the major consideration seems to have been whether the representative of one of the Council's permanent members could get to and from the Marianas in time for the weddings of his daughters.

Even at the ceremony where the Marianas Covenant was signed, the role of the United Nations was downplayed to observation of the plebiscite. When the

United States Representative outlined the ten steps remaining before the "final chapter" of the Marianas Commonwealth was written, there was no mention of the need for the United Nations Security Council to agree to termination of the Trusteeship Agreement. On the contrary, the tenth step, "Proclamation by the President of the United States that the Trusteeship has been terminated," leaves the implication that the United States may indeed look upon termination as a unilateral act. The implication is similar to that contained in the Solomon Report. Then, as now, the implication that the United States might act unilaterally brought strong objections from the State Department, particularly the United States Mission to the United Nations.

Actually, the omission of further reference to the United Nations was quite deliberate. The Marianas representatives have sought to de-emphasize the United Nations largely because of fear that the United Nations might derail the Commonwealth as a result of its opposition to fragmentation. But the Marianas view coincided with the personal views of Chief United States Negotiator Haydn Williams who, according to several Interior and State Department sources, held the United Nations in extremely low regard. Williams, said one official, had "this thing" about the United Nations.

For the Micronesians, the international legal factors which govern self-determination were to prove far less important than the practical realities of international politics.

*What right does a small number of people
have to shape the destiny of the world?*

—A high-ranking military officer

*We fought for them, we've got them,
we should keep them. They are necessary
for our safety. I see no other course.*

—F. Edward Hébert

IV

The Military
And Micronesia

Most young Americans probably don't know very much about Micronesia, except that it is "somewhere in the Pacific." But thousands of American men fought and died in Micronesia and surrounding waters in World War II. Mention Kwajalein, Ulithi, Saipan, and Peleliu and you are likely to waken the memories of millions of Americans who by newsreel, radio and newspaper followed the advance of American forces across the Pacific toward Japan after that country launched a surprise attack against Pearl Harbor from Kwajalein in the Marshall Islands, one of the eastern-most atolls in what were then referred to as "the islands of mystery."

Between the spring of 1942 and the fall of 1944, American forces struggled for control of Micronesia. Some of the island fortresses erected by Japan in violation of its obligations under the League of Nations Mandate were attacked directly; others were bypassed, leaving their Japanese defenders helpless, cut off from food and new supplies, and, more importantly, in no position to assist Japanese forces elsewhere. Before the Micronesian campaign was over, American forces had engaged in some of the costliest battles of the war. At Saipan, 3,272 Americans died and another 10,952 were wounded. The battle at Peleliu lasted ten weeks and left 1,864 dead and 6,459 wounded. The battle for Kwajalein was briefer and less costly—still, 372 died and 1,582 were wounded. Tinian cost 389 dead and 1,816 wounded; Eniwetok, 195 dead and 521 wounded. All told, 6,288 Americans died and 22,810 were wounded in Micronesia. Japanese casualties were, of course, even heavier. More than 5,000 Japanese died on Tinian alone. An additional 3,000 were unaccounted for; many had committed suicide rather than be captured. And there were the Micronesians, innocent victims who little understood why a battle was being fought on their islands. Five thousand died, or 10 per cent of a Micronesian population estimated at 50,000.

Micronesia's capture did not end its role in the war. Ulithi, which in the *National Geographic* is noteworthy largely for the cultural oddity of bare-breasted women riding Honda motorbikes, became an important naval base at which the force was assembled for the eventual invasion of Okinawa. Peleliu, Angaur, Saipan and Tinian became important naval and air bases.

By far the most important bases were those on Saipan and Tinian. On Saipan the military built two large airfields, Kobler and Isley, both capable of handling B-29's, as well as facilities for servicing naval and air forces. Tinian became the world's largest airfield; even by modern standards it was formidable. Tinian's North Field had four parallel runways, each 8,500 feet long. West Field had two 8,500-foot runways and a 6,000-foot runway. In addition, there were smaller runways, some as long as 4,700 feet. By way of contrast, runway requirements for today's C5A's and B-52's are 8,800 feet and 10,000 feet, respectively.

To support the armada of B-29's and personnel stationed at Tinian, thirty-four miles of new paved roads were constructed (including a dual-laned highway named "Broadway"). Thirty-five miles of road previously built by the Japanese were radically improved. In addition, a huge breakwater was built at the harbor to accommodate scores of ships laden with supplies, bombs, and other ammunition. Almost 200,000 men were stationed on Tinian alone. That was the number needed to support the 29,000 missions which B-29's flew from Tinian to Japan.

The hustle and bustle that was Tinian base is no more. Fewer than 1,000 Micronesians live where thousands of soldiers once worked feverishly. The only significant structures remaining from the war are the building which served as headquarters for General Curtis Le May and a bombed and shelled building used by the Japanese for communications but used today as a place to slaughter the cattle which graze among Tinian's deserted runways and roads.

From a military point of view, Tinian was built to last. Even now, thirty years after the war, Tinian's coral runways can clearly be seen from the air and are in remarkable condition, although the jungle threatens from all sides and some tangen-tangen trees have managed to take root. Even today Tinian probably has more miles of paved roads than the other islands of Micronesia combined. Tinian stands as mute testimony that those who built it as a military stronghold anticipated the island's heavy use in a prolonged assault on Japan itself. Tinian's builders obviously did not know, or if they knew, did not place much faith in the bomb which on August 6, 1945, was loaded on a Tinian-based B-29, the Enola Gay, and a few hours later rained terror over Hiroshima. Tinian's builders probably would not have believe that on August 10, 1945, one day after the flight of another Tinian-based B-29, Japan would sue for peace and World War II would come to an end.

The unexpectedly sudden defeat of Japan and the rapid demobilization of American forces had an immediate effect on Micronesia. Japan's military fortifications and Japan's war machinery lay in ruins. Japan's fleet, bottled up in the picturesque Truk lagoon, lay on the lagoon floor—virtually ignored for twenty-five years until the 1970's when, with the introduction of jet transportation to the territory, the sunken fleet became an attraction for touring scuba divers. Few military buildings survived: among them fortress-like communications buildings at Truk, Palau and Tinian which, though obviously heavily bombed, are today used as a high school, an airport check-in terminal, and slaughter house.

Japanese civilian structures were also devastated. Today a few buildings, Japanese lanterns (particularly on Koror in Palau), retaining walls, and hospital and prison ruins at Saipan are all that remain of the thriving cities the Japanese built in Micronesia for Japanese settlers. Many of these structures fell before the islands were secured, but particularly in Palau, where Shinto shrines were evidence of Japanese influence, many buildings were needlessly destroyed by American forces after the islands were secured. One old Micronesian hand who served in the naval government tells of deliberate orders by a well-intentioned United States military officer to destroy buildings in Palau simply because they were Japanese built. "We're going to tear this stuff down and show the Micronesians what the Americans can build," the officer is quoted as saying. He may indeed have thought that the United States would institute a massive rehabilitation program, but the opposite was to be true. The Japanese settler economy lay in ruins, and Japanese citizens were repatriated to Japan and Okinawa. In the rush to demobilize, even the mighty base at Tinian was dismantled. Scrap metal, the debris of war, became Micronesia's second most important export.

Once the war was over, Micronesia, which had been a dependent of Japan under the League of Nations, became a dependent of the United States under the United Nations.

In 1945, the American military wanted to have hard-won Micronesia placed under American sovereignty but was bitterly opposed by the Department of State. However, the United States did gain virtually unlimited use of Micronesia for military purposes with the establishment of a strategic trust—the compromise that postponed the issue of annexation.

State, joined by the Department of the Interior, was critical also of the idea of military administration of civilian populations and fought hard against the formal assignment of Micronesia to the Navy in 1947. There were even proposals for administration by the State Department. In the end, Navy got the assignment, largely because they had been put in charge of American Samoa and Guam already and had been administering Micronesia since the end of the war.

Navy's initial victory was not to last long. President Truman was committed to civilian administration, and in 1950 and 1951 he transferred first Guam and then American Samoa from Navy to Interior. Effective July 1, 1951, he did the same for Micronesia. However, part of the transfer of Micronesia to Interior was also short-lived. Navy pulled an end-run and succeeded in breaking off part of the Marianas. Ruth Van Cleve provided the following account of the Navy's victory.

Sometime between June 29, 1951, when President Truman signed the order transferring all of the Trust Territory to Interior, and November 10, 1952, there was perpetrated, in the hyperbolic language of former Director of the Office of Territories James P. Davis, "the worst end run in the history of the United States Government." It is alleged that the Navy, smarting under its loss of jurisdiction in Guam, Samoa, and the Trust Territory, importuned President Truman privately, specifically through the persuasive Admiral Arthur W. Radford, to transfer back to the Navy the northern Marianas islands of Saipan and Tinian. Following whatever prompting, President Truman did on November 10, 1952, transfer Saipan and Tinian back to the Navy, and the interested Interior officials first learned of it when they read the executive order the next day in the *Federal Register.*[1]

The precise reason for the continuation of miliary rule in the Marianas was not announced at the time, nor has it been since. But it is now known that there was a $28 million CIA base on the island of Saipan. This base was used between 1951 and 1962 for training Chinese nationalists who still believed Chiang Kai-shek's forces would recapture the mainland and, reportedly, later for training Vietnam advisors. Although official confirmation of it can be found in the Pentagon Papers, the CIA's Saipan operation was originally one of the items which the United States government sought to censor through court order from the book *CIA and the Cult of Intelligence* (New York: Knopf, 1974) by Victor Marchetti and John Marks, former employees of the CIA and of the State Department.

For Micronesians, the establishment and subsequent abandonment of the CIA facilities was to have far-reaching effects. First, the Marianas were separated off with definite economic advantages and henceforth would press for separation from the remainder of Micronesia. Second, the existence of the clandestine facility meant restricting entry into the Marianas area, except Rota, for "security reasons." Restricting entry into the Marianas, in effect, meant closing Micronesia, for the Marianas were Micronesia's port of entry, its most immediate link to the outside. Under these circumstances, efforts at economic development through tourism there or elsewhere were hamstrung. The CIA's departure in 1962 had even larger effects. The Trust Territory government, which had previously been based outside of Micronesia in Hawaii and later on in Guam, looked upon the newly abandoned facilities as a cheap, in fact free, and ready-made location for "interim" headquarters and a response, albeit not ideal, to the United Nations recommendations that government headquarters be moved to Micronesia proper.

But this windfall had a number of unfortunate effects for Micronesia, most of which could have and should have been foreseen. First, a more centrally located capital—Truk was the planned site—would have been a major force for unity. A central location would have meant shorter lines of communication, more frequent travel to the capital by residents of the districts, and the advantages of education and development in the heart of Micronesia. However, the location of the capital in an area geographically close to the American territory of Guam with its military-inflated economy and the concentration of still more of the advantages of development in Saipan increased the tendency of the people of the Marianas to wish to reintegrate with their fellow Chamorros on Guam and to

---

[1] Ruth G. Van Cleve, *The Office of Territorial Affairs* (New York: Praeger, 1974), p. 10.

think of themselves as better than other Micronesians. "Better off" would be a more accurate description. Except for the nearly abandoned roads on Tinian, Saipan has Micronesia's best roads, schools, communications, shipping, commerce and transportation. And its people, even more than in the rest of Micronesia, learned that the best jobs—those held by Americans—were white collar, or at least government jobs, whose availability at headquarters was plentiful. In such circumstances agriculture was de-emphasized and an artificial and expensive economic structure was substituted.

In the forties and fifties, Micronesia was no longer important to the military except to deny the area to other powers, to conduct weapons tests, and to hold for future contingency purposes. These objectives were achieved without the erection of a single base and without the stationing of either naval vessels or armed personnel, except Coast Guard personnel stationed at Long Range Radio Aid to Navigators (LORAN) stations, and the few personnel assigned to testing facilities. There were not even enough Coast Guard personnel to catch more than a few of the Korean, Okinawan, and Japanese fishing vessels which frequently intruded into Micronesian territorial waters.

NUCLEAR TESTING: BIKINI AND ENIWETOK

Ironically, the nuclear device which ended Micronesia's role in the war was later to return Micronesia to the world's headlines. Bikini and Eniwetok Atolls became important United States atomic bomb test sites, necessitating the relocation in 1946 of 166 people from Bikini and in 1947 of 146 from Eniwetok. Some of the people were relocated several times as successive locations proved undesirable. The people of Bikini lagoon first moved to Rongerik where they suffered from severe shortages of food and water, then to a Kwajalein camp, and finally to the island of Kili—from thirty-six islands with over two square miles and a tranquil lagoon to a single island located 475 miles south with less than one-half square mile of land and no lagoon. For Micronesian fishermen, the new location meant an unaccustomed struggle with the pounding waves of the Pacific in order to get the fish which were an essential part of their diet. They became increasingly dependent on supplies brought by Trust Territory ships which, however, could not approach the island four months of the year because of high wind and waves.

Testing in Bikini ended in 1958 and all atmospheric nuclear testing was banned by the Nuclear Test Ban Treaty of 1963. Although the Bikini people longed to return to their homes, Defense retained the islands for some unspecified use. However, it was not until 1968 that State, Interior and the Atomic Energy Commission overcame Defense objections and announced that the Bikini people, now numbering 750, would be returned after the necessary rehabilitation of the islands had been completed.

The rehabilitation of Bikini was an extensive undertaking. The entire island was bulldozed to reduce radiation, debris was removed, and old coconut trees were destroyed. Almost 90,000 new coconut trees were planted and construction was started on forty of eighty planned homes and supporting public facilities. Some things could not be rehabilitated. One of Bikini's twenty-seven islands had been completely destroyed by a 1950 hydrogen bomb test and a large portion of the reef destroyed, thus permitting the entrance of sharks to the once tranquil lagoon. And crabs remained too "hot" to eat safely.

The construction of housing ran into difficulties. Funds ran out after the completion of only forty homes and the return of only three families. The people became concerned about the level of radioactivity of the islands and, most important, held out for additional financial payments for having moved in the first place. In mid-1975, Bikini was still inhabited by only three Bikini families and by Marshallese construction workers whose principal job is to keep the buildings in good repair.

In 1972, it was announced that Eniwetok, now two islands smaller as a result of forty-three nuclear tests, could also be returned to its former residents—at the end of 1973, the announcement said. As it turned out, Defense had further plans for Eniwetok. According to newspaper reports, the United States Air Force initiated, in April of 1972, a series of TNT explosions designed to simulate the effect of hydrogen bomb explosions on land. These explosions left craters of up to 50 feet deep and 300 feet around. Government sources described the tests as aiding in the effort to better understand the geology of nuclear craters and coral atolls. No mention was made of the permanent damage which would result. Fortunately, Micronesia was saved from further damage when a Federal District judge in Hawaii, issued a temporary and then permanent injunction against the planned tests for environmental reasons. However, the judge's order was too late for Aumon Atoll where, the test director admitted, an excavation 6 feet deep covering 19 acres was left in Micronesia's scarcest resource: land.

The plan to return the people of Eniwetok ran into an additional snag. The cost of rehabilitating the island was estimated at $40 million in 1972, but a Defense Department request for an initial $4 million was turned down when a majority of the membership of a subcommittee on appropriations questioned spending $40 million on 450 "natives." Thus, no work has begun on the rehabilitation of Eniwetok, although the islanders, assisted by Micronesian legal services lawyers, continue to press their case.

Such destruction of land and relocation of people wasn't the only undesirable effect of post-World War II military operations. In a 1954 hydrogen bomb test, eighty-six Micronesians on Rongelap were caught in a storm of radioactive fallout after a sudden wind blew clouds in their direction. The people of Rongelap have since received $10,494 each in compensation from the United States government. In addition, the Rongelapese have received constant and excellent health care from United States scientists. On the other hand, the United States made an ex gratia payment of $2.3 million to Japan for the twenty-three Japanese fishermen caught in the same incident. Micronesians are quick to note that the amount given to Japan was approximately $100,000 for each fisherman.

KWAJALEIN ATOLL

Kwajalein Atoll, also in the Marshalls, was to feel the far-reaching effect of military operations again, this time under the guise of a "civilian" contractor. While the rest of Micronesia was struggling on a budget of less than $10 million, a large part of which was used to cover the salaries of American administrators, the Pentagon decided in 1947 to construct what eventually became a billion dollar missile test facility on Kwajalein Atoll. From the Vandenburg Air Force Base in California, missiles are fired 5,000 miles across the Pacific to impact or be "intercepted" by Spartan and Sprint missiles in and over Kwajalein, the world's largest atoll. Kwajalein is an important facility, as attested by the presence of Soviet "fishing" vessels on test days. "We know when a test has been called off and it's safe to go fishing," said one Micronesian official. "All we have to do is watch the Soviet ships. They get their word from their 'fishing boats' off California even before Kwajalein."

For Micronesians, the Kwajalein test facility brought mixed blessings. At least 148 islanders were forced to relocate to nearby Ebeye Island. Seventeen years later, the military "leased" the island for ninety-nine years at the rate of $10 per year. But Micronesians didn't think much of that agreement after they saw what was done to the island and became more knowledgeable about the monetary value of their land. A renegotiation of the lease in 1970 resulted in payments of $420,000 per year, with possible further renegotiation later. It is a standard joke among American military men that they have already purchased the land several times.

There are usually fewer than twenty or thirty United States military personnel stationed on Kwajalein. The facility, which is run by a civilian contractor, has had as many as 5,000 other American employees, including dependents. For the American contract employees, all the amenities for American expatriates are present, including air-conditioned housing, movies, a golf course, and shopping and laundering facilities. But Kwajalein also has all the attributes of a military base, with the usual resulting tensions. Kwajalein is off-limits to Micronesians outside working hours. Micronesians are ferried in and out to perform unskilled labor. They claim (and American officials deny) they are searched each way and that the unfortunate Micronesian who misses the last ferry is locked up for the night. The Micronesians may stare at but not use the golf course or self-service laundry. The PX is a problem, as it is worldwide. Except for one day of the year, the day they receive their annual bonus, Micronesians are prevented from shopping in Kwajalein's well-stocked PX. Even though the stores on Ebeye suffer serious shortages as a result of poor cargo ship service to Ebeye, Defense officials argue, with some justification, that Micronesian merchants would complain if Micronesians were accorded regular access to the PX.

The United States military has built houses to replace the shanties initially built on Ebeye. Miraculously, there has been no new major disease such as polio, which left 196 crippled and 11 dead when it spread from Ebeye to the rest of the Marshalls in 1963. However, all agree that Ebeye is an overcrowded and disgusting slum right in the middle of "paradise." Lamented one American official, "The stench is so bad you can hardly walk the street."

Micronesians are lured to Ebeye by the possibility of high wages and, so far, steady employment. At the behest of Congresswoman Patsy Mink of Hawaii, Congress extended federal minimum wage legislation to Kwajalein, mostly to help the large number of Hawaiian laborers. Only about 500 Micronesians are employed on Kwajalein, but the number of people per Ebeye household grows steadily as more and more Micronesians abandon outer island life and head for Ebeye to live with relatives. Today, almost 8,000 people, one-third of the entire population of the Marshalls, live on Ebeye. Problems of overcrowding, pollution, juvenile delinquency—all the problems of decayed urban communities—are multiplying there at an astounding rate.

These problems and the restrictions on Micronesians seem to be fully recognized at district and Trust Territory headquarters. A significant exception in early 1974 was the Trust Territory government liaison representative for Ebeye, a long-time American employee who lived and worked amid the comforts of Kwajalein and who, all sources agreed, had overstayed his time. "Things are going very well here," he told an interviewer. "And there is none of the friction and resentment of restrictions to which United Nations Visiting Missions have referred." Only minutes before, a highly regarded Micronesian, being trained for the liaison position, and who, as a result, has become the only Micronesian who lives on Kwajalein, had painted a starkly opposite picture. Early in 1975, the Micronesian "trainee" was still waiting to assume his post.

Micronesians have also benefited from the Kwajalein installation. A tax of 3 per cent on all salaries goes into the Trust Territory coffer. As in the Marianas, the irony is that the presence of an income-producing facility in economically poor Micronesia also has a detrimental effect. The people in the Marshall Islands, the island chain and political district in which Kwajalein is located, believe that a larger share of revenues generated at Kwajalein should be kept by the Marshall Islands district and not sent to the general treasury at Saipan—a kind of revenue sharing. Unless this is done, the Marshallese, who also produce more than 50 per cent of Micronesia's major export, copra, have threatened to withdraw from Micronesia. Their threat remains even though a level of revenue sharing was approved by the Congress of Micronesia in 1974. But an economy based on the Kwajalein missile range may prove to be short-lived, or, at best, uncertain. Although Kwajalein is designated by the United States as one of the areas which would remain under United States control in a self-governing Micronesia, there are rumors that successful Strategic Arms Limitations Talks (SALT) would seriously affect the scope of activities at Kwajalein and therefore Micronesian employment opportunities. Such rumors are, however, denied by the military, who state that a SALT agreement would not prohibit research and development. But employment at Kwajalein can be expected to vary sharply. For example, it is estimated that the conclusion of Safeguard testing would reduce the United States population at Kwajalein to below 3,000, down sharply from the 1970 population of 5,000.

CHANGING UNITED STATES POLICY: FROM DENIAL TO USAGE

The administration of John F. Kennedy saw the end of the caretaker philosophy followed by the United States in Micronesia between 1945 and 1961. A new policy was formulated to assist in the transition of the Trust Territory from its international status to the status of a territory under United States sovereignty. Interestingly, though there were numerous studies of future United States base requirements and Micronesia always appeared in the list of contingencies, throughout the Kennedy and Johnson administrations, no concrete base plans were developed for Micronesia.

Beginning in the late 1960's, shifting power relationships in East Asia caused the United States to reassess its approach to a changing Asia. The most important aspect of the present focus on Asia was set forth in the so-called Nixon Doctrine in July, 1969. As summarized in a report of the Secretary of State, Nixon stated:

> The United States will keep all its treaty commitments. We shall provide a shield if a nuclear power threatens the freedom of a nation allied with us or of a nation whose survival we consider vital to our security and the security of the region as a whole. In cases involving other types of aggression we shall furnish military aid and economic assistance when requested and as appropriate. But we shall look to the nation directly threatened to assume the primary responsibility of providing the manpower for its defense.

The Nixon approach did not declare United States military withdrawal from Asia. It did provide a rationale for reducing the size, number, and role of United States military installations in Vietnam, Thailand, Korea, Japan and the Philippines. Nixon made no mention of establishing bases in Micronesia, even though he outlined his plans during a refueling stop on Guam; nor was the Nixon Doctrine drafted to "fit" the Trust Territory. But the military quickly cited the President's statement as justification for activation of then vague contingency plans for Micronesia. In the minds of most Department of Defense officials interviewed, United States troop reduction in Asia makes Micronesia more strategically important to United States security.

Micronesia also fit well into the philosophy, first apparent in the early sixties, that United States military bases would be moved to island areas if, as seemed likely, increasing nationalism made the continued presence of bases untenable in some countries. Planning for a base at Diego Garcia in the Indian Ocean started in 1963 on just such a hypothesis. The theory was that isolated islands with small or no populations and limited resources would be less subject to adverse political movements and would not automatically involve the United States in another nation's conflicts. Similarly, when it first appeared that United States bases and unfettered operations in Okinawa might be imperiled by the reversion of Okinawa to Japan, and, at the same time, nationalist sentiment rose in the Philippines, potential Micronesian bases took on a more concrete form in strategic planning.

In 1969, when the United States first began negotiations for use of Micronesian land, the military sought maximum flexibility in its planning. It refused to indicate specific land areas it might use and insisted on an unlimited right to eminent domain even in the face of known and steadfast opposition in Micronesia. Not until it was clear that no progress on status could be made without a clear indication of military land needs did the Departments of State and the Interior prevail upon Defense to submit its land requirements to an interagency body of the National Security Council. By this time, however, the military had been reassured that bases in Okinawa were not immediately imperiled.

STATED MILITARY REQUIREMENTS FOR THE 1970's

An analysis of United States efforts to acquire additional military facilities in Micronesia will be discussed in a chapter devoted entirely to the status negotiations. However, it is necessary at this point to discuss the specific, initially stated requirements of the United States military in assessing the strategic importance of Micronesia. The qualification "initial" is important because essential military needs for the United States proved to be flexibile in a downward direction. The

United States gave its general requirements during the third round of negotiations and later outlined more specific requirements, first for five districts and then for the Marianas.

In the Draft Compact of Free Association first issued in August, 1962, the United States and Micronesia (excluding the Marianas) agreed that the United States should hold "full responsibility for, and authority over all matters which relate to defense in Micronesia." This responsibility included the defense of Micronesia and "the right to prevent third parties from using the territory of Micronesia for military purposes." More generally, the United States would be allowed to establish military bases on Micronesia for "the security of the United States, and to support its responsibilities for the maintenance of international peace and security." The parties also agreed that the United States could conduct "all activities and operations on the lands and waters in the territory of Micronesia in the exercise of this responsibility and authority." The last general agreement between the United States and Micronesia would give the United States the option to request the use of Trust Territory areas to satisfy future defense requirements.

Annexed to the Draft Compact was an outline of specific defense needs in Micronesia. The United States wished to maintain "continuing rights to occasional or emergency use of all harbors, waters and airfields throughout Micronesia," as well as "continuing rights to use existing Coast Guard facilities."

In the Marshall Islands, the United States specifically asked for "continuing rights for the use of lands and waters associated with, and currently controlled as part of the Kwajalein Missile Range, the land portion of which encompasses approximately 1,320 acres." In the Bikini Atoll, the United States sought "continuing rights for use of 1.91 acres of Ourukaen and Eniman Islets, and the use of the pier, airfield and boat landing on Eneu Island." Finally, upon the return of Eniwetok Atoll to the Micronesians, the United States sought to retain use rights there.

In the Palau Islands, the United States sought "access and anchorage rights in Malakal Harbor and adjacent waters, together with the rights to acquire forty acres for use within the Malakal Harbor area which is composed of submerged land to be filled, and adjacent fast land." The United States asked for rights for "the joint use of an airfield capable of supporting military jet aircraft (the proposed airfield at Barreru Island reef, or Babelthuap airfield—Airai site), the right to improve that airfield to meet military requirements and specifications, and the right to develop an exclusive use area for aircraft parking, maintenance and operational support facilities." On the island of Babelthuap, the United States wished to reserve the "right to acquire 2,000 acres for exclusive use, along with the right for non-exclusive use of an adjacent area encompassing 30,000 acres, for intermittent ground force maneuvers."

The bulk of the United States requests, as spelled out in the second round of the United States negotiations with the Marianas, were in the Mariana Islands. The United States wanted to purchase facilities on three islands, all of which are located in the proximity of Guam: Farallon de Medinilla, Saipan, and Tinian.

The United States requested the use of Farallon de Medinilla for target range purposes. The island was then being used by the Department of Defense as a bombing range. It is uninhabited and the United States said that it would be used only for air-to-ground and ship-to-ground target practice.

On the island of Saipan, United States military interests centered on the use of so-called military retention land which the United States took from the Japanese after World War II. Approximately 4,996 of the island's total of approximately 30,000 acres, including Kobler Field, which serves as Saipan's commercial airport, is in retention land. The military said it required the retention of Isley Field for military purposes, although civilian activities would be allowed. The United States would relinquish rights to 4,100 acres of retention land, retaining almost 900 acres. Five hundred acres around Isley Field were required for reasons the United States considered "not hypothetical but contingent." "It will be needed immediately," said the United States representative, "if we are to move out of some other location or if another location could handle a new requirement." The planned use of this area was for "aircraft maintenance and repair facilities as well as limited logistical support." Near the village of Tanapag, the United States would release some of the 320 acres of retention land presently used for commercial development, provided that the area was used for harbor-oriented purposes.

With regard to Tinian, the United States presented a detailed seven-stage plan for the construction of a base. As outlined in May, 1973, construction of the base would cost $144.6 million, plus an estimated $13.5 million for relocation of San Jose village. Ultimately, the base would have 930 Air Force and Navy personnel, supported by 2,370 others. Up to 1,000 persons would be involved in four stages of the seven-stage development plans.

The Department of Defense wished to *purchase* the entire island of Tinian, but use only two-thirds, or 18,500 acres. Plans called for a new airfield on Tinian. San Jose Harbor was sought by Defense on the grounds that "it is the only site reasonably suited to harbor development." Joint use of the harbor would be allowed 90 per cent of the time. The village would have to be relocated for reasons of safety. Areas within a "safety zone" of the harbor would be allowed the people of Tinian for agricultural and recreational purposes. Warehouses would be built; the church would be permitted to continue its function; and citizens would be employed at the dock. Finally, the Defense Department would control development of the civilian community on the remaining one-third of the island "in order to prevent undesirable conditions and consequences which could possibly result from the presence of a major military base." The planning of the civilian community would be a "joint military/civilian effort."

Military requests for lands and waters in the Trust Territory were more than a casual list prepared by the Department of Defense. Each request had been carefully tailored to reinforce strategic justifications for continued United States occupation and, in the initial request, each branch of the United States military saw to it that it got some facilities in Micronesia.

DEFENSE JUSTIFICATIONS FOR MICRONESIA

A seasoned Pentagon official sat at his desk, and spoke about the United States military role in the Pacific for the 1970's and beyond. He responded to specific questions with regard to strategic theory—What does the military define as our first line of defense? How far back are we prepared to retreat? "I have no idea," he replied. "I wish we could be certain."

He talked at length about the sweeping political changes in Asia, the shifting power relationships. He expressed concern over United States troop reductions and withdrawal from United States military bases stretching from Indochina to Japan. Throughout the conversation, he was troubled that despite American presence in the Pacific, there is no longer any hard and fast line of defense as defined by accepted military strategic theory.

This encounter with the Defense official was typical of subsequent interviews. An ever present concern of the military is the fear of uncertainty and coping with that uncertainty is neither superficial nor unrealistic.

The concern for United States military preparedness in the face of uncertainty has fostered the development of two important strategic concepts: first, the United States should retain possession of the Pacific Islands; and second, the United States should remain the most resilient and formidable military power in the world.

In 1945, it was the sense of Congress that the United States should retain permanent control of the Pacific islands, entrusting them to the military in defense of United States security. Agreeing with military officials, Congress felt that giving up the islands would be an irresponsible breach of national security that could lead to another war. Congressman F. Edward Hébert of Louisiana, who would from 1971 through 1974 become the powerful head of the House Armed Services Committee, expressed the views of Defense officials and Congress in 1945 when he said, "We fought for them, we've got them, we should keep them. They are necessary to our safety. I see no other course."

There was also a feeling among the military that retention of the Pacific islands was realistic and practical considering the military investment expended in their capture. Congress shared the feeling that no one had the right to give away land which had been bought and paid for with American lives. The passing of time does not seem to have altered the conviction of the military and some congressmen that the Pacific islands must be kept. As noted below, many Pentagon officials and congressmen today echo the sentiment expressed by Hébert in 1945.

The second military concept resulting from the fear of uncertainty has been more readily apparent to the casual observer in recent years—that the United States should remain a first-rate power with superior strategic capability.

Many Department of Defense and military officials are increasingly concerned that the United States will become a second-rate power. Defense officials fear that the United States has been lulled into complacency by such things as détente and the SALT agreements, leading to widespread troop reduction in foreign bases. They fear that the public remains dangerously uninformed about the realities of growing Soviet superiority in all phases of nuclear strategic capability and particularly naval power. "Soviet naval buildup," defense experts say, "is a major element in the shifting balance of military power." As a 1970 Blue Ribbon Defense Panel, appointed by the President and the Secretary of Defense stated in their report: "The road to peace has never been through appeasement, unilateral disarmament or negotiation from weakness. The entire recorded history of mankind is precisely to the contrary. Among the great nations, only the strong survive. Weakness of the U.S.—of its military capability and its will—could be the gravest threat to the peace of the world."

The reality of uncertainty and the emphasis on superiority coupled with the propensity never to give up anything willingly all lay behind the long and sometimes shifting list of strategic justifications for United States military presence in Micronesia.

Denial

In the late 1960's and the early 1970's, a number of Micronesian studies by military officers were published at war colleges in the United States. Many of these officers had access to classified information and were able to interview key military strategists. Without exception, these studies have indicated that the major immediate strategic justification for retaining Micronesia is to *deny* the use of the Trust Territory to a third power, and perhaps secondarily, to *prevent* denial to the United States. Indeed, except for testing, denial has been the major United States strategic objective in Micronesia.

Theoretically, denial does not require military occupation. Since World War II the United States has relied on the legal sanction of the United Nations and the Trusteeship Agreement to deny the territory to others and to insure its military access to Micronesia. Would an end to the legal sanction of the United Nations necessarily mean that the denial objective is no longer obtainable? Are there alternatives to United States military presence which still adhere to the principle of denial?

The Micronesians have favored United States military presence in the Trust Territory for the peace it has brought to the islands and the belief that continued United States protection is necessary. They have also maintained that potential use by the American military is probably Micronesia's greatest economic asset. For these reasons, the Micronesians have indicated a willingness to continue to accommodate the United States military provided they receive adequate compensation—compensation which they believe has been lacking in past years. Assuming that the United States would find it in its best interest to offer adequate compensation to the Micronesians, the possibility would exist for continuing denial to others and potential access for the United States.

In the event of the termination of the Trusteeship Agreement, the alternative in keeping with denial would be the neutralization or demilitarization of the region by international agreement. (A unilateral declaration along the lines of the Monroe Doctrine might be unsaleable in 1975.) Few military officials place much faith in neutralization, fearing infiltration by Communist powers who might be less scrupulous than the United States in observing Micronesian neutrality. That fear, however, seems unjustified to other defense experts. One high Pentagon official ventured the view that "neither the Soviets nor the Chinese have an interest in Micronesia; and even if an interest were present, the threat of United States power would serve as a strong deterrent." This would seem to be an accurate evaluation judging from the mild Soviet and Chinese reaction thus far to the ongoing negotiations with the Micronesians and the United States proposals for military facilities in the islands. On the contrary, both the Soviets and the Chinese may look upon clear American interest in Micronesia as protection against the aggressive intentions of each other.

The military fears neutralization for another reason—it would require foregoing access to lands they consider essential to United States security even though Micronesia is currently unused except for testing. While it is true that neutralization would prevent third power access, it would also prevent United States military access—a bleak prospect in the minds of military strategists.

Fallback (Contingency)

Some Defense Department officials agree that while military bases in Micronesia are not immediately essential to United States security, they would become essential if bases in Okinawa, Japan and the Philippines were no longer available. The assumption is made, probably correctly, that United States use of

Taiwan has been or will be sacrificed for improved United States-Chinese relations. Similarly, with the fall of Vietnam, Thailand will seek some accommodation with North Vietnam and China and shut down United States bases in Thailand. Further, while outright expulsion of the United States from Asian bases might not occur, restrictions on the use of nuclear weapons and offensive operations might necessitate fallback to the Trust Territory. In Japan and on Okinawa, for example, the ability of the United States to launch combat missions and to use nuclear weapons has been restricted severely and might remain so, short of an attack on Korea or Japan itself. In addition, the United States can no longer store weapons used in chemical and biological warfare on Okinawa. Finally Defense officials see a possible need for facilities on United States controlled soil in the Pacific.

Contingency planning attempts to prepare for every eventuality. Defense experts have repeatedly asserted that the Department of Defense must prepare for the *worst* contingency. "Contingency planning is fully 50 per cent of our justification for Micronesia," said one military official at the Hawaii headquarters of the commander in chief of United States Pacific forces (CINCPAC), "but we have to be careful in advancing it because contingency arguments don't get appropriations."

Sprinkled liberally among Pentagon comments about the possible loss of United States bases in Japan, Okinawa, and the Philippines are doubts about the political situation in each location. There is concern about Japanese "leftists." Okinawa is a "hotbed of leftist sentiment," said one United States official, and you never know when this sentiment will "strike the right chord." Even before the fall of Vietnam, similar references were made by the military with regard to the Philippines where the United States has bases under a lease which runs until 1991: the political situation in the Philippines was described as "tenuous"; the Philippines government was said to be becoming "belligerent" in dealing with the United States military; and Clark Field was described as becoming a "no-man's land for Americans."

While fallback and denial are the main justifications for the United States military in Micronesia, Defense officials have supplied various other rationales for United States military expansion in the islands.

Forward Defense

Some experts see the need for a forward position in Micronesia to defend Hawaii against Asian attack. They contend that if Hawaii and Wake Island are the first line of defense for the United States, the enemy could easily reach the United States mainland. On the other hand, if Micronesia were not militarily accessible, the distance between the nearest United States military forces and potential Asian attackers would be much extended. The military could not quickly reach Asia from Hawaii or the West Coast of the United States. One officer predicts a problem of credibility with our allies if the Department of Defense makes its forward line of defense in Hawaii rather than Micronesia. "How much can the United States reassure its allies or deter its enemies," he asked, "if we are not closer to Asia?"

According to Defense, a forward base in Micronesia would be equipped and fully able to withstand an enemy assault which might threaten Hawaii or our allies. "Days are vital in conventional warfare," said one General, "and the islands [Micronesia] would provide ship and aircraft refueling and resupply that is necessary to maintain forward defense."

The Defense Department considers Micronesia an important forward defense position for another reason not generally stated by the military. There are strong feelings within the Department of Defense about the possibility of another island-hopping World War II-type conflict and the need to meet the enemy as far away from the United States as possible. "We have to remember that the center of the United States is somewhere in the Pacific, not in Kansas," said one United States military officer.

Admiral John McCain, former Commander in Chief, Pacific, and former head of the United States military mission at the United Nations, strongly advocated Micronesia's retention on a forward defense rationale:

> ... one of the points I continually stressed was to do something with the Trust Territories [sic]; because if the Trust Territories are not kept under the immediate control of the United States, the next fallback position is Honolulu, and that's a long way back. The Trust Territories, if properly used, will put the United States in a position not too remote from advanced bases in the Philippines and other forward bases.

Similarly, Hanson Baldwin, former *New York Times* military writer and a man with close Pentagon connections, advanced the case for military retention of Micronesia in a 1970 book, *Strategy for Tomorrow.* Baldwin, who covered the war in the islands, argues that if the United States is to maintain any forward position in the west Pacific, "retention of these Trust Territory islands—indeed, their outright ownership by the U.S.—is essential."[2] Stating that political conditions make continued use of United States bases in Japan and Okinawa "tenuous at best," Baldwin concludes that formalization and perpetuation of United States sovereignty in the Trust Territory is one of the "strategic imperatives" we face in the Pacific unless the United States is prepared to withdraw its defense line to Hawaii.

---

[2] Hanson Baldwin, *Strategy for Tomorrow* (New York: Harper & Row, 1970), p. 279.

Dispersal

Dispersal of forces is normally considered a major means of defending oneself in conventional and nonconventional warfare. With its 2,000 islands, Micronesia is the perfect place to disperse forces. "At a time when communications are vital, as they would be during warfare," said one officer, "several communications installations would be advantageous."

Others concur on the necessity of dispersal in the nuclear age. With an extensive nuclear capability in the hands of potentially hostile powers, it is necessary to have many bases to make it difficult for the enemy to destroy all or most military installations in a single blow. According to one defense expert, many bases would facilitate an effective counterattack upon an enemy attempting to achieve a quick victory by surprise attack.

Spillover

While massive facilities already exist on United States-owned Guam, the military argues that Guam is too far away from Asia and not adequate to handle future military needs. Brigadier General Hanket, director of the Far East Division, Joint Chiefs of Staff, stated that Guam was "oversaturated" with Air Force and Navy personnel and that facilities there have been developed to the maximum. In the event it became necessary for the military to move its installations from other Asian bases, Tinian in the Mariana Islands would aid in absorbing the spillover.

Other Defense officials believe that future expansion of Guam is limited by the desire of Guamanians for economic development. Presently, much of the land and many of the better roads remain off limits to the Guamanians. Although Guamanians are ambivalent, it is commonly held that transferring some military facilities to Tinian would be an economic asset to Guam. Guamanians could then concentrate on building an economic structure based on tourism or some other industry.

Unforseen Resources

Oil interests have already begun to look into the possibility of constructing transfer, storage and refinery facilities worth up to $1.5 billion at a protective, circular reef north of Babelthuap in the Palau Islands which not only has no inhabitants, but also has no islands. The spot would seemingly be ideal for storage of oil from the Middle East or South Asia and distribution to Japan or the United States. Also, in the mid-sixties a Texas oil entrepreneur, Fred Fox, became interested in Micronesia partially because of his wartime service there but also because he speculated that oil could be found in the islands.

Today there is an increasing demand for tin and rubber from the western Pacific area. Australia and Indonesia are sources of raw materials for the United States and Japan. The military has noted recent worldwide interest in Indonesia because of its oil, raw material, minerals, and its strategic location by the Malacca Straits. Areas around Indonesia are considered politically unstable by the Defense Department. Therefore, they contend, United States military presence would help to stabilize the situation and protect United States interests.

Most defense experts agree that the Pacific basin is vital to world commerce, and that the United States should strengthen its position in the western Pacific. A recent Defense justification for remaining in the Trust Territory is to maintain control over ocean resources in the three million square miles covered by Micronesia. "If sea farming were developed, Micronesia would be the biggest pastureland in the world," said one Deputy Assistant Secretary for Defense. "Because no one knows the worth of resources to be found in Micronesia," said another Defense official, "its strategic importance cannot be defined. ... The area will possibly be extremely important to the United States and therefore we ought to keep a strategic position in Micronesia to maintain the flexibility we might need."

Storage

The military considers the western Pacific a potential storage area for material and fuel. Land is scarce on Guam and Japan, and there is said to be no room for large storage areas. Defense officials believe that Micronesia is better suited for storage. The military maintains that storage depots in Micronesia could double as refueling stations for transports en route to Asian ports from the United States. The use of the islands as supply depots would rule out the need to store large amounts of fuel in more vulnerable ports like Korea.

Assuming the Seventh Fleet will remain in the area, there is a need, according to the military, for repair facilities for United States ships requiring regular maintenance. The repair facilities on Guam are adequate for minor repairs on small ships only. Furthermore, the Navy has been cutting back on the number of ship-tenders which supply the Fleet, making it "necessary that bases be available in the Western Pacific which are readily accessible and well-stocked with supplies."

In addition, Micronesian land under American sovereignty provides storage space for nuclear weapons or even chemical and biological weapons, none of which can be stored in such places as Japan and Okinawa.

Research and Development

The missile testing range on the eastern edge of Micronesia is considered essential for research and development of antiballistic systems. Nike-Zeus,

Nike-X, Sentinel, Safeguard, "Site defense" all stand for antiballistic missile systems which one after another have been tested at Kwajalein. The Kwajalein lagoon is said to be ideal for missile research because it is easy to recover missile projectiles which fall into surrounding waters. The Pentagon has stated that Kwajalein will be needed indefinitely. According to Pentagon officials, there will be no reduction in the research and development facility as a result of the SALT agreements. They argue that Kwajalein is important to the military because there are no better alternatives.

The military considers Kwajalein a "must" for the United States due to the expense of the equipment already there. The facilities are seen as "unique" and "extremely difficult to duplicate."

Training and Practice

Finally, the Department of Defense is making plans to put a Marine training facility and maneuvers area on the island of Babelthuap. According to officials, the United States is running out of readily accessible training areas in the Far East. In addition to Babelthuap, Tinian has been suggested as a multipurpose facility for Marine maneuvers, communications and tracking stations, and long-range reconnaisance activities.

In 1974 and 1975, the military began actual small scale training maneuvers on Tinian. Training, however, seems to have been an incidental objective, for the exercises more clearly served to show the islanders that training was not necessarily injurious and was sometimes advantageous such as when the visiting forces interrupted their exercises to help the islanders make civic improvements. Secondly, this training program, once established, would constitute a deprivation for the military if discontinued.

ANALYSIS AND CONCLUSIONS

Military planning for Micronesia has proceeded largely on the basis of Defense Department assertions, particularly those of the Navy and the Air Force, that Micronesia was essential to American security and to the maintenance of international peace and security. There was a lively debate between Defense and State. State took the position that Micronesia was worth holding onto provided the political costs, particularly at the United Nations and in Micronesia, were not too high. State also took a more optimistic view than Defense about the reliability of United States bases in Japan (including Okinawa) and the Philippines, provided Defense was reasonably responsive to pressures in those countries to reduce excessive United States military holdings. However, over the years Defense assertions went almost completely unquestioned or ignored by most of the other governmental agencies whose views would have to be taken into account.

Interior officials tended to accept with little question Defense arguments about Micronesia's strategic importance and about most other military operations in the area. Defense, they believed, is responsible for military assessments and Interior's role was mostly limited to administration, except for those occasions, as in Ebeye, when insensitive relocation created overwhelming problems in housing, sanitation, and health. Interior officials take a different view once they are out of office. Three of the Interior Department officials most intimately connected with Micronesia during the Kennedy-Johnson years, and a former Assistant Secretary of the Interior under Nixon, as well as William R. Norwood, high commissioner of Micronesia from 1966 to 1969, all now question the strategic importance of Micronesia and past military operations in the area.

Nor was there any questioning of administration plans in the Congress, or for that matter much occasion to critically question military plans. No military legislation of direct application to Micronesia was submitted for enactment. None of the money spent initially for planning future military bases was specifically authorized and appropriated and thus subject to congressional scrutiny. Rather, that money came from general planning funds or from reprogrammed Air Force and Navy funds. This is not to say that there was no congressional attention devoted to military plans and their effect on Micronesia's political status. The Interior and Insular Affairs Subcommittees on Territories, particularly on the House side, were periodically briefed on Micronesia's military importance. They, too, tended to accept Defense assertions without critical scrutiny. Defense officials assert that the ranking members of the Armed Services Committee and members of the committee staff were consulted and approved of military plans for Micronesia. Committee staffers may have been consulted, or informed. However, F. Edward Hébert, then chairman of the House Armed Services Committee, told an interviewer on September 23, 1974, that while some "upstarts" on his committee might have been consulted, he had not been. There is little evidence that members of the Foreign Relations Committees of Congress were consulted.

Ironically, the first formal congressional views since the forties on the use of Micronesia for military purposes came about by accident. In the course of an investigation of American military bases in Korea, staffers of the House Defense Appropriations Subcommittee became skeptical of Defense plans for Micronesia. Largely as a result, the House approved the 1974 report of the Appropriation Committee that there was no justification for building bases in Micronesia so long as numerous other facilities were available in the Far East.

There is no evidence that Defense planners placed these stated needs for military facilities in Micronesia in the context of Defense or overall administration economic priorities. The United States was in the process of closing, not opening, military bases at home and abroad. Instead of needing ship repair personnel and facilities, for example, the Navy cut back on such activities in Guam, much to the dismay of the Guamanians. The reactions of the Office of Management and the Budget or the Congressional Appropriations Committees were clearly not anticipated. For when it came time to request funds, the administration decided in late 1974 against immediate base construction.

In addition to this general criticism of the military's planning for Micronesia, there are several specific reasons why Micronesia is not essential to United States defense and security—the array of defense justifications notwithstanding.

Micronesia Not Needed as Fallback

The United States continues to maintain reasonably stable relationships with the two Asian countries—Japan and the Philippines—in which the most important United States bases are located and therefore does not need Micronesia as a fallback position. State Department officials in Washington and at the American embassy in Japan say there is no evidence that American bases in Japan are in danger of forced withdrawal or would be unduly restricted. On the contrary, the reversion of Okinawa and relinquishment of some of the excess American facilities in Japan and Okinawa during the early seventies have reduced political pressure in Japan. Differences with Japan during that period resulted from other United States actions, said a State Department official, referring to problems created over textiles, trade relations, and unilateral actions on China.

Former Undersecretary of State for Political Affairs, U. Alexis Johnson, has said that restrictions in Japan have not severely hampered United States military operations there. In testimony before a Senate committee, Johnson stated that restrictions had not been imposed to keep American aircraft or naval vessels from stopping at United States bases in Japan, whether en route to or returning from combat operations. Johnson might also have added that United States bases in Okinawa, for better or for worse, are an integral part of Okinawa's economy, making it unlikely that Japan would take precipitate action against United States military facilities in Okinawa.

Moreover, United States officials believe Japan will remain a close ally of the United States. They refer to public statements of Japanese officials concerning the role of the United States military in Japan, which includes preserving peace and security in the Far East. Whereas the United States has reduced the number of troops stationed in Japan, the Japanese hope for the continued presence of United States carriers and tactical power. Even on the most sensitive issue, storage of nuclear weapons on Japanese soil, there seems to have been a softening of the original Japanese position.

Furthermore, Defense Department plans for American bases in Japan do not indicate that the military is overly concerned about its tenure. Plans are underway to modernize and enlarge American petroleum terminals at Sasebo; and in

October, 1973, the President declared Yokosuka Naval Base to be the homeport of the aircraft carrier *Midway*. As a result, about 1,000 families have been moved from the United States to Japan.

Far from wanting to kick the United States out, the Japanese were somewhat concerned that initial military plans for Micronesia might imply a change in the way the United States looked on its military obligations toward Japan. Because of this concern, the United States military has stressed the limitations of Micronesia as a site for bases so as not to undermine Japanese confidence in American protection, or give anti-United States groups in Japan, Okinawa, and the Philippines the impression that those facilities are no longer essential and that active political pressure would force the United States to withdraw. Indeed, Robert S. Ingersoll, then ambassador to Japan and now Deputy Secretary of State, is reliably reported to have been sufficiently concerned that he made a special effort to discuss the implications of Micronesian facilities for Japan and Okinawa with Pentagon officials. Ambassador Ingersoll's concern was well placed. According to a Japanese Foreign Office official, perplexed Japanese military officials had already raised serious questions about American intentions in Micronesia and their implications for Japan.

Largely because of an historic special relationship, the United States has had large military holdings in the Philippines. The United States still has two major military facilities there: Clark Air Force Base and Subic Naval Base, both of which the United States occupies under a mutual defense treaty rent-free until 1991. The facilities on both bases are extensive and, partly as a result, the United States economic impact in the Philippines has been tremendous. According to the *New York Times* of April 18, 1975, about 14,000 Americans and 54,000 Filipinos are employed at Subic and Clark. Together they spend as much as $150 million annually, about 10 per cent or more of the country's gross national product.

Since the mid-sixties, the United States and the Philippines have sought to reduce strains in their relationship. Economic arrangements and the 1947 military base agreements have received special attention. As a result, the duration of the military base agreement was reduced in 1966 from ninety-nine to twenty-five years, a base labor agreement was negotiated in 1968, and in 1969, a custom's agreement. In 1971, in response to Philippine requests, the United States agreed to explore modernization of the basic agreement itself. In addition, in 1971, the United States turned over to the Philippine government the Sangley Point Naval Air Station in Manila Bay and LORAN stations operated by the United States Coast Guard in the Philippines. A steady reduction in the size of United States holdings in the Philippines can be expected as the Philippine government tries to make an accommodation with post-Vietnam Asia, to grapple with economic and political forces at home and to attain a greater measure of control over the level and nature of United States military operations on Philippine soil.

Despite the adjustment in United States-Philippine relations, members of the Joint Chiefs of Staff have described military presence in the Philippines as an "ongoing proposition." There is no doubt that the Joint Chiefs continue to hold this view even after the Philippines saw the need to review their relations after the fall of Vietnam. State Department officials, replying to comments by the military that the Philippine government is becoming more belligerent toward the military, have said that "any anti-military noises on the part of the Marcos government are merely part of a bargaining strategy." Even after the Philippines called for a re-examination of their defense pact with the United States, a senior American diplomat told the *New York Times*, "Until now the Philippines have suffered one key fault . . . the Filipinos never learned how to be a squeaky gate."

But, United States overseas bases in the Pacific extend beyond Japan and the Philippines; Micronesia is not the only fallback. Even after withdrawal from Thailand is complete in 1976, the United States will still have bases in Taiwan, South Korea, New Zealand, and Australia. In addition, there are major facilities on Guam, over which the United States has sovereignty. It would appear unlikely that the United States would engage in any activity which would result in a simultaneous expulsion of the military from these bases. It is also highly unlikely that the United States would engage in any activity which would be restricted by all these countries or by even a substantial portion of them. If this did occur, it would be a prima facie case for a thorough re-evaluation of policy. Indeed, the inability of the United States to enjoy the full support of its allies or to conduct military operations without restriction was a necessary sobering influence on United States policy in Vietnam.

Partial losses could be absorbed by other facilities if the United States were forced to withdraw from some of its bases. When asked the effect if the United States gave up a lot of facilities in Japan, the Philippines and elsewhere in Asia, Admiral B. A. Clarey, then Commander in Chief, Pacific Fleet, told the *U.S. News and World Report* in April, 1972, "In the unlikely event that we gave up bases in one area, we would simply concentrate in other areas. . . . We would use Subic Bay in the Philippines more if we gave up bases in Japan. . . . We have a lot of capacity at Subic. Or we could come back to Guam." Admiral Clarey thought it "unlikely in the foreseeable future" that the United States would lose bases in Japan, Okinawa, and the Philippines. Such a situation would "represent a major political change out there, which would affect more than just the Fleet. It would affect the whole American posture in the area."

There are, of course, no current plans to concentrate United States Asian and Pacific military might in Micronesia, but that is the implication of planning based on the total loss of current bases in East Asia. Such planning has an air of unreality, especially since forward defense needs of the United States can be met by other means. It conjures up the image of the United States as a malevolent giant sitting off the coast of Asia waiting to come to the aid of countries unconcerned about their own defense. Henry Kissinger emphasized the *mutual* importance of United States bases when—in the wake of pressure on United States bases by Turkey, Thailand, Greece, Spain and the Philippines—he bluntly told an Atlanta audience (June 24, 1975): ". . . no country should imagine that it is doing us a favor by remaining in an alliance. . . . No ally can pressure us by a threat of termination; we will not accept that its security is more important to us than it is to itself. . . . We assume that our friends regard their ties to us as serving their own national purposes, not as privileges to be granted and withdrawn as means of pressure. Where this is not the mutual perception, then clearly it is time for a change."

While military officials have emphasized the contingency nature of Micronesia, they have also prudently stated that the "modest" facilities proposed in Micronesia would not—could not—replace the extensive United States naval and air facilities in Japan, Okinawa, and the Philippines. Among other things, Micronesia does not have the developed economy or the large pool of skilled and unskilled labor necessary to repair and service modern military equipment. The military facilities initially proposed on Tinian, for example, would require large numbers of construction workers. The proposed joint Navy-Air Force base on Tinian would have required imported labor during and after construction. There are only 779 people—423 male and 356 female as of June 30, 1972, excluding commuters from Saipan—on Tinian. Micronesia, said one official, is a "poor man's fallback," to be relied on as a last ditch attempt to retain a foothold in East Asia. Deputy Secretary of Defense William P. Clements told a September 16, 1973, Tokyo press conference that the need for the Tinian base complex is in the "out years," meaning fifteen to twenty years from now.

Indeed, there is a psychological argument for continued United States presence closer to Asia. If the United States wishes to follow a policy of active military, economic, and political involvement in Asia—which it apparently does even after the debacle in Indochina—it undoubtedly is helpful to have actual military forces in the region rather than based on Hawaii or on the United States mainland. But this does not mean that the United States should build up its forces in Micronesia. Rather, if only for psychological reasons, there is a strong case for keeping some of the current United States bases in East Asia, recognizing, of course, the necessity to make necessary adjustments in their size and purpose.

Japan, for instance, could not be expected to feel more secure knowing that American forces and nuclear protection are to be removed from the Japanese defense perimeter and relocated 1,000 miles south in Micronesia. Some Asian experts have even suggested that both China and the Soviet Union would prefer that the United States retain credible, albeit reduced, forces in East Asia as a deterrent against precipitant actions by one of the communist giants against the other; or against other countries in the area; or Soviet efforts to upset the delicate balance in the area by getting a foothold.

Modern Armaments Change Strategy

There are already massive facilities available on United States-owned Guam. These facilities and the existence of sophisticated new weapons, aircraft and ships obviate the need for new military installations in the Trust Territory.

It is argued that Guam is too far away from Asia and not sufficient to handle future military needs. During the Vietnam war, "Guam almost tipped into the Pacific from the weight of B-52's at Anderson Air Force Base," stated one military officer. Economic development pressure on Guam limits the possibility of future expansion there, said another military official. We need additional space for dispersal, said another.

The argument that Guam is too far away from Asia is particularly ironic since during the Vietnam war B-52's daily made the journey from Guam to targets in Indochina. In fact, economic costs, not technical capability, led to the build-up and use of bases in Thailand instead of Guam during the Vietnam war. While it is certainly true that it is more *convenient* and less costly for the United States to have big bombers as close as possible to targets, it does not mean that they must be at the closest point. For example, if United States military authorities decided that the United States *must* maintain a bomber force capable of hitting targets in China and Siberia, such forces could be maintained on Guam or as far back as Hawaii, Alaska, or even the West Coast.

The same situation applies to United States ballistic missile subs, six of which are now homeported at Apra Harbor on Guam, and to United States antisubmarine (ASW) land-based aircraft. On-station time for United States ballistic missile subs would be shortened if there were no room on Guam. On the other hand, the United States has mobile sub-tenders and will be introducing the Trident sub into the fleet in the late seventies. The Trident will carry a missile of greatly increased range, increasing the optimum-maximum distance between a sub and its target. The need for forward submarine bases would be lessened.

Similarly, the range of ASW land-based planes—which are a major part of the United States effort to keep the sea lanes open to commerce—can be extended by inflight refueling, as the Russians do over the Atlantic Ocean. Again, this obviates the need for having a string of island air bases. The United States has a fleet of fifteen aircraft carriers on which these planes can be stationed. The Soviet Union has no aircraft carriers.[3]

As to overcrowding and saturation of current military facilities on Guam, a number of observers expressed strong doubts. Much of the military land on Guam was unused even at the height of the Vietnam war. A number of B-52's and other aircraft were relocated to bases on the mainland after the conclusion of United States participation in the Vietnam war. Further, Congress has given preliminary approval to military plans for a new generation of bomber, the B-1, which would probably require only half as many planes as are required with B-52's. In addition, carrier-based fighter bombers capable of carrying nuclear weapons can reach many Asian targets, as can land-based F-4's. Finally, argued one former Pentagon analyst, the bomber is no longer the main force in the United States strategic arsenal and is of less strategic value against China, for example, because of that country's "thick" ground-to-air as well as air-to-air bomber defense system. The United States is much more dependent on the other two parts of the United States nuclear triad, intercontinental ballistic missiles and submarine-launched missiles, to protect its national security.

Since World War II, the United States has built a sizable carrier-based navy in the Pacific. The Seventh Fleet already consists of 35,000 men, three aircraft carriers, two cruisers, and about twenty destroyers. The destroyers are being modernized, and funds are committed to build thirty-seven new DD-963 destroyers that have a range of approximately 6,000 miles at cruising speeds. In addition, the United States has committed funds to a fourth nuclear-powered aircraft carrier and to twenty-eight new 688-class nuclear-powered hunter-killer submarines. These nuclear-powered ships have virtually an unlimited range of operations. With Hawaii in the east Pacific and Japan, Okinawa, Australia, New Zealand, and the Philippines in the west Pacific, Micronesia takes on the appearance of an outmoded stage coach stop that is by-passed by modern trains.

Several Guamanian lawmakers have found military protestations about "saturation" and economic development pressures on Guam unappealing and "hypocritical." Over 33 per cent of Guam is presently controlled by the military, and 25 per cent of that land is unused. They argue that the military was long responsible for Guam's economic stagnation, and even today the military actively opposes or delays major projects which might assist the economy.[4]

There remains, with regard to Guam, the dispersal argument. Dispersal of military facilities is desirable to prevent damage from a single attack, to force the

---

[3] According to the Institute for Defense Analysis, the Soviets have two helicopter carriers and are building two aircraft carriers. They plan to have three 40,000-ton aircraft carriers by 1980; however, none is expected to be used for heavy aircraft.

[4] Guamanians themselves are not consistent in their desire to see the military reduce its role on Guam. In May, 1975, the Guam delegate to Congress implored the Secretary of Defense to maintain the Guam Naval Repair Facility as its previous high level and to review

enemy to disperse his attack, or to provide alternate weather locations. Obviously, the military planners do not rate dispersion as the first priority in current military plans for Micronesia. Dispersal arguments are undermined by geography. Tinian, where plans called for a large joint naval and air facility, is within sight (five minutes by plane) of Saipan and 150 miles from Guam, where two other major United States airbases are located. The weather in all three bases is likely to be the same. In short, a major facility on Tinian grossly ignores the rules of dispersal.

The Department of Defense has maintained that Micronesia is essential to United States security by providing logistical support in contingency planning and forward defense strategy. At a time when the Department of Defense debates "limited nuclear warfare" as opposed to "unlimited nuclear warfare," it appears strange to speak of conventional means of military buildup. Nevertheless, Defense continues to plan in accordance with conventional methods, knowing that the ultimate use of United States nuclear capability would mean total annihilation. But even in a conventional sense, sophisticated aircraft and ships capable of enormous capacity and range cast doubt on the need for new facilities in Micronesia.

Some members of Congress have publicly stated their skepticism about the need for the United States to retain all current fixed bases or to establish new ones. Former Senator Fulbright, noting the "great change in weapons systems" stated, "if we are going to have an ABM and missiles, why do we have to have Clark Air Force Base?" Senator Symington, ranking Democratic member of the Senate Armed Services Committee and former Secretary of the Air Force, thought many developments, principally the Polaris sub, had eliminated much of the necessity for bases.

Symington was also skeptical of the fallback policy when he said, during 1970 Senate subcommittee hearings on United States Security agreements,

> I do not think we have to have so many islands in the Pacific to back up Korea. The Philippines back them up, Okinawa backs them up, Taiwan backs them up, Japan backs them up, the Polaris sub backs them up. How many places do you have to back them up before you break your own back?

Military "Requirements" Constantly Changing

Finally, changing statements of United States military needs and constantly changing strategy of the United States in negotiations cast doubt on the judg-

---

the decision to lay off several hundred employees. Guam sees a continued role for the military, first to assure greater protection than they got in World War II and, second, as a mainstay of their economy until other sources of income are developed.

ment that Micronesia is essential to either United States military needs or to the maintenance of international peace and security.

At first, the United States insisted on a virtually unlimited right to eminent domain and "permanent" control of Micronesia. All of Micronesia was said to be strategically important and the military did not wish or was unable to designate specific requirements. Consistent with this view, high ranking military officials swooped down on Micronesia with vague but grandiose plans for military facilities. Marine Corps Commandant Lewis Walt probably created everlasting concerns in Palau as a result of his insensitive remarks about United States land needs in that district. For example, he envisioned using large sections of Babelthuap for Marine Corps training.

Advocacy of unlimited needs was later changed to designation of specific military land needs and acceptance, in principle, of Micronesia's right to "opt-out," indicating that the United States saw a time when Micronesia as a whole might not be strategically important or at least saw a way to protect its real strategic interest, denial, by means other than permanent association (such as a mutual defense treaty). Giving the five districts of Micronesia the right to "opt-out" came about only after the Marianas had broken away from the other islands and appeared agreeable to providing land if it became a "permanent" part of the United States. The point was made bluntly by a Deputy Assistant Secretary of Defense who asked an interviewer, "Who cares about the rest of Micronesia as long as the United States has the right to build bases in the Marianas?"

There is strong evidence of bickering between State and Defense Department experts about United States military needs in Micronesia and about the political position the United States should take in light of those needs. From the time of the recommendation of the Solomon group in 1963 until the Defense Department was overruled by President Nixon in the fall of 1973, Defense has maintained that Micronesia was of such strategic importance that the option of independence should not be included on a plebiscite. "What right," demanded one high-ranking military officer, "does a small number of people have to shape the destiny of the world?" Interior initially, but reportedly not later, accepted the Defense view. On the other hand, the State Department has argued that the credibility of the United States would be sufficiently on the line that the political importance of including an independence option outweighed the risks of its selection. In any event, State Department officials argued the Micronesians were unlikely to select independence.

Similarly, when the strategic importance of Micronesia was reviewed in the summer of 1973, Defense presented a long list of reasons for Micronesia's strategic importance. On the other hand, the State Department took the position that access to Micronesia should be retained only if the financial and political costs proved reasonable.

The State Department concluded that if there was great resistance, for example, in Palau, the United States was "buying trouble" if it insisted on obtaining land in that district. And, indeed, Palau is an example of sharp differences between State and Defense, and perhaps even within Defense. Palauan leaders are on record as strongly opposed to United States military operations in their district. Actually, Palauan leaders say they're not opposed to a United States military presence in Palau *if* their public lands are first returned and *if* the United States negotiates with Palauans for specific land use.

Originally, said one State Department source, there was no real requirement for facilities on Palau. Palau had been "tacked on." At first Navy had written to the Deputy Undersecretary of State U. Alexis Johnson to emphasize the Navy view of Palau's importance. Johnson responded, rather unenthusiastically, that Palau might be too expensive politically but that the United States would make its best efforts. Navy then persuaded Defense and the Joint Chiefs of Staff to shift ground and to claim that Palau was "equally important." A subsequent Defense Department letter to the Deputy Secretary of State is said to describe Palau as "essential, an irreducible minimum." But the State Department again was described as less than enthusiastic. Deputy Undersecretary Porter, who had replaced Alexis Johnson, responded that Defense could not unilaterally change United States policy. The majority view continued to be that the United States "would go for Palau only if it was not too expensive." Arguments over Palau, said State, should not be allowed to delay an agreement on Micronesia, lest the "seeds of erosion" destroy everything.

Even with regard to Tinian the United States position changed drastically. Within little more than a year, the Department of Defense went from a proposed multimillion dollar base development program in all of Micronesia, costing several hundred million dollars, to a "modest" airfield and port facility on Tinian, to a long-term lease for training areas on Tinian. "Why was this done?" asked Congressman Robert Sikes at a March, 1975, Defense House Appropriations Subcommittee hearing. Secretary of Defense Schlesinger replied that "basic military land requirements for Micronesia have remained constant for the past five or six years; the plans to develop military facilities on Tinian have changed in the past two years. Plans for a training and logistic support base were developed in the 1970-72 timeframe when certain factors clouded the outlook for our future posture in the Western Pacific and seemed to require the early development of alternative facilities." Among other things, Schlesinger refers to initial military concern about the Okinawa reversion, and the uncertain political climate in Japan and the Philippines. He does not account for the fact that concern within the State Department was not nearly as great. Nor does he state why contingency plans for Micronesia continued long after uncertainty regarding Okinawa had disappeared.

Useful But Not Essential

There is little evidence that Micronesia is *essential* to United States security or to international peace and security. (In January, 1974, CINCPAC officials were able to identify only one classified use of a new base on Tinian, presumably storage of nuclear weapons.) Micronesia's importance in 1975 remains as it has been since 1945: the area must be denied to any hostile power. This objective does not justify the rigid position which the United States used in negotiations aimed initially at the development of a permanent relationship with the Micronesians and the construction of a major new base in the Pacific. Rather, at a time when the United States is reducing military bases at home and abroad and is under severe budgetary pressures, the United States could have used Micronesia's arrival at the juncture of self-determination as a way of assuring that the people of those islands, already pawns in two world wars, were further removed from international conflict. This might have been accomplished by an international agreement which would have neutralized the area. There is no evidence that the United States, particularly the cautious military, gave serious consideration to neutralization. Only with regard to missile testing in the Marshalls would such a proposal have affected current American military use of Micronesia and, as already noted, that use has an uncertain future.

There might be distinct advantages in such an approach which might outweigh any loss of American facilities in Micronesia. Although the Soviets have expressed little interest in Micronesia, they have not discounted the potential use of other mid-South Pacific islands. Eugene Mihaly, a former advisor to the Congress of Micronesia, argued in *Foreign Affairs* in July, 1974, that supply and maintenance points in the mid- and South Pacific have "the same attraction to the Soviet Union that Diego Garcia has to the United States in the Indian Ocean." "Given the number of small and impoverished Pacific island states," said Mihaly, "it would seem just a matter of time before one or another state finds a Soviet base arrangement irresistible." The prospect of United States and Soviet fleets encountering one another in such close proximity presents political ambiguities of a delicate nature. The negotiations between the Soviets and the Americans have reached a crucial stage in an attempt to forge détente between the two powers. The ultimate goal of détente is to *limit* the arms race: but military build-up in the Pacific by the Soviets and the United States would surely lead to a naval arms race between the two countries. Competition of this nature would have a negative impact on the stability of the Pacific area and on the chances for permanent détente.

While Micronesia is not essential to the United States, it is clearly *useful*. It may be worth retaining access for training, storage, research and development, and even for a future base if costs are not excessive. Although not even Pentagon officials placed much faith in their initial estimate of $144.5 million as the cost for building a base on Tinian, for the Pentagon the base costs are not high in the context of a $90 billion budget. Even in absolute terms, Micronesia is cheap. Rehabilitation of World War II docks and runways costs considerably less than new construction. The relatively small amount of money to be paid for land leases and grants for operations to the Micronesian government compares most favorably with Pentagon expenditures for bases in Spain and elsewhere.

On the other hand, given Micronesia's poor economic prospects, the financial costs for the relationship which the Pentagon seeks must be looked upon as expenditures which will continue indefinitely. Rather than push unquestioningly for an economy based on uncertain military needs, it would be better to develop a firm base for Micronesia's economic support.

Costs must be measured in political as well as economic terms. What will be the effect of the effort to achieve Pentagon objectives in terms of the relationship of the United States to the Micronesians, of American standing in the United Nations and of American adherence to long held principles such as self-determination? Such political costs are more difficult to measure than financial outlays but they are no less real. Few Micronesian leaders were initially opposed to determining their future political status within United States strategic constraints. Even at times of exasperation with the United States, Micronesian leaders admitted that they had little recourse, either because of their need for American economic assistance or because they were resigned to the combination of United States power, a disinterested and uninformed United States Congress, and a disinterested and powerless United Nations. But as the negotiations proceeded Micronesian leaders in every district became convinced that military considerations were so dominant that the United States had little concern for intangible political considerations, especially if they remained within manageable proportions. This assessment was shared by all districts including the Marianas which, however, came to realize that the dominant military considerations could work toward their immediate advantage.

*   *   *   *

Thus, it was with a constantly changing and exaggerated assessment of Micronesia's real strategic importance to the United States and to international peace and security that the United States began negotiations with the Micronesians on their future political status. American thinking, at least among the dominant group which professed to be pragmatic and hardnosed, distinctly placed military considerations above humanitarian considerations, despite international trusteeship obligations. As a matter of fact, there is little evidence that defense officials ever recognized that the Micronesians themselves had rights. The United States, said Secretary Schlesinger, before the Defense Appropriation Subcommittee in 1975, looked on the negotiations "only to change the form of the [trusteeship] agreement while retaining the basic objectives and responsibilities we have had for nearly thirty years." For Schlesinger and the military, the impetus for the negotiations was not an effort by the Micronesians to exercise their right to self-determination but "international and political" considerations. American officials rationalized, to the extent they saw any need to do so, that the small, powerless and poverty-stricken Micronesian population had to sacrifice its right to decide its own future to the greater good as perceived by the United States. Military considerations dominated the negotiations.

There are only 90,000 people out there.
Who gives a damn?
                              —Henry A. Kissinger,
                        as quoted by Walter Hickel

. . . and Micronesia would become the
newest, the smallest, the remotest non-white
minority in the United States political
family—as permanent and as American,
shall we say, as the American Indian.
                              —Lazarus Salii

V

United States-
Micronesia
Negotiations

In 1963 it was thought that Micronesia could rather easily be made a permanent part of the United States and at acceptable international political costs. Micronesians were not politically conscious. Those who were were favorably disposed toward the United States, partially out of gratitude for American economic and educational assistance and partially because of the new feeling of political freedom which United States administration had introduced. In fact, American policymakers believed that Micronesians would overwhelmingly select permanent association with the United States in any plebiscite, a judgment shared by most observers, among them E. J. Kahn in his sensitive book, *A Reporter in Micronesia*.

American policy was to strike while the iron was hot, hold a plebiscite at the earliest possible date, and to insure a favorable and credible outcome, take rapid economic, educational, and political measures which would promote the attainment of policy objectives. Almost the opposite took place. Educational and political development moved ahead, but Micronesia's economic plight remained the same, for in one sense economic development was intimately connected with Micronesia's political status.[1] On that the United States vacillated. In turn, educational development increased Micronesian political consciousness and worked against early attainment of intial United States political objectives. Micronesia's political elite might have been satisfied with a status equivalent to or even lower than other United States territories in 1963, but Micronesian expectations steadily increased.

THE MICRONESIANS PREPARE

By August, 1966, one year after the establishment of the Congress of Micronesia, the leaders of the new territory-wide legislature, increasingly aware of the opportunities open to them and prodded by the United Nations, made their first move toward self-determination when they petitioned President Lyndon Johnson to establish a Micronesian status commission.[2] But while the Department of State first opposed the idea, and then while Interior and State bickered over the mandate of such a commission, a year passed. It was not until August, 1967, that Johnson submitted a joint resolution to the United States Congress recom-

---

[1] United States investors were not attracted to Micronesia. Japanese investors were kept out by the United States pending settlement of the territory's political status. Micronesian businessmen, even those operating as fronts for Japanese, were unable to make long range plans because of the uncertain plans of the United States military which, in Saipan, for example, controlled about 5,000 acres on the island.

[2] The Department of Interior made a similar suggestion at this time. Interior officials hoped that a status commission would not only help resolve some difficulties concerning the interpretation of "self-determination" for Micronesia but also serve to draw more high-level attention to the Trust Territory.

mending a status commission, to be composed of eight members of Congress and eight public members (including Micronesians) and a chairman selected by the President. The resolution called for a plebiscite by June 30, 1972!

As already noted, the commission legislation proposed by Johnson was approved by the Senate but never really got off the drawing boards. The action by the Senate was already outdated. A month before the Senate Interior Committee action, a committee of Micronesian legislators had rejected the idea of Micronesian representation on a United States organized and directed status commission. Micronesians were willing to cooperate with the United States commission, to testify and to exchange information but did not wish membership. More important, action on United States territorial policy had become the virtual prerogative of the House, specifically of Wayne Aspinall, chairman of the House Committee on Interior and Insular Affairs. The bill never got a hearing in the House. Aspinall, for reasons discussed in Chapter VIII, adamantly opposed the status commission.

The Micronesian Negotiators

The Congress of Micronesia decided not to sit back and passively watch further delay in the resolution of Micronesia's status. On August 8, 1967, three weeks before President Johnson submitted his commission proposal to Congress, the Micronesian legislature established its own commission to undertake four major tasks: (1) to recommend procedures and courses of political education in Micronesia; (2) to study the range of political status alternatives open to Micronesians; (3) to recommend ways of determining Micronesian views on their future political status; and (4) to undertake a comparative study of self-determination in Puerto Rico, Western Samoa, the Cook Islands and other territories.

The Micronesian Political Status Commission consisted of a representative of each of the territory's six districts and at its initial meeting elected as its chairman Senator Lazarus Salii of Palau, a young political science graduate from the University of Hawaii. Between its organizational meeting in November, 1967, and the submission of its interim report on June 26, 1968, the Political Status Commission held three sessions, each lasting a week.

The Interim Report

The interim report reflected a moderate and cautious approach to the status question. It examined nine possible political status alternatives ranging from those theoretically possible to those which were practical. Practicality won out and some theoretical alternatives were dismissed even though the commission "fully realized that many of the theoretical alternatives should have been considered to provide an academic base. . . ."

In essence, the questions before the Micronesians then were the same as they are now. What is the geographic scope of the area or areas whose status is to be determined? Is it the single political entity which since 1920 formed the League of Nations mandate and since 1947 the United Nations Trust Territory? Or is it two or more geographic areas whose only previously unifying force (aside from isolated island location, poverty, sparse population, and weakness) had been mutual dependence on an external power? And of the several political status alternatives available to Micronesia which was preferable?

One aspect of the question "Which political entity?" was resolved rather quickly and has received little formal consideration since: Micronesia could theoretically "expand"—that is, join forces with other political units in the Pacific. But besides Japan, the most logical areas were islands which guarded their own new status jealously. Moreover, with the possible exception of Guam and phosphate-rich Nauru, other Pacific islands faced economic problems similar to those of Micronesia and would have brought additional language, cultural, and physical problems as well. The possibility of union with Guam was set aside for later, in-depth exploration. Japan was mentioned and dismissed, a strong indication of Micronesian antipathy toward Japan as a result of Japanese administration. Perhaps equally important was a strong suspicion that Japan desired to reap maximum commercial benefits from Micronesia without taking on the economic and political burdens which accompany close association.

With regard to separatism, the commission decided to leave its final position to a later date but it reached these tentative conclusions: (1) a divided territory would bring no greater political, economic, or social advantage than a unified territory; (2) further enquiry into division was effectively "concluded" since both the United States and the United Nations had expressly stated on numerous occasions that "fragmentation" of the territory was "out of the question" as a public policy; (3) a budding sense of nationalism was growing among younger Micronesians; and (4) Micronesia's size and the possibility of economic specialization would enable each district to "complement" the other.

The commission wrote of four broad categories of political alternatives open to Micronesia: independence; a "free associated state" or protectorate status; integration with a sovereign nation in the form of a "commonwealth,"[3] unincorporated territory, or incorporated territory; and remaining a trust territory. Although it was stressed that observations were "preliminary and tentative," the advantages and disadvantages of each status were briefly discussed with no conclusions or recommendations except that a substantial amount of research remained to be done.

---

[3]The report placed Puerto Rico in this category but incorrectly states that Puerto Rico has "the option to sever their ties with the United States at any time and become independent." (Interim Report, p. 23.)

The major portion of the interim report was devoted to an analysis of the methods by which selected territories had achieved "self-government"—Puerto Rico, Western Samoa, the Cook Islands, the Philippines, and Guam. In its comparative but, in the commission's own word, "superficial" analysis of the five territories, the commission reached two principal conclusions. First, while self-sufficiency is a "prerequisite for a healthy, progressive government," *none* of the territories examined was self-sufficient prior to attaining its new status nor had the new status necessarily resulted in self-sufficiency. Second, "a metropolitan nation which is apathetic to the political status question can be aroused to take an interest by agitation for change from within the territory, but other factors seem to have affected the same kind of arousal in the United States with regard to Micronesia." In the commission's views what apparently "aroused" the United States was not humanitarian concern for the Micronesian people, but "an increased awareness of the United States' strategic needs in the Pacific and an increased level of pressure from the Trusteeship Council of the United Nations."

Report of the Future Political Status Commission

One year later, in July, 1969, the commission submitted its second and final report to the Congress of Micronesia, a report which was noticeably more outspoken than the interim report. The commission had clearly acquired a sense of direction and was more definitive in its observations and recommendations. It called for "a government of Micronesians by Micronesians and for Micronesians," and spoke of future status as the "imperative primary issue." Openly critical of the United States, the commission wrote of the "frustration," of the "sad irony . . . of life on islands strewn with unexploded bombs and other debris of the Second World War," of the lack of a clearly defined objective on the part of the United States, and of the slow pace followed by the United States in taking effective action to bring Micronesians toward "self-government or independence." Also noted was the failure of the United States to replace Americans with Micronesians in senior positions as rapidly as possible and an ineffective economic development program which "lacked the sense of urgency." However, the commission was quick to admit that both politically and economically "the United States had not been lacking in good will," and as the report progresses, an increasingly moderate tone is apparent as the Micronesian commission envisions "not an end but a redefinition, renewal, and improvement" of Micronesia's relationship with the United States.

"We believe that we have acquainted ourselves with every alternative we might possibly face, that we have studied and contemplated every reasonable political arrangement for Micronesia" reads the report's confident statement of intent. Although recognizing that "independence . . . is the political status most in accord with the intent of the Trusteeship Agreement," the commission based its conclusion on "two inescapable realities"— the need for Micronesian self-government and long-standing American strategic interest in the area—and therefore recommended "that the Trust Territory be constituted as a self-governing state and that this Micronesian state—internally self-governing and with Micronesian control of all its branches including the executive—negotiate entry into free association with the United States." The commission defined "self-government" as "direct and unconstrained involvement of the Micronesian people in the foundation of their government and, specifically in the preparation, adoption, and subsequent amendment of the basic documents of government. . . ."

In a statement reminiscent of the eloquence of America's Declaration of Independence or Africa's little known Lusaka Manifesto, the Micronesians explained the rationale for their recommendation:

> We choose a free state because the continuation of a quasi-colonial status would prove degrading to Micronesia and unworthy of America. Difficulties and problems will surely arise, but the administering authority in these islands must become an authority administered by Micronesians. At the same time, we choose an associated state because we recognize the historically unique partnership between Micronesia and the United States. In recommending free association with the United States, we seek not an end but a redefinition, renewal and improvement of this partnership.

> Whatever our particular evaluations of the American administration in Micronesia may be, we feel that one contribution has been indelible, one achievement almost unqualified: the idea of democratic, representative, constitutional government. Our recommendation of a free associated state is indissolubly linked to our desire for such a democratic, representative, constitutional government. We endorse this system—which was brought to us by America and which we have come to know as an essentially American system.

> Yet our partnership with the United States and our endorsement of the American democratic system must be joined by our wish to live as Micronesians, to maintain our Micronesian identity, to create a Micronesian state. Such a state, we believe, would be a credit to America and to ourselves. As a self-governing state in free association with the United States, our past twenty years of partnership would be raised to a new level in a compact, not between guardian and ward, but between more nearly equal friends.

But the commission recognized that even as a self-governing entity Micronesia would continue to need support from the United States

> . . . for representation and protection in international affairs, for material and human assistance in the affairs of government, both in times of crisis and in day-to-day operations. As a self-governing state, Micronesia's needs will be as great or greater than as a territory. We do not underestimate the problems we will face. We do not wish for any lessening of American concern for Micronesia or of American presence in Micronesia.

From the beginning, however, the commission expressed the view that Micronesia also had something to contribute to a new United States-Micronesia relationship of an associated free state.

> How, then, will America benefit by entering into association with Micronesia: How can Micronesia hope to reward continued American contributions to its development? We would point out— without the slightest suggestion of self-righteousness—that there was an element of trust, of moral obligation, involved when the United States undertook responsibility for these islands, and that such an obligation, which was begun when these islands were in ruins, should not be ended when they are reaching for political maturity.
>
> Yet there is one item of material value which Micronesians can offer the United States—an item which is most precious in Micronesia and to Micronesians: the use of their land. Micronesians recognize that their islands are of strategic value, that the United States may require the use of some areas for purposes of military training and defense. We have seen the strategic value of these islands, have seen them used for nuclear experiments and missile testing. Our experience with the military has not always been encouraging. But as a self-governing state in free association with the United States, we would accept the necessity of such military needs and we would feel confident that we could enter into responsible negotiations with the military, endeavoring to meet American requirements while protecting our own interests.
>
> Relinquishing use of land, accepting the presence of large numbers of military personnel, accepting the risk of treatment as a target area by a hostile power in war are not conditions to be lightly undertaken. But as a self-governing state we would be far more prepared to face these prospects than as a Trust Territory.

The commission recognized that achievement of its desired status necessitated long and complex negotiations with the United States and that the United States might be called upon to make "unprecedented provisions and accomodations." But as the Marianas group would later argue, the Micronesians believed that the United States had dealt "flexibly and imaginatively" in its previous territorial policies. The United States had "shown a willingness to evaluate each territory as a separate case—and Micronesia surely is that."

The commission looked forward to successful negotiations toward free association but left no doubt about their alternative course:

> ... it is the second alternative mentioned in the Trusteeship Agreement, an alternative which might bring economic hardship and administrative difficulties. That alternative is independence. Independence is not the alternative we now recommend, but if it should prove impossible to renew our partnership with the United States as an associated free state, the Political Status Commission feels that independence would be the only road left open to us.
>
> In the times to come, we will look to the United States for friendship and aid; but, whatever our relationship with the United States, whether as an independent nation or an associated free state, we must also look to

Micronesians, look to ourselves. We maintain that the basic ownership of these islands rests with Micronesians and so does the basic responsibility for governing them.

But the principal Micronesian recommendation as the first step in achieving a new status was not to be met. The commission recommended that the United States Congress pass enabling legislation along the lines of similar legislation used for Puerto Rico. Such legislation, the commission thought, would indicate Congress's endorsement of the movement toward self-government in Micronesia and would be a "basic test" of future United States policy. If so, the United States flunked the test. Not only did the Congress not pass enabling legislation but also even President Johnson's study commission failed passage. United States-Micronesian negotiations would begin without any indication of the formal views of the United States Congress. Thus, any agreement reached in negotiations with the executive branch of the American government would risk repudiation by Congress.

THE NEGOTIATIONS BEGIN

From the Micronesian point of view, they were finally on the road to a future political status of free association or independence. After two years of careful study they felt well-prepared to meet the United States delegation at the first round of talks held in Washington in October, 1969. But it was apparent that the United States delegation was not equally prepared. The change from a Democratic to a Republican administration in Washington brought sweeping changes in personnel not simply at politically sensitive policy-making levels but also at middle and lower management levels. Within months every official in Interior's Office of Territories had been changed, some precipitously and unceremoniously. The civil servant director of the Office of Territories was replaced by the seventy-three year old widow of a former Republican congressman from Hawaii. (She "never did figure out what the score was," said one of her former superiors at Interior.) At State and Defense, normal assignment rotation had taken a similar toll. In addition, staff from the seventh floor (the location of State's senior officers), particularly those assigned to the National Security Council Undersecretaries Committee, assumed responsibility from those lower-level officials most knowledgeable.

Partially as a consequence of these changes in personnel, the history of the bitter arguments, hesitant initiatives, and attempts at resolution of Micronesia's status were forgotten, at least at the policy level. But there was also an arrogance about the new administration which made it assume that nothing done by the prior administration was of any value. Nixon's administration did not bother to

exhume President Johnson's proposal for a joint United States-Micronesian status commission but, as already noted, started pulling together a position under
the aegis of the Undersecretaries Committee of the National Security Council,
then headed by Elliot Richardson at the Department of State.[4]

The new Secretary of the Interior, Walter Hickel, later wrote of his own lack
of knowledge about Micronesia. He, like Harrison Loesch, the Assistant Secretary of the Interior for Land Management who was assigned the task of bargaining with the Micronesians, believed that the United States had made no prior
effort to resolve Micronesia's status—that consideration for a future status came
only with the urging of the Micronesians. In *Who Owns America?*, Hickel writes:

> The story behind my trip started in the middle of February, less than a
> month after I became Secretary of the Interior. My staff brought to my
> attention a report that the United States was likely to be seriously criti-
> cized during the next session of the United Nations General Assembly for
> mishandling its responsibilities in the Trust Territory. I directed that all
> available information be summarized for a presentation to me. The infor-
> mation on the Trust Territory indicated that we *had* been lax in caring for
> the needs of the people of the Territory. The report showed desperate
> needs for better education and health facilities and—most important—for
> some mechanism allowing the voice of the Micronesians themselves to be
> heard in the decision-making that affected them.
>
> I assigned a number of my staff members the responsibility of preparing
> recommendations we might make to Congress for improving conditions for
> the Micronesians. I also dispatched members of my staff to Saipan and
> throughout the Territory to meet with its leaders to get their assessments
> of some of their more basic problems.
>
> As the matter developed, I became more and more convinced that there
> was a need for me to visit Micronesia personally and determine first-hand
> what could be done to help these people.[5]

The President agreed and in May, 1969, Hickel made a dramatic, special
public relations trip to Micronesia aboard a presidential plane. He encouraged
the Micronesians to prepare for negotiations, and, in his own words, exhorted
them to "dream big dreams." "You will help develop the legislation," Hickel
continued, "which will end the trusteeship and build a lasting political partnership with us." Hickel's speech left the Micronesians ecstatic. Hickel recalls that
he pledged immediate steps to improve the Micronesian judicial system, ease
tariff barriers and travel restrictions, establish major educational and health programs and invite new investment capital to the islands. "For years," he continued, "you have had little voice in your government. This is wrong. Only when

---

[4] As Assistant to the President for National Security Affairs, Kissinger was a member of
the Undersecretaries Committee. But Kissinger attended only the first two or three sessions.
At those he arrived late and left early.

[5] Walter Hickel, *Who Owns America?* (Englewood Cliffs, New Jersey: Prentice-Hall, Inc.,
1971), pp. 204-5.

the people lead their government can that government be great and the people prosper."[6]

A member of Congress who arrived in Saipan shortly after Secretary Hickel's address to the Micronesians reflected, "I was aghast at the Secretary's speech. . . . Hickel made promises he couldn't possibly keep. . . . It was a premature speech. The Nixon administration had just begun. . . . It seems every new administration starts out believing that they can correct the errors and inabilities of past administrations but they proceed to talk themselves into the same problems."

Not surprisingly, the first round of negotiations with the Micronesians held in Washington in October, 1969, was "a funny round," former Assistant Secretary Loesch recalls. "We had no position." The purpose, Loesch said, was to "explore Micronesians' feelings without any proposals of what we would do." The Micronesians are said to have been outraged that the United States spent more time entertaining them than in substantive discussions. Yet, two months earlier (August 10, 1969) the new High Commissioner, Edward Johnston, had addressed the Congress of Micronesia in his first state of the territory address: "We [the United States] are *prepared and anxious* [emphasis added], from this moment forth, to discuss with this Congress . . . the exact nature which this partnership should take." The United States was anxious to secure permanence of the relationship, but apparently not anxious to discuss or negotiate, and certainly not prepared.

But the first round would not be the only round where the United States came unprepared. Throughout the status negotiations, the United States side complained about receiving last minute approval of negotiating instructions "from the airplane" of Henry Kissinger, Nixon's chief foreign policy adviser. The sixth round broke down because the United States delegation said it did not know what the Micronesians meant by independence, even though the Micronesian delegation had always had the mandate to negotiate free association *or* independence and the Congress of Micronesia had publicly reaffirmed the independence aspect. (Actually, the United States representative had been instructed *not* to discuss independence.) And six days before the seventh round of negotiations were to begin, the United States delegation still had no final negotiating instructions because President Nixon had not yet approved them. Significantly, the United States would not be so ill-prepared at the time of the Marianas request for separate negotiations. The United States was able to grant the request on the day it was made.

If the purpose of the first round from the United States point of view was to explore Micronesian feelings, the Micronesian delegation let them be known. In

---

[6]*Ibid*, p. 206.

addition to two published reports on their status desires, they had developed eleven topics for discussion and presented them to the United States.

1) Micronesians wished to draft and adopt their own constitution;
2) Micronesians wished assurance that no confiscation of land and no military bases would be established in the islands without full consultation and consent of the government of Micronesia and fair compensation; that land currently held, controlled or possessed by the United States under lease or other arrangements would be renegotiated;
3) The United States, subject to certain exemptions, limitations, and conditions, would conduct Micronesia's external affairs and provide protection from outside aggression and consult with Micronesia before entering into international obligations with respect to Micronesia;
4) Micronesia would agree not to allow any other country to enter into Micronesia for military purposes;
5) The United States would agree to an early settlement of Micronesia's postwar damage claims;
6) The United States would remove all barriers to the free movement of Micronesians into the United States;
7) The United States would agree to remove all barriers to the free movement of goods from Micronesia into the United States;
8) The United States would fully consult with the government of Micronesia in matters of shipping, civil aviation and communications;
9) Micronesians would have access to the United States Ninth Circuit Court and the United States Supreme Court;
10) Micronesia would continue to have access to banking facilities in the United States, to the use of United States currency and postal services; and
11) The United States would guarantee financial aid to Micronesia.

The United States delegation agreed in principle with the eleven points with two outstanding exceptions. Because land was so scarce, its control was one of the most important issues throughout the negotiations. Whether a future relationship should be permanent or in the form of a revocable compact was also a point of disagreement.

These major differences would lead the Micronesian Political Status Delegation to report after the next round of negotiations:

> ... the difference between current United States and Micronesian positions is profound. From the beginning, it has been clear that the United States and Micronesian Delegations have very different notions of what would constitute true self-government in Micronesia and what would be a sound future partnership between Micronesia and the United States.

The "very different notions of what would constitute true self-government in Micronesia" basically narrowed down to two questions. Should the Micronesians be able unilaterally to terminate the arrangement if later they should decide to become independent? How much control would the Micronesians exercise over internal developments?

Thus the negotiations brought out in public the debate which had raged in the bureaucracy. The Micronesians took essentially the position which had been advocated by the Department of State while the official United States negotiators took that of the Departments of Defense and of the Interior.

THE COMMONWEALTH PROPOSAL

The second round of talks was held in Washington from May 4-8, 1970, but in January Assistant Secretary of the Interior Loesch had met with the Micronesian delegation in Saipan during the special session of the Congress of Micronesia. Informally, Micronesia got its first look at what the United States would call the "commonwealth" proposal. Under this proposal, the United States would gain permanent control and sovereignty over Micronesia, and after some preliminary procedural hurdles, would be free to do what it wished, including acquire land under eminent domain.

The commonwealth proposal had been drawn up in late 1969 by an interagency group of the National Security Council Undersecretaries Committee following a meeting at the office of Secretary of State William P. Rogers. Those who attended are said to have included Henry Kissinger, President Nixon's Assistant for National Security Affairs, Secretary of State William Rogers, Secretary of the Interior Walter Hickel, High Commissioner Edward Johnston, and Assistant Secretary of the Interior Harrison Loesch. At that meeting Kissinger adopted Defense's argument that Micronesia could not have a degree of self-government which included control of their land. Other minimum Micronesian demands such as the right unilaterally to alter the relationship were obviously out.

Hickel disagreed with Defense and Kissinger. According to Hickel's account, he "might have gone along with almost anything less than the argument for eminent domain—such as negotiated purchase or lease of land. We had established military bases in Turkey and Spain without right of eminent domain. What right did we have to invoke eminent domain on the Micronesians?" Hickel's account of Kissinger's response is readily quoted by Micronesians: "There are only 90,000 people out there. Who gives a damn?"[7]

_____

[7]*Ibid*, p. 208.

The United States commonwealth proposal, in the form of draft legislation, was informally presented by Loesch, who, in his own words, knew he was "dead as a duck." Loesch had taken the proposal to the home of Micronesian Status Commission chairman, Lazarus Salii, put it on the table, and apologized, "This is what I was sent out with. Don't blame me." The reaction Loesch expected was the one he got. The draft bill was "almost totally objectionable" to the Micronesians. It was labeled a "commonwealth," apparently to make the status *sound* similar to that of Puerto Rico, whose status the Micronesians had generally spoken of approvingly, but according to the bill, Micronesia would have become an unincorporated territory of the United States like Guam or the Virgin Islands. The Micronesian delegation felt the "commonwealth" offer directly clashed with the Trusteeship Agreement, with the mandate of the Congress of Micronesia and with the basic premises upon which the Micronesians had opened discussions in Washington. Maintaining that the internal self-government of Micronesia should be "reserved solely to the people of Micronesia" and that they were totally opposed to any United States legislation providing for the internal government of Micronesia, the Micronesian negotiators flatly rejected the proposal as a "camouflaged offer of outright territorial status."

Even the manner in which the United States presented the commonwealth proposal was inconsistent with Hickel's promise that Micronesians would assist in developing legislation on their future. Instead, the United States was saying, "this is what you ought to do." The usually mild-mannered Salii reacted sharply:

> The U.S. offers us a new name: This Trust Territory would become a Commonwealth. But the United States would control our future. Micronesia would become a permanent part of the United States' political family—that is the phrase they use—but eminent domain would remain eminent domain; veto would remain veto; Kwajalein would remain American and Ebeye would be Micronesia. And Micronesia would become the newest, the smallest, the remotest non-white minority in the United States political family—as permanent and as American, shall we say, as the American Indian.

During the four months between the January meeting in Saipan and the May status talks, the Interagency Group further developed the commonwealth proposal—a proposal which Leosch would later describe as "a disaster."

In preparation for the May, 1970, negotiations, the Micronesians had prepared a list of four basic principles which would guide their effort to negotiate free association with the United States: sovereignty in Micronesia resides in the people of Micronesia and their duly constituted government; the people of Micronesia possess the right of self-determination and may therefore choose independence or self-government in free association with any nation or organization of nations; the people of Micronesia have the right to adopt their own constitution and to amend, change or revoke any constitution or governmental plan at any time; and free association should be in the form of a revocable compact, terminable unilaterally by either party.

As formally explained by the United States delegation, the "commonwealth" proposals had the following essential provisions:

1) *Structure of Government*: Micronesia would become a "commonwealth" of the United States—a "part" of the United States; in "permanent" association with the United States—a relationship neither as close as a "state" nor one implying future evolution as in the case with an "unincorporated" territory. Some powers would be reserved to Micronesia; others shared with the United States government and a "few" others reserved "primarily" to the federal government.

2) *Structure of Government*: As with all "other political subdivisions of the United States," there would have to be (a) a republican form of government; (b) a bill of rights; and (c) three separate branches of government.

3) *Powers of the Commonwealth*: Micronesia would be able to control economic development, education (so long as it remained free and equal), and pass all local legislation. Powers on local matters would be extensive "within the limits of Micronesia's dependence on financial support from the federal government."

4) *Shared Powers*:
   A. *Legislative*. Legislation passed by the United States Congress would take precedence over local legislation. Micronesia would have a nonvoting delegate in the United States House of Representatives.
   B. *Judiciary*. A federal district court for Micronesia would be established with the possibility of appeals through this court to the United States Supreme Court.
   C. *Taxes* generated in Micronesia would be matched by the United States and could be locally controlled. The United States Congress would be authorized to appropriate additional funds for specific purposes.
   D. *Land and Property Control*. The United States would retain the right of eminent domain but with extensive protective procedures "unique to the Commonwealth, with no other political subdivision of the United States being accorded the same extent of review and consultation, in particular, the right of review by the legislature."

5) *Areas Reserved to the Federal Government*:
   A. *Foreign Affairs*. Foreign affairs would be conducted by federal government except where "consistent with national policy." Areas of possible "commonwealth" activities include cultural, commercial contacts and tourism. Where policy was directly involved, Micronesian views would be welcomed and would receive sympathetic attention.
   B. *Defense.* The United States would have total responsibility.

C. *Citizenship, Travel and Trade.* Micronesians would become United States "nationals" but could become citizens by "simple application" to the federal court. Micronesians would have free access to the United States and the same would be true of Micronesian goods.

The clash between the Micronesian principles and the United States offer was obvious and in the Micronesian view "profound." Specifically, while finding much to commend in the "commonwealth" proposal, the Micronesians, as expected, rejected it because they would not be able to control their land, laws or future status.

In attempting to conceal the fact that the United States policy was solidly against not only independence for Micronesia but also, in fact, any status that restricted United States powers, the United States delegation quibbled over definitions, contradicted itself, and in general treated the Micronesians as if they knew little and hadn't prepared for the negotiations. The Micronesian delegation had expected disagreements; what they hadn't expected was the low esteem in which they were held.

For example, the United States representative quibbled over the definition of "free association" although in the United Nations the United States had itself been a leading exponent of "free association" for small territories as an alternative to independence. In fact, in Trusteeship Council reports, the United States had repeatedly inserted references to United Nations General Assembly Resolution 1541 which was the basis of the Micronesian definition of "free association." Moreover, internal United States working papers cited Puerto Rico as an example of the use of "free association" in the political development of United States territories. Yet, according to the Micronesian report, the United States representative even stated that the United States was not obligated to offer "free association" since the term was not used in the Trusteeship Agreement. Neither, retorted the Micronesians, was the term "commonwealth."

Similarly, when the Micronesians asked what, in view of the strategic interest of the United States, was the attitude toward independence for Micronesia, the United States representative avoided any forthright discussion of what was really an essential issue for the United States. Instead, in a long, rambling and imprecise statement, he said that Micronesia was not ready for independence, would not be "for some time to come," and the United States was not prepared to undertake specific programs nor to adopt a specific time-table to show when Micronesia would be ready for independence. In what can only be described as a hypocritical statement, and incidentally a hint of American thinking on the possible division of the territory, the United States representative said, "The United States would, in fact, be derelict to its obligations under the Trusteeship Agreement if it were to prejudge the outcome of that act of self-determination by the people of Micronesia *as a whole.*" (Emphasis added.)

Clearly, the executive branch wanted a territorial status. This view was mirrored in Congress as well. The first two rounds, as well as the commonwealth proposal, had naturally been influenced by Wayne Aspinall, a "hardliner on possible future political relationships—he was on a colony or territory kick at the time," recalled Loesch. But the Micronesians' outright rejection of the United States proposal complicated matters because the basic American assumption—that the Micronesians would accept any status offered by Washington and in fact that they wished to become a part of the American political family—was shot down. Because their perception was shattered, United States officials began to gain an awareness of the real problems to be confronted in the negotiations.

There were bureaucratic problems as well. Loesch had essentially a free hand in representing Interior's position to the Interagency Group, but other representatives from the various agencies were often not able to speak for their own departments. In Loesch's opinion, the NSC representative was a "dumbhead, a junior." At one point it took nine months just to get the Undersecretaries Committee to meet to discuss Micronesia. In addition, considerable friction remained among those offices responsible for Micronesia's administration. The Interior Department's Office of Territorial Affairs harbored resentment toward the Trust Territory government. There was also a feeling in the United States negotiating delegation that Trust Territory employees, because of a desire to hold onto their jobs, hindered the talks and Interior's Micronesianization program.

Harrison Loesch admitted that during his tenure the main problem regarding self-determination for the Trust Territory was bureaucratic infighting, inertia, and laziness. Agencies who had input in the decision-making process seemed more concerned about their own particular position than about what happened to the Micronesians. The irony was that while putting the status question off, Washington officials nevertheless thought they were securely holding onto Micronesia. But this was not the case. Micronesians leaders had been influenced by Western ideals and by distinguished political advisers from New Zealand and the United States who had been hired by the Micronesian legislature. Intellectually, Micronesian leaders had moved farther and farther away from the likes of the "commonwealth" proposal. The United States hope for a "permanent and lasting" relationship with Micronesia backfired and United States officials were not prepared to deal with the resulting difficulty.

THE OFFICE OF MICRONESIAN
STATUS NEGOTIATIONS

Not until sixteen months later, in October, 1971, did United States-Micronesian talks resume. The political situation in Micronesia had greatly deteriorated. The Mariana Islands representatives began to look upon commonwealth as their long sought closer association with the United States and regretted its rejection. They found more cause for disagreement with the other districts of Micronesia when the Congress of Micronesia passed territory-wide tax legislation and stipulated that the funds collected would go into a general fund for use throughout Micronesia. In essence, the economically better off Marianas (and Marshalls) were to help pay for programs in poorer areas of Micronesia. In that so-called "summer of discontent," the building of the Congress of Micronesia was destroyed and the home of the high commissioner was damaged by arson. Finally, in February, 1971, the Marianas District Legislature voted to secede from Micronesia "by force of arms if necessary" in order to join the United States "with or without the approval of the United Nations."

In response to the worsening political climate in Micronesia and in an effort to obtain information filtered through neither the Trust Territory government nor the Department of the Interior, the position of Status Liaison Officer was created. John Dorrance, a foreign service officer and a specialist in Pacific island affairs at the American embassy in Australia, was appointed to the new post of political adviser to the high commissioner in Saipan. Later, Dorrance would continue to handle Micronesian affairs from the State Department's Australia, New Zealand and Pacific islands affairs desk, after his replacement by another foreign service officer.

On June 24, 1971, President Nixon, in the words of his announcement, "demonstrated his continuing interest in the political status deliberations" by appointing Haydn Williams as his personal representative with the rank of ambassador to conduct negotiations, on a part-time basis, on the future political status of the Trust Territory with the Congress of Micronesia and other Micronesian leaders. Negotiations were taken out of Interior's hands and put into Williams's by the establishment on July 28, 1971, of an Office of Micronesian Status Negotiations to support Ambassador Williams.

The Office of Micronesian Status Negotiations is an inter-agency group located in the Department of Interior but separate from Interior and the Office of Territorial Affairs. The overriding role of Defense is evident. Officials assigned to the office included an office director who was a Navy captain, an Army colonel who was next in line, two legal advisors, and one public affairs officer. There is an informal understanding that the top two positions are occupied by military men because, as one official put it, of the "substantial interest of the Department of Defense." "Let's face it," he said, "if it weren't for that Defense interest, the negotiations would have been over long ago." The changeover in personnel was great. In the short span of three years, there were two office directors, both Navy men. In just under four years the position of deputy United States representative, a full-time position, was filled by three people. This special office further removed Interior from responsibility for status negotiations. The State Department had long sought such a change as a means of elevating policy above bureaucratic infighting. However, according to a former director of the Office of Territories, the Department of State, Interior, and Defense were "simply astonished" at this move, for they had no prior warning. Williams himself is reported to have expressed surprise at his appointment.

Williams's background is a combination of the military and diplomacy and, some contend, the CIA. He was a member of the faculty and assistant dean of the Fletcher School of International Law and Diplomacy, where he earned his MA and PhD; Deputy Assistant Secretary of Defense for NSC affairs and plans, then for International Security Affairs; and president of Asia Foundation, a position he still holds today. The Asia Foundation, located in San Francisco, was created in the 1950's to provide "proper training and education" for "promising" foreign leaders. Reports in the *New York Times* and *Ramparts* that the Asia Foundation was receiving major backing from the CIA led to extensive suspicions, particularly among young Micronesians and returned Peace Corps volunteers, of Williams's past associations. There is no evidence, however, that Williams's work on Micronesian matters was connected in any way with the CIA.

Various government officials have described Williams as "sensitive to protocol," "aloof," "basically non-communicative," and as a man with no shortage of self-esteem. At one point, a State Department official, concerned about what he called Williams's "attitude of exploitation", expressed the hope that Williams could be replaced. According to the *Newsletter* of the Friends of Micronesia, the Micronesian negotiating team nicknamed him "crocodile,"—one who grins but bites. [8]

The fact is that neither Williams nor his office enjoys a warm relationship with the Micronesian or even with the Marianas negotiators. Micronesians resent Williams's constant and formal use of his title, The President's Personal Representative, speculating that Williams never discussed Micronesia with President Nixon or even with Henry Kissinger. In fact, Williams admitted to never having discussed Micronesia with Nixon and to never having had a detailed substantive discussion with Kissinger.

In a 1972 (Second Quarter) *Micronesian Reporter* article, P. F. Kluge gave a bleak account of the proceedings of the fourth round held in April, 1972 at Koror, Palau, the second round for Williams:

> The meetings, it soon developed, were rigid confrontations, in which one side would read a prepared position paper at the other. The other side would acknowledge receipt of the paper—sometimes with thanks, sometimes without—and we would all return to our rooms and prepare for the next meeting.

---

[8] A similar name was used, but it was used affectionately, by State Department officials when referring to W. Averell Harriman.

It was a stiff, formal routine, a world of lawbook phrases, measured politeness, and Xerox machines working overtime and it changed very little as negotiations proceeded. . . . Whether the United States Delegation ever got close to Micronesia, whether it ever developed some special feeling for the islands, I cannot say.[9]

Williams's assistants believed that the office should have "loosened up." They complained that after negotiation rounds had ended and some Americans would have liked to have relaxed with the Micronesians, Williams assigned extra tasks which could easily have been done on return to Washington. Former negotiator Loesch, though cautious not to interfere with Williams, thought that the Micronesians probably found Williams "cold and secretive" and thus had trouble negotiating with him. "Williams," he said, "thought it was terrible to take a drink with the guys." Loesch himself tried to develop personal relationships with Micronesians and joked, "I often wished I had taken them up on some of their drunken offers."

Williams's deputy, James M. Wilson, a foreign service officer, according to several sources, had even less rapport with Micronesians and at one point he engaged in a public dispute with Felipe Q. Atalig, representative of Tinian in the Congress of Micronesia. One official from the Office of Micronesian Status Negotiations admitted that Wilson was highly opinionated, that he was the most difficult man to work with in the office, and that he was despised by the Micronesians.

The negotiations appeared to be between hostile countries rather than close associates. For example, strained relations resulted from the dictatorial manner in which the Office of Micronesian Status Negotiations handled initial Micronesian efforts to educate the Micronesians about the political decisions they would have to make in deciding their future status. A program had been prepared by Carl Heine, a highly respected Micronesian government official. It was approved by the high commissioner and by Mary Vance Trent, the State Department's liaison officer in Saipan, and sent to Washington, ostensibly for information purposes. The program was hurriedly and summarily stopped by Williams's office. Williams maintains that the original program was qualitatively inadequate; the Micronesians contend that the extensive changes demanded by the United States slanted the educational program toward the political status desired by the United States. In any event, agreement was finally reached on the development of a political education program after one of the frequent Hawaii summit meetings, but Micronesian legislators still express resentment that the United States, through the Trust Territory government, controls political education.

Still another point of conflict was Micronesia's own "Watergate," or at least the so-called "executive privilege" aspect. The Congress of Micronesia charged

---

[9]P. F. Kluge, "Looking Back," *Micronesian Reporter* (Second Quarter, 1972): 17-20.

three Trust Territory government employees with contempt when in early 1974 they provided information regarding land to American negotiators but refused to provide similar information to the Congress of Micronesia.

Finally, the feeling of mistrust between the Micronesians and the United States was further complicated. There is some concern that former Peace Corps volunteers who served in Micronesia have "sold out" by taking jobs in Washington, although at least one of them was concerned enough about a possible conflict that he consulted with his Micronesian friends before taking a position with the government. Three former volunteers worked in the Office of Territorial Affairs and one worked in the Office of Micronesian Status Negotiations. Micronesians and former volunteers now working for the Congress of Micronesia suspect that government-employed former volunteers aren't really concerned about the Micronesian people. On the other hand, United States administrators and negotiators are deeply suspicious of Americans, and particularly Peace Corps volunteers and poverty lawyers who are pro-Micronesian.

Despite suspicions and personality problems, the new measures by the executive branch did produce results. The Office of Micronesian Status Negotiations provided a center for information and viewpoints. Micronesian proposals were given more consideration and study when one office could devote full time to the negotiations. The next round of negotiations would reflect these improvements.

A NEW APPROACH: SERIOUS NEGOTIATIONS BEGIN

Prior to the second round of talks, the Congress of Micronesia, hoping to make its position clear, had endorsed four basic principles and legal rights as the essential premises of future negotiations. For the Micronesians, these were to be the minimum, non-negotiable requirements for future relationship with the United States. The United States, on the other hand, had never clearly listed defined objectives to be reached through negotiation.

The major change in renewed negotiations, held at Hana, Hawaii in October, 1971, with the Micronesians, was in the United States approach. This time it was apparent that the United States had carefully studied the Micronesian position. In Williams's own words, "rather than presenting a United States blueprint for the future political status of Micronesia, the United States sought to concentrate on those issues of greatest importance to them [the Micronesians] and their future." It had taken the United States two full years to get around to discussing with the Micronesians the three key issues which the United States had itself privately identified and which the Micronesians made explicit at the first and second rounds of negotiations. These were: control of laws, control of land, and control of future status. Two other issues would remain lurking in the background: finance and Micronesian unity. In his opening statement, Williams correctly stated the first two Micronesian concerns. Curiously however, in his report to the President, the important issue of control of future status would be rephrased to read, "full protection for their own values, traditions and cultural heritage," thereby obscuring a crucial issue.

The United States also made explicit its three basic interests against which any agreement would be tested: 1) The United States general concern for the long term welfare of the "peoples" of Micronesia; 2) The United States general legal and moral obligations under the Trusteeship Agreement; and 3) The United States "larger Pacific role and other commitments with respect to the peace and stability of the Pacific Ocean area."

The vague and elastic nature of United States interests was to prove a major stumbling block. Among other things, the question was raised anew as to the implications of United States strategic interests on the range of options available to Micronesia. When asked to clarify this at the second round, the United States delegation had refused. But there was an implied answer, at least, in the statement of the three basic United States interests: United States strategic interests required a continued United States presence in Micronesia.

Since this third and highly successful round there have been four more rounds.[10] Round four, held in Koror, Palau, in April, 1972, saw basic agreement reached on the issue of termination. Outside the formal talks of round four, the United States announced its decision to negotiate separately with the Mariana Islands. In August, 1972, round five was held in Washington, and tentative agreement was reached on the preamble and three titles (internal affairs, foreign affairs, and defense) of a Draft Compact of Free Association. The Micronesians suggested that the next talks focus on the United States response to Micronesian proposals on the level of United States financial assistance as well as on transitional arrangements; however, the sixth round in Barbers Point, Hawaii, in September and October of 1972, broke down over the issue of independence.

More than a year passed between the sixth and seventh rounds. In addition to disagreement on negotiations on independence, three other issues had accounted for delay: United States negotiations with the Marianas; disputes over the return of land; and the dispute with Williams over the content of the political education program. And by the seventh round, held in Washington in November of 1973, the level of United States financial assistance and the issue of the Marianas brought about another breakdown. After that breakdown, the United States and Micronesia began to emphasize informal private discussions between the leaders of the Micronesians and two or three representatives of the United States. Informal negotiations proceeded in fits and starts. Preliminary agreement over

---

[10]See Appendix I for a description of the major developments of each round.

finances was followed by disagreement over land followed by a breakdown over finances. All along there was disagreement on the Marianas.

CONTROL OVER FUTURE STATUS

In spite of its rhetoric, the United States was never under any illusions about what the Micronesians wanted—the right to unilaterally declare its independence—or about what the United States perceived to be the implication of that right. The United States believed that Micronesia's ability to unilaterally terminate its association with the United States would endanger the third "basic" United States interest in Micronesia: its commitments with respect to the maintenance of peace and security in the Pacific area. Certainly the objectives of the military would be endangered by "free association" —a status which would not bring the much sought guarantee of long-term security in Micronesia. Under free association the United States military would be just as vulnerable as in Japan, the Philippines, or any place where the United States did not have sovereignty.

At the renewed talks held at Hana, October, 1971, the Micronesians forcefully reviewed their position. "Free association" offered an "acceptable compromise" between the desires of the Micronesian people and the "exigencies of the situations" in which Micronesia and the United States found themselves, said Lazarus Salii. Free association, Salii continued, would afford Micronesia a status which had most of the characteristics of full independence and which could be translated into independence if and when the Micronesians chose, but it would also "offer the United States optimal protection of any interest it may have in our islands, whatever they may be." Salii summarized: "We are here to secure independence for our people. We are willing to discuss arrangements wherein that independence has minor limitations placed upon it—limitations as contained in the Free Association proposal. We are not interested in discussing more limiting arrangements."

Salii's opening remarks were explicit; in the afternoon he described control of future status and control of laws as "primary" with the former taking precedence, while land and funding were "subordinate." But the United States discussed land first and did not get around to control of future status for two days, by which time the Micronesians had sent a pointed and formal reminder of their opening remarks:

October 6, 1971

Ambassador Williams:

We would like to remind you that the Micronesian delegation is not authorized by the Congress of Micronesia to compromise or negotiate the right of either side unilaterally to terminate any future association or compact arrived at between Micronesia and the United States. Our question then is: Is the United States Delegation authorized to negotiate on this basis, or are you required by your mandate from your government to insist upon termination only by mutual consent? If you are prepared to accept the principle of unilateral termination, we can discuss procedures which will assure an orderly termination should this take place.

(Signed) Lazarus Salii

Williams responded that he did not wish to be evasive about the scope of his instructions. But the whole truth was that the United States was not prepared to accept unilateral termination. United States strategy was to present sufficient concessions in other areas to keep the talks going. Williams proposed a procedure whereby after a period of years each side would promptly consider and negotiate in good faith those changes, including termination, desired by the other. But it added up to mutual consent. And Williams, obviously aware that his response fell far short of Micronesian demands, twice virtually pleaded with the Micronesians to recognize that negotiations involved give and take and to accommodate United States interests on land and control of laws. Perhaps, Williams later suggested, the Congress of Micronesia might change its insistence on unilateral termination in light of United States concessions in other areas.

Unilateral termination remained, in Salii's words, "the single most important area" of basic disagreement. The United States negotiators left Hana impressed with Micronesian determination on the termination question. But the military also left with a renewed belief in the importance of termination by mutual consent, for the Micronesians also proposed (and withdrew at the next round of talks) that all leases for military land terminate with the termination of the relationship.

At the Micronesians' suggestion, termination was the key question for discussion when the fourth round of negotiations was held at Koror, Palau, April, 1972. The initial United States statement seemed to indicate no change in the United States position. Williams reaffirmed the virtues of the United States position on termination by mutual consent but he added that the United States did not intend that the Micronesian people "should be forced to remain locked forever in a relationship that is detrimental to their best interest and one that remains in effect against their freely expressed will."

But it was the Micronesians who took the initiative on the issue. The Congress of Micronesia, said Salii, had authorized his side to "attempt to arrive at a tentative agreement which in its judgment is best suited to the needs, interests and aspirations of the people of Micronesia." Unilateral termination remained one of the governing principles "deemed essential" to preserve Micronesia's "sovereign rights" and to permit changes in a relationship if the interests of either party required. But, Salii continued, the Micronesians recognized "the importance to the United States of being able to plan on a long range and continuing basis." The Micronesians recognized "the importance of a stable relationship and the American concern for its ability to carry out its responsibilities for the maintenance of peace and security in the Pacific area." Salii then proposed four termination features which he said would preserve the "essential principle of unilateral action but, at the same time, accommodate the security and planning concerns of the United States *and* Micronesia" (emphasis added): 1) An initial period of *five* years during which the compact could not be terminated except by mutual consent; 2) After the initial five years the compact could be unilaterally terminated by either party on one year's notice given prior to January 1; 3) Notice of termination by Micronesia could be given only after a vote of the Congress of Micronesia and subsequent approval by a majority of Micronesian voters; and 4) Immediately on notice of termination the parties would "negotiate in good faith" a security agreement providing for terms and conditions under which the United States might continue to maintain previously agreed-upon military base plans.

On April 11, during an afternoon session, Haydn Williams again presented the long-held United States position on the subject of unilateral termination:

> The events of the past few months have reinforced the need both for continuity and security in the relationship we are discussing. Important changes are occurring, or are certain to occur, in the Pacific and in our relations with countries in this region of the world. In this swiftly changing atmosphere, who can tell what U.S. security interests may be in the years to come? What we cannot guarantee is that today's assessment of our strategic interests will hold good indefinitely. . . . For this very reason, we consider bilateral termination of our future relationship an important benefit for you, as well as us.

Nevertheless, Williams went on to approve, somewhat begrudgingly, of the unilateral termination provision:

> Despite the continuing firm belief of the United States that the best interests of both sides would be better protected by a procedure for termination by mutual consent, the United States is nevertheless agreeable to working out a unilateral termination procedure, which would be written into the proposed Compact of Association, provided our basic interests in foreign affairs and defense have been agreed to.

The procedure suggested by the United States allowed unilateral termination after fifteen years instead of five as the Micronesians had proposed and after a more complicated and difficult procedure than that proposed by the Micronesians. For example, the United States stipulated approval by two-thirds of each house of the Congress of Micronesia and by two-thirds of the electorate. And, for the first time, the United States formally *suggested* fragmentation. Procedures should be written in the compact, suggested Williams, to accommodate other arrangements since "there may exist or arise sentiment among . . . [Micronesians] for allowing individual districts the option of association with the United States despite a Micronesia-wide vote for a change of status." Moreover the United States added the proviso that such a termination arrangement was possible only if basic United States interests in foreign affairs and defense were agreed to.

Even though no agreement could be reached on *procedures* of termination at Koror, agreement had been reached on the principle of unilateral termination. And the Micronesian desire for free association was an established fact—or so it was thought.

Independence had steadfastly been the Micronesians' alternative in case free association was not possible. Independence was a growing force in Micronesia, particularly in Truk and Palau, and among Micronesian students at the University of Hawaii and of Guam. In addition, when the Congress of Micronesia met at Ponape in 1972, it had before it only the partially completed Draft Compact drafted at the fifth round. It was a compact in which Micronesia's concessions were explicit but which did not include, for example, United States financial commitments to Micronesia. Thus, the Draft Compact was vulnerable to attack, particularly from independence advocates. In its special session in Ponape during the summer of 1972, the Congress of Micronesia adopted a resolution authorizing and directing the Micronesian delegation to conduct negotiations with the United States regarding the establishment of an independent nation and to continue negotiations toward free association. In their final report prior to negotiations, the Micronesians had said that free association was their second choice and independence their first. Free association, however, had been thought to be the most practical alternative. Some therefore thought the new Congress of Micronesia directives were not different from previous instructions, although they emphasized independence a little more.

At the sixth round, Salii explained that the Congress of Micronesia did not like the way the talks were moving. There was, he said, an "important and growing sentiment" in Micronesia for independence on its own merits. Although free association was still the mandate, the Micronesian delegation was bound to negotiate for independence so that an alternative of independence would also be before the people of Micronesia when they voted in a plebiscite on their future political status.

United States officials feel there were other reasons for this new approach. They think that Salii, finding himself in trouble in his home district after the fifth round of talks, wanted to show that there had been significant accomplishments in the negotiations and that he could handle the Americans. Thus, he had introduced the incomplete and tentative Draft Compact for approval by the Congress of Micronesia which wisely refused to ratify it. Salii would later comment about the Ponape directive that "it wasn't really clear in our own minds how we were going to handle free association and independence at the same time." United States officials claim that Salii came to the sixth round under pressure to "hardline" the United States but that the Micronesian position was so confused that Senators Nakayama and Amaraich, previously two of the most ardent supporters of independence, were not prepared to push independence.

The United States delegates did not take the Ponape directive seriously; they pictured the new approach as more of a personal move by Salii than a serious demand by the Congress of Micronesia and also felt that the Micronesians, wishing to stretch for negotiating room, had used the "threat" of independence as a bargaining tool.

Perhaps in an effort to assert more authority, the "threat" of independence would be used again. Shortly before the seventh round, one member of the Micronesian negotiating team commented, "If the United States fails [to meet Micronesian demands] then we opt for independence."

At Barbers Point in September and October, 1972, the United States delegation claimed that it did not know what the Micronesians meant by independence and had no instructions on how to handle the issue. The fact is the United States delegation was specifically instructed to avoid a discussion of independence. In addition, in a not too veiled threat (which would later lead to United Nations chastisement) the United States let the Micronesians know that United States strategic requirements would not countenance independence. Thus the talks broke off indefinitely. They did not resume until a year later and even then, it was so clear that the level of United States financial assistance was directly tied to the termination issue that financial assistance was the focus.

The United States position on independence was not resolved until the eve of the November, 1973, negotiations between the United States and the Joint Status Committee of the Congress of Micronesia. President Nixon approved inclusion of the independence option in a plebiscite for Micronesia.[11] In so doing, the President came down on the side of the Department of State, the United States Mission to the United Nations, and some lower level Pentagon and Interior officials who have consistently argued that whether the inclusion of an independence option is legally required is irrelevant. The independence option is a practical political necessity.

LAND

Land and its acquisition had long been a major point of friction between the Micronesians and the United States administrators. The inhabitants claim that a

---

[11] It should be noted that United States military land requirements were already assured by separate negotiations with the Mariana Islands.

substantial amount of land was either confiscated by the Japanese or acquired at unreasonably low rates by the Japanese and the United States. Almost every United Nations Visiting Mission has urged the United States to take steps to settle long-standing land disputes. Given the scarcity of their land, the role of land in Micronesian culture, past experience with foreign land acquisition and the uncertain and unlimited nature of future military needs, it was not surprising that Micronesians summarily rejected eminent domain provisions of the "commonwealth" proposal of 1969.

Two kinds of land have been the subject of dispute:

1) *Public lands*—land owned or maintained by the Japanese as government or public land; land formerly owned by Japanese individuals, agencies, and corporations, and land acquired by the Trust Territory government for public purposes. Theoretically, public land is being held for use by Micronesians who would also decide on the manner of its disposition. Public land amounts to 60 per cent of total land in Micronesia and is distributed as follows: Yap, 3 per cent; Marshals, 13 per cent; Truk, 17 per cent; Ponape, 66 per cent; Palau, 68 per cent; and the Marianas, 90 per cent. According to the United States, the largest percentages are found in districts with the largest islands, "primarily because these larger island areas were acquired and used by the Japanese for agricultural and industrial purposes."

2) *Retention land*—land reserved or used by the United States government. The amount of retention currently totals 3.8 per cent of the total land in Micronesia. But the figure has been larger. A total of 21,141 acres had been turned over to the Trust Territory government including all military retention land held in Yap, Palau, and Truk. But Defense still controls more land than any United States agency: 3,031 acres under use and occupancy agreements in Kwajalein, Eniwetok, and Bikini Atolls and 8,882 acres on Tinian and 4,943 acres on Saipan for a total of 13,825 acres in the Marianas. An additional 519 acres is in use by the Coast Guard (500 acres), and the Post Office (6 acres) and the National Weather Service (13 acres).

As part of its new approach at the third round of negotiations, the United States backed off its insistence during the first two rounds that the United States ultimately have an unrestricted right to eminent domain. For the first time, the United States outlined a formula whereby specifically stated United States military land requirements would be agreed on prior to a change in status. Any future United States needs would be in accordance with Micronesian laws and "mutually agreed on procedures". In addition, the Micronesians would agree to negotiate in good faith for emergency and temporary land use.

The United States, said Williams, had "gone to considerable lengths" to keep its military land requirements at a minimum. There were no military land requirements in Yap, Ponape or Truk. In other districts the United States outlined the following requirement:

- *Marshalls:* No additional land was needed in the Marshalls in addition to existing missile range facilities at Kwajalein. There facilities were described as "important and integral" to military research. And while consolidated tests might lead to smaller land needs, there was "no prospect" that the need for missile testing would disappear or even diminish in the near future.

- *Marianas:* The United States had definite requirements, primarily on Tinian where the United States wished the "flexibility" to rehabilitate some existing airstrips and to build supporting structures and "other facilities." By "consolidating" future activities mainly on Tinian, the United States would be in a position to release a "significant portion" of the 4,000 acres it held on Saipan. In addition, the United States thought it "essential" to have use of Farallon de Medinilla Island, for which a use and occupancy agreement was then being negotiated with the Trust Territory government.

- *Palau:* There was no immediate need for land in Palau but the United States wished four options: 1) forty acres of submerged and adjacent land to establish a "very small naval support facility at Malakal Harbor," configured to support naval ships calling periodically at Palau; 2) an unspecified amount of land on Babelthuap to build structures and store material; 3) the right to hold "intermittent" training exercises ashore for ground units (exercises would be for "only a few limited periods every year" and property owners would be fully compensated for property use and damage); and 4) the right to build or to use jointly a civilian airport to support operations under the options.

In return for its land needs, the United States promised a fair and adequate compensation and reminded the Micronesians that some other benefits would accrue such as harbor dredging and improved road, port, and communications facilities.

Thus on the subject of land, the United States made a major change at Hana. Lands would be under full Micronesian control; their major fear, unknown and unlimited military acqustion, was eliminated. Even by Micronesian standards the United States land requests did not appear large. Indeed, a consultant to the Micronesians recalls that they were surprised at United States modesty and may also have been disappointed since modest land needs would surely mean more modest financial support.

In the fifth round, sharp differences began to develop over the methods of returning land to Micronesian control and to the potential presence of the military. The Palau legislature indicated that the military was not welcome. Still others, including the speaker of the Palau legislature and a prominent chief from Babelthuap, believed that discussion of possible military use of land should take place only after land had been returned to the people of Palau, implying that the United States was withholding land in order to blackmail Micronesians into agreement. "It's not that we don't like or distrust the Americans," the speaker told an interviewer. "Americans are good people—after you learn now to deal with them. And we now know the rules of the games." In any event, in late 1972, the Palau legislature demanded the return of public land to the chiefs of Palau to hold in trust and made the return a precondition to resumption of the talks (which had been stalled on the question of independence). The Palau position became the Micronesian position and it was only after the United States indicated agreement on disposition of land that the abortive seventh round of negotiations took place in Washington, in November, 1973. As if to reinforce Micronesian views, a delegation of both elected and traditional leaders from Palau were on hand to hear the United States statement of land policy.

At the outset, the United States announced that public land would be turned over to each district prior to termination of the Trusteeship Agreement after passage of implementing legislation by the Congress of Micronesia. However, the United States insisted on a number of "safeguards." Clearly the most important was the United States requirement that title to public land which had been requested by the United States for military purposes would not be changed until a commitment had been made to meet United States land needs. The Micronesians objected to leases as preconditions for the return of public land, noting that they were already committed in principle to meet United States defense requirements.

However, the United States announcement that land would be returned to each district was sufficiently responsive to lead to renewed negotiations—only to have the new negotiations promptly break down over finances. But the land question was far from resolved. The United States, through the Trust Territory government, asked the Congress of Micronesia to pass legislation implementing the new land policy. Twice in 1974 the Congress of Micronesia passed land legislation, but without all of the "safeguards" contained in the United States policy announcement. Twice the high commissioner vetoed the legislation. Among other things, the Congress of Micronesia insisted that public lands be returned to the Congress of Micronesia and then to the Districts; that the right of eminent domain rest with the Districts and not the central government; that agreement to meet military land needs not be a precondition for the return of land; and that land questions previously "settled" but controversial be subject to review. The United States opposed these conditions largely because they would endanger or at least make more difficult the attainment of United States land objectives, not only in the five districts but in the Marianas as well.

As in other instances, the United States had the authority to make its will law by executive order. At a meeting in Honolulu in November, 1974, representatives of the Interior Department met to "consult" with Micronesian representatives on United States land actions. The United States informed the Micronesians that an executive order would be issued implementing land transfers along the lines of the November, 1973, United States policy announcement. The Micronesians promptly walked out and negotiations were again at an impasse and again on *the* item of central importance to Micronesians and their culture—land.

CONTROL OF LAWS

Control of their own internal affairs had been one of the principal Micronesian objections to the so-called commonwealth proposal which the Micronesians had rejected. For, unlike the Commonwealth of Puerto Rico or even the commonwealth which the United States would later work out with the Marianas, the initial United States commonwealth proposal retained for the United States large measures of control over Micronesian internal affairs. Even the basic law governing Micronesia would have been passed by the United States Congress in the form of an organic act.

At the third round, the United States reversed its position. Ambassador Williams said that the Micronesians would be able to write, adopt and amend their own constitution and write, adopt and amend legislation governing Micronesian internal affairs. The constitution would be consistent with the basic understandings and terms of a compact between the United States and Micronesia. There would be provision for the protection of fundamental human rights. However, circumstances in Micronesia might dictate some provisions and procedures which might differ from what might be done in the United States. For example, the Micronesians might wish provisions to protect their land from purchase by other than Micronesian citizens. Finally, the compact would specifically state those areas where responsibility was delegated to the United States. There would be no other United States responsibility except by mutual consent.

The United States representative recalled that the Micronesians themselves had suggested in 1970 that the United States handle foreign affairs and defense and that "it would be therefore necessary for the United States to retain sufficient powers" in those areas to enable it to fulfill its responsibilities. Indeed, the United States representative acknowledged that his government looked with favor on the allocation of authority contained in the agreement between the United Kingdom and the West Indies Associated States of 1967, although during the second round United States negotiators had feigned ignorance of that arrangement.[12] The United States delegation suggested that there were services in health, education, public works and postal and currency which Micronesia might wish to request from the United States which would require agreement as to rules and regulations. For example, if United States postal services were used, United States postal laws and regulations would be applicable in Micronesia.

The Micronesians were delighted with the new United States proposals that Micronesians govern their internal affairs. However, they asked for clarification of the suggestion that some United States laws would be applicable. They recognized the rationale for the application of American laws where United States responsibility or services were made available but suggested that authority derive from Micronesian laws parallel or identical to American laws. They envisioned practical problems otherwise, as when American law enforcement personnel might seek to make arrests in Micronesia or if a Micronesian were tried in American courts in the United States. In his response, the United States representative acknowledged potential conflicts but suggested that the best approach was for each side to decide which services would be used and then to work out procedures to resolve potential conflicts.

There was no detailed discussion of the issue of control of laws from the fourth to the seventh rounds, except that at the fourth round, Salii suggested in a summary of agreements already reached in principle that United States law would be applicable only if specified in the compact or as otherwise agreed in connection with specific United States services and programs.

DEFENSE AND FOREIGN AFFAIRS

The Micronesians noted that the United States had not spelled out its approach to foreign affairs and defense or the powers that United States would require in Micronesia to fulfill foreign affairs and defense responsibilities. The Micronesians however had hardened their own views: Micronesia had to have the "determinative voice" in defense and foreign affairs without which it could not be truly sovereign.

1) Micronesians had to give their consent before any international legal obligation was reached in their name or was made applicable to Micronesia.

---

[12] Great Britain was to have responsibility for "any matter which in the opinion of Her Majesty's government in the United Kingdom is a matter relating to defense."

2) The United States would seek concurrence before taking "steps which would have a direct impact on Micronesia's interest."

3) Micronesia would reserve the right to reach agreements on its own behalf with nations other than the United States, and with international institutions in matters of economic, cultural, educational, social and scientific character. In particular, Micronesia would reserve the power to: (a) negotiate and conclude trade agreements; (b) seek economic assistance from other countries and from international institutions; (c) seek technical assistance and employ nationals from other countries and from international institutions; and (d) apply for membership in United Nations specialized agencies or similar international organizations.

4) They wanted a Micronesian attached to those United States embassies which handled a high volume of Micronesian business.

5) Micronesia would establish its own tariff schedules and other mechanisms to control imports. Among other things, they thought it necessary for balance of payments reasons for the United States to accept restrictions on entry of United States goods, but to allow unrestrained entrance of Micronesian goods into the United States.

6) They wished free entry to the United States and the right to seek employment but thought their small size should allow them to restrict Americans in Micronesia on a most-favored-nations basis.

7) The Micronesians wished prior consent before storage of dangerous materials.

In response to these views, the United States delegation pointed out that there was already legislation pending which would give Micronesians preferred status in the United States. They believed that the Micronesians might better restrict immigration and tourism indirectly (e.g., tourist facilities, rates, etc.) rather than by direct restrictions on American citizens. Similarly, legislation was pending to allow the free entry of Micronesian goods into the United States. The United States would expect reciprocity; however, there were ways such as excise and sales taxes which the Micronesians could use to hold down imports provided such taxes did not discriminate as to country of origin.

Although there was an effort to emphasize areas of agreement, there is little question that the United States was disturbed that the Micronesians wanted so much responsibility in foreign affairs and defense, especially since they also insisted on the right to unilaterally declare their independence. "We would be less than forthright," said Williams, "if we did not state clearly that there remain some fundamental differences or at a minimum, misunderstandings between us which must be resolved prior to your change in status. These differences do effect our legitimate interests, our responsibilities, and our obligations." He continued:

The fundamental divergence is this: You have described and proposed a relationship which would be so loose and tenuous, and the protection of U.S. interests so circumscribed and qualified, as to raise serious doubts as to whether my Government could be responsive. I am not speaking simply of my present negotiating authority but, more fundamentally, of feelings in both the Executive and Legislative Branches of my government as measured by my consultations and their reactions prior to our coming to Hana, Maui. These feelings also reflect the consideration of the views, attitudes, and interests of other Pacific nations with respect to the need for political and economic stability in the Pacific Ocean area. We know that you too share and have a vital stake in this matter.

The United States did not see the proposed agreement as a treaty but a "binding compact with legal definition of its own and recognized as such by both parties and by the world community." It would be an "agreement between two parties and between two peoples concerning the respective power and responsibilities of each within, and only within, those areas covered by the agreement. The basic division of power and responsibilities would flow from the force of the voluntary and freely expressed agreement of each party to the compact, rather than being assigned from one party to another." The United States did not envision approval of the compact only by the United States Senate, as in the case of treaties, but submission to both Houses in view of the financial implications of any agreement and the fact that appropriations measures must originate in the United States House of Representatives.

The United States delegation particularly had difficulty with Micronesian requests that they maintain what the United States representative called a "veto" in foreign affairs and with their request for prior consent on the storage of dangerous weapons. The United States envisioned close and continuous consultations but said the Micronesian proposals would "substantially vitiate" the authority of the United States in the two areas which the Micronesians had all along proposed would be left to the United States. The United States delegation said that advance revelation of dangerous material movement and storage was "counter to the strategic and tactical interests of the military" but suggested that Micronesian apprehensions could be allayed by looking at the limited nature of United States land needs.

The questions of defense and foreign affairs were discussed again at the fourth round. Again the United States reiterated that it desired prerogatives in defense along the lines of the West Indies Act, i.e., while the United States would "consult" on matters directly related to Micronesia, it required full and final authority in defense and in foreign affairs to carry out its threefold responsibility: defense; denial; and use of Micronesian waters and soil to support United States military obligations in the Pacific. The United States delegation saw significant value in a status of forces agreement aimed at eliminating military/civilian conflict.

The Micronesian response was again agreeable in principle to delegating authority for defense to the United States. But they rejected sweeping authority such as that contained in the West Indies Act and several times sought standards and criteria to insure that there would not be any "unduly expansive interpretations as to defense matters." They wished prior consent, for example, if the United States changed the use of a facility from missile testing to storage of chemical and biological weapons. On the other hand, they would not object and sought no control over whether military facilities were used for a specific policy objective. As Salii put it:

> ... we recognize that the Government of Micronesia would retain no veto power as to the situations and circumstances under which the United States might elect to utilize these military facilities. The determination of when and under what circumstances [the United States] will require use of these bases will reside within the exclusive control of the United States Government.

The United States delegation just as repeatedly stated that it could not accept the severe limitations which the Micronesians seemed to be placing on defense and which the United States saw as hampering its fulfillment of its three basic defense responsibilities. The United States was willing to *consult* on possible changes in use of Micronesian bases and to insure that defense activities did not adversely affect Micronesia's environment. However, it objected to any requirement that Micronesian approval would be necessary if the use of a facility was changed (e.g., missile testing to chemical weapons storage).

In the final analysis, in addition to agreements already reached, the two sides compromised on the issue of changing the use of bases. The United States undertook to consult and seek Micronesian consent to any military uses which differed significantly from the use specified in leases.

The United States sought to spell out its desired role in foreign affairs. It desired "full authority" (by which it meant that it would be responsible for Micronesia's foreign relations) and would "represent Micronesia in all official government-to-government relationships and in international organizations and conventions which required official government representation and participation." Micronesia's policies and positions in "areas touching upon foreign affairs would have to be consistent with or at least not in conflict with American foreign policy." In the event of a dispute, the United States wanted the "primacy of overall United States foreign policy considerations" to be clear. For example, the United States would not wish Micronesian control of their own tariffs to include preferential trade arrangements while the United States was promoting non-discriminatory world trade within the General Agreement on Trade and Tariffs framework.

On the other hand, the United States did not want Micronesia to be isolated from the world community. The actual exercise of foreign affairs in many areas of closest concern to Micronesia would be "delegated" to Micronesia. The United States would encourage and assist Micronesian contact with foreign countries in commercial, cultural, technical and educational areas. Micronesia would be free to seek technical and economic assistance from regional and international organizations and to participate directly as members or associate members in appropriate regional and other international organizations (e.g., the Economic Commission for Asia and the Far East) of special interest to Micronesia and, in certain "limited key areas of major and special importance" (e.g., airline routes in Micronesia), prior Micronesian consent might be required. But the United States made clear that, in the final analysis, any Micronesian participation in foreign affairs must be within the "broad concept of plenary United States responsibility for foreign affairs."

The Micronesians responded that they were prepared to recommend that the United States be "invested" with authority to act on Micronesia's behalf in view of what the United States had described as its "larger role in world affairs," but wished to retain authority to conduct their own affairs in the areas of trade, international organization, regional associations and the like. For example, they saw no reason why they should not be free to enter into direct agreements with foreign countries on the free reciprocal entry of goods and people. Finally, they proposed to utilize United States services related to representative and protective services.

In general, the Micronesians made a distinction between external affairs which involved security matters and areas involving their economic, education and cultural development. They were willing to delegate the former with reservation (e.g., they opposed weapons storage) but not the latter. As Salii explained:

> It is essential that the Compact and the new relationship which it brings into existence recognize the fundamental sovereignty of the State of Micronesia. Intrinsic to the concept of sovereignty is the authority of a country over both its internal affairs and its foreign relations. Recognizing the security interests of the United States, which are not identical with those of Micronesia, the Micronesian Delegation is prepared to recommend to the Congress of Micronesia that full authority be delegated to the United States for the conduct of the external relations of Micronesia which bear significantly on international security matters. On the other hand, the Government of Micronesia must reserve to itself the authority to negotiate and consummate arrangements that relate to matters of trade, economics, foreign investment and cultural affairs that are not directly relevant to security and defense matters.

The United States representative found the Micronesian division of authority "directly counter" to the United States need for "full authority." The Micronesian proposal was unacceptable because it contained "a corollary giving Micronesia the right to decide what agreements bear on United States interest and which ones affect only local matters." The United States representative saw, for example, the possibility of political penetration as the result of trade missions, of policy conflicts on items such as free trade and, in general, of numerous disputes as to authority.

The United States representative suggested that since both sides were in general agreement that Micronesian international activities would have to be consistent with United States foreign policy and security interests, their differences really related to the questions of formal and official intergovernmental relations. The Micronesians in turn agreed to leave government-to-government agreements to the United States, provided such agreements were initiated at the request of Micronesia and were concluded with Micronesian participation and consent. The Micronesian government would be free to negotiate and sign contracts which do not involve direct intergovernmental obligations and responsibilities. (These could even include agreements with government-owned banks.) Micronesia would also participate in appropriate regional and international organizations.

Both the defense and foreign affairs provisions were subsequently included in the Draft Compact written at the fifth round in Washington. Neither provision was to receive much direct discussion at later rounds, although there was extended discussion of a mutual defense pact which would come into effect on termination of the compact. Indirectly, both defense and foreign affairs remained at issue, not so much as to their provision but as to whether the United States should play such a large role and, particularly, have access to land use if the United States financial offer were not correspondingly generous.

FINANCE

It appeared at the third round that the Micronesians and United States negotiators were in agreement on the role of finance in the negotiations. Lazarus Salii labeled future funding as subordinate to the issues of control of future status and control of laws. Williams agreed that any "future relationships should not be dictated by financial considerations" and later added that financial questions were subordinate to other questions to be decided. However, the real United States position was sandwiched between its statements of seeming agreement with the Micronesians. In Williams's words, "the form, substance and continuity of a future association will have a direct bearing in the long term on our financial relationship."

At the third round, the United States was diplomatic and elliptical in presenting its view on the connection between permanence of the relationship and the level of financial support. At the fourth round it was more direct. Recalling his earlier remarks at Hana about form, substance and continuity, Williams added: "Under a close association there is a greater likelihood that the United

States Congress and the American taxpayer will be willing to accept the responsibility of long-term and abiding commitments to the people of Micronesia. It stands to reason, conversely, that the more tenuous the relationship, the more difficult it will be to assure continuing and adequate budgetary support and the availability of federal programs and services."

Unofficially, United States officials were even more blunt. One member of the United States negotiating team accused the Micronesians of wanting to limit their relationship with the United States to "an office where Micronesians can pick up the check." A Micronesia which could unilaterally change the relationship could not expect, the official remarked, to get the same financial support it would have had under a "commonwealth" status.

But the United States was not alone in camouflaging its real position on financial matters. The Micronesians seemed to de-emphasize financial considerations, particularly the tie between finances and the nature of the relationship. In fact, the Micronesian position was the exact opposite of the position of the United States, a fact which was to become clear when the talks broke down at the seventh round in November, 1973. For the United States, financial levels depended on the nature of the political relationship; for the Micronesians, the nature of the political relationship depended on the level of United States financial support.

The two sides also disagreed on the conceptual approach of how to calculate United States financial payments after trusteeship. The United States wanted to calculate on the basis of how much Micronesia would "need" for support and development, the nature of future financial policies and institutions, and the possible continuation of current United States programs and services. For example, at the third round, possibly in an effort to lower Micronesian expectations, the United States cited the existing magnitude of United States assistance as the only tangible indicator of the amount of support which the United States Congress might approve in the future. Estimated United States expenditures were said to exceed $75 million, broken down as follows: $60 million annual appropriation; $7.4 million in Office of Equal Opportunity, Health, Education and Welfare, Peace Corps, etc. programs; $1.8 million by the Post Office; $1 million by the Coast Guard; plus expenditures by the Department of Defense on excess material, ship loans, and Civic Action Teams. The $75 million appears to be slightly inflated, for the United States apparently included approximately $2.5 million earned by Micronesian employees at Kwajalein and approximately $2 million realized from sales and income taxes at Kwajalein.

On the other hand, the Micronesians looked upon their "strategic location" as their only natural resource. The United States was being asked to pay for the purchase of that commodity as well as to meet moral financial obligations arising out of trusteeship. Their position was similar to the "strategic rental" concept in the Solomon Report of ten years earlier. The Micronesians proposed that financing be divided into four basic areas:

1) Continuing economic support to be provided Micronesia during its transition from trusteeship to "economic independence";
2) Compensation on an annual basis for the agreement by Micronesia to deny the use of its land and waters to military forces of any nation other than the United States;
3) Annual payment for the continuing right to use specified land and waters for United States military bases and operations; and
4) Payment for specific rentals for military use of land and territorial waters and options on specific land and territorial waters.

The Micronesians suggested that the United States provide $50 million annually for the first category, economic support, and another $50 million annually for the three categories of compensation for military privileges, plus an unspecified amount of transitional assistance. The Micronesian request was substantial, but as Senator Daniel Inoyue had pointed out earlier, the Micronesians were aware that the United States was then paying Spain as much as $100 million annually for base rental.

The Micronesian request for a guaranteed $1 billion over ten years (adjusted in the event of inflation and devaluation) was significantly higher than earlier United States suggestions of about $75 million annually for an unspecified period. However, having itself broached the financial question, the United States was unwilling to discuss specific figures, preferring to hold out until the Micronesians were more specific about the nature of the new relationship. But it was clear that a chasm separated United States and Micronesian views on the amount of United States financial support. "I would be doing you a disfavor," said Williams in a statement inserted into the record, "if I were to leave this [financial] issue without stating candidly that our views on the future level and categories of United States support are far apart."

How far the two sides were apart would remain unclear for another year and a half when the talks at the seventh round immediately broke down over the question of finances. This time it was the Micronesians who would link finance and the nature of the association.

Subsequently, during informal talks in Washington, the United States for the first time suggested an annual payment of $40 to $43 million, in addition to services of the Federal Aviation Agency, the Post Office, and the Weather Bureau. (The two sides were unable to agree on the value of the United States proposal—$40-41 million, said the Micronesians; $43 million, said the United States.) The figure was significantly below the $100 million plus figure advanced by the Micronesians at the fourth round and well below the $75 million budget for all of Micronesia, which the United States originally suggested was a "tangible indicator" of the amount the United States Congress might support. "It has been and remains our position," said Salii, "that we cannot usefully discuss the remaining details of the proposed Compact of Free Association until it becomes clear that there is a substantial likelihood that we can reach agreement on the question of financial support."

The United States proposal "for the six districts" was unacceptable, said Salii, and the United States had been unwilling to improve its offer despite a Micronesian offer to reduce their request by $20 million and to accept a "significant diminution" in federal programs. The "wide gap" and "apparently unyielding" United States stance, said Salii, made it impossible to proceed with discussions about a compact unless it was on the basis of "a significant curtailment" of the degree of authority to be delegated to the United States in the areas of foreign affairs and defense.

Buried in Salii's statement was the third major difference between the two sides on financial questions. The United States proposal was for a five district Micronesia, since the Mariana Islands District was already engaged in advanced negotiations with the United States for a so-called commonwealth status. On the other hand, the Micronesians continued to negotiate for six districts, never having accepted the Marianas negotiations as legal.

The United States did not budge in its response to a virtual ultimatum. The United States proposal, Williams stated, was based on its estimates of Micronesia's future needs: Micronesia's desire to work toward economic self-sufficiency; gradual economic development taking into account the need to preserve Micronesian traditions and culture; less costly, simpler and decentralized government; reduced dependence on expatriates; exclusion of the Marianas. In fact, Williams argued, on the basis of these criteria the United States proposal of $43 million, excluding payments for use of public land was above United States projections of Micronesian needs and represented United States efforts to continue to support Micronesia at substantially the same level as during the closing years of the Trusteeship. In addition, Williams concluded, new sources of income such as additional taxes, bilateral and multilateral assistance and private funding would become available to a freely associated Micronesia.

INFORMAL NEGOTIATIONS

The Washington finance negotiations ended abruptly and bitterly. A series of informal and unofficial negotiations with limited participation on each side would replace the formal rounds of talks. United States and Micronesian negotiators met quietly and briefly at Guam, Hawaii and California. At the same time, the United States unilaterally took a number of steps to improve the negotiating climate. The most important step took place in January, 1974, when Secretary of the Interior Morton announced that the United States would no longer automatically exclude countries other than the United States from investing in Micronesia. Instead, the initial decision on investment applications would be left to each district. Final approval would be left to the high commissioner, who was to base his approval "on the security of the area and the general welfare and development of the Micronesian people." Thus, the United States still maintained control over undesirable investment whether Japanese, Chinese or Soviet. In addition, Morton asked the high commissioner and his staff to draw up a five-year program of capital improvements and to develop plans for their construction.

Both announcements had a potentially revolutionary effect on Micronesia's future—they might have been highly praised in Micronesia, and they were, in fact, welcomed by some. But the foreign investment announcement was widely questioned, and, in some instances, strongly denounced. Micronesian leaders objected to such an important announcement without prior consultation, especially since the Congress of Micronesia was in session. Micronesian officials and businessmen argued that machinery had not been established to implement the new policy. Said Senator Edward Pangelinan, head of the Marianas negotiators: "I think they've opened a Pandora's box and I don't know how we're going to control this monster." Prominent businessmen in Truk and Palau suggested that Micronesians did not have the technical knowledge to enable them to evaluate sophisticated foreign proposals or to compete with foreign businesses; others, particularly in Yap, feared an adverse cultural impact from a heavy influx of tourism. Finally, Micronesians particularly objected to the Madison Avenue nature of the announcement: a filmed speech, hand-carried to Micronesia by an Interior Department official, then hand-delivered to district headquarters by the director of public affairs, and then shown and broadcast simultaneously throughout Micronesia. With all that coordination, said one official, they could have consulted us if they had cared.

Lost in all the commotion was Morton's announcement on capital improvement. Intentionally or not, the five-year capital improvement program provided a formula for a resolution of the impasse over finances. At meetings in the spring of 1974 at Carmel, California, and later at Guam, it was agreed that the effective date for termination of the Trusteeship Agreement would be delayed until 1981, that is, until after initiation and completion of a $416 million capital improvement project. Thus, the burden of financing needed capital improvement was made a part of the continuing United States Trusteeship obligations instead of a major and pressing problem of a new Micronesian government. Now both the Micronesians and the United States could present a respectable cost figure to their respective constituencies. In addition, the two parties agreed to the following financial provisions (in constant dollars) of a fifteen-year compact:

1) A United States grant to Micronesia of $35 million annually for the first five years; $30 million annually for the second five years; and $25 million annually for the tenth through fifteenth year. (Section 401)
2) A United States grant for capital improvement of $12.5 million annually for the first five years; $11 million annually for the the next five years; and $9.5 million annually for the next five years. (Section 404a)
3) The United States will provide economic development loans amounting to $5 million annually for fifteen years, subject to the terms of long-term, low-interest loan agreements. (Section 404b)
4) The United States will provide services of the United States Postal Service, the United States Weather Service, and the Federal Aviation Administration (FAA). No dollar figure is given, but the United States had previously estimated the value of postal services to all of Micronesia at $1.8 million. The Weather Service put its services for 1975 at $2,161 and the FAA budget at $144,495. No mention is made of the services for the Coast Guard.

In total, the United States agreed to provide, over fifteen years, a total of $690 million, broken down as follows:

U.S. Grants	
First 5 years	$175 million
Second 5 years	$150 million
Third 5 years	$125 million
Capital Improvements	
First 5 years	$62.5 million
Second 5 years	$55 million
Third 5 years	$47.5 million
Development Loans	$75 million

Once again, what appeared to be agreement did not turn out to be true. During its spring 1975 session, the Congress of Micronesia rejected the financial package as inadequate. But dissatisfaction on financial matters was only part of the problem. The Micronesians continued to object to the United States land policies, to the extent of American control on foreign affairs, and to the United States policy on the Marianas. Finally, disillusioned at the impasse and at their own powerlessness, the Micronesian spokesman told the 1975 meeting of the Trusteeship Council that free association was no longer the basis of an agreement. The trustee and its wards had reached an impasse.

. . . After a quarter century of American administration, our people have come to know and appreciate the American system of government. The concept of democracy has been very important and significant to us . . . . We desire a close political union with the United States of America—a membership in the United States political family.

—Edward Pangelinan

We've been had.

—Andon Amaraich

VI

The Marianas Break Away

The United States decision in 1951 to administer the Marianas separately from the other districts was taken for United States military reasons, not for any separatist sentiment in the Marianas. For more than ten years following the separation, however — even following return of the Marianas from the Navy to Interior — the Marianas expressed the desire for a "close and permanent affiliation with the United States" through referenda, resolutions adopted by the district legislature, petitions to the United Nations, endorsement of the 1970 "commonwealth" proposal, and direct representation to the United States government. Given their small population, the Marianas had pushed for a bicameral instead of a unicameral legislature at the time of the formation of the Congress of Micronesia. However, they had already concluded that this classic means of protecting small units from the decisions of the majority was insufficient for their purposes. Much opposed territory-wide tax legislation had already been enacted despite opposition from the Marianas. There was every possibility that once they were a part of a new Micronesia unit they would be even more vulnerable to what they saw as unfair legislation passed for the benefit of more populous districts. The Marianas representatives on the Micronesian negotiating team had become increasingly dissatisfied after the Micronesian delegation flatly rejected the "commonwealth" proposal. They were particularly adverse to inclusion in a unit that could some day terminate its relationship with the United States.

Thus, it came as a surprise to no one when, at the close of the fourth round, representatives from the Marianas formally requested separate negotiations with the United States. Culture, geographic distance from other districts, and relatively greater economic development and aspirations set the Marianas off from the rest of Micronesia. Most important, previous separate administration by the United States (entirely for United States military purposes) contributed to the desire for separation from the rest of Micronesia.

The inhabitants of these islands are largely of Chamorro descent, although about 4,000 of the total population of 12,500 are Carolinians.[1] Mariana Islanders tend to look down on other Micronesians—even on the Palauans, who are said to look down on everyone. Their neighbor, Guam, though geographically part of the Marianas, became an unincorporated territory of the United States in 1898. Guam's relatively modest economic achievements have always loomed large to the people of the substantially less well-off Marianas District and have been attributed to Guam's close association with the United States. The Marianas decided they wanted the same for themselves. As their request said, "The United States has brought to our people the values which we cherish and the economic goals which we desire."

---

[1] An additional 2,500 residents of the Marianas are "foreigners," i.e. , Micronesians from other districts and American civil servants.

In the longstanding Marianas drive for close association with the United States, the idea of "reintegration" with their fellow Chamorros on Guam was rejected, for the immediate future and probably indefinitely. In a 1969 referendum Guam's voters rejected reintegration. Like budding nationalists elsewhere, the leaders of the Marianas did not welcome loss of their political identity in the larger and already established political unit of Guam. They saw *themselves* as governors and senators and concluded that such positions would surely be held by Guamanians with "reintegration." Reintegration came to be viewed as "political suicide"; people believed the Northern Marianas would be "swallowed up" by better developed and more educated Guam.

In the Marianas view, Guam's status as an unincorporated territory was colonial, and it was thought that the Marianas could do better. They had a protected position as a United Nations ward; the American military really wanted facilities there (and might not be able to have them elsewhere in Micronesia). Thus, the Marianas had a unique bargaining position. At a February, 1974, meeting on the subject of Guam and Micronesian status at the University of Guam, Edward Pangelinan, a graduate of Howard University Law School and chairman of the Micronesian Status Delegation, openly denounced the status of Guam and even that of Puerto Rico as inadequate. The Marianas, he said, wished to develop a new kind of relationship with the United States.[2]

The Marianas took advantage of their unique bargaining position at the fourth round of negotiations; there the United States formally accepted the principle of unilateral termination. On April 11, 1972, Marianas representatives on the Micronesian delegation, Edward Pangelinan and Herman Guerrero, presented to the United States delegation a letter and a statement of position, which they said were transmitted "with approval of the members of the Joint Committee on Future Status." This was the first known formal communication regarding separate negotiations. The question was whether the United States would consider conducting separate negotiations with the Marianas. The statement of position began simply, "The people of the Mariana Islands District desire a close political relationship with the United States of America."

The United States representative was able to approve the request the afternoon it was presented to him. Preliminary contact with representatives of the Marianas had been extensive, although the amount and timing remain unclear. What is clear is that, although up until 1972 United States policy had been clearly against separation, the State Department representative in Saipan, John Dorrance, had begun to explore informally with Marianas representatives the possibility of separate negotiations on numerous occasions. The deputy United States representative, Arthur Hummel, had himself explored the question as well during a visit to Saipan.

---

[2] See Benjamin F. Bast, ed., *The Political Future of Guam and Micronesia* (Agana: University of Guam Press, 1974).

MICRONESIAN REACTION TO SEPARATE NEGOTIATIONS

According to several Micronesian delegation sources, the Micronesians never approved of separate negotiations or even the transmittal of a request, as the letter from Pangelinan and Guerrero asserted and as United States representatives were to repeatedly assert, at least initially, in defense of separate negotiations. The Marianas representatives had indeed first taken their letter to the Micronesian delegation and had asked them to present the letter to the United States representative. The Micronesian group then had a long debate over whether to transmit the letter themselves, approve the transmittal by the Marianas, or disapprove the transmittal. The Micronesians decided not to transmit the letter to Williams, stating that they had no authority to approve or disapprove of transmittal by the Marianas representatives, but adding that the group had no control over actions taken by Pangelinan and Guerrero in their individual capacities either.

In fact, the Micronesians virtually ignored the fact that separate negotiations were requested and approved by the United States. The Micronesian delegation communique of the fourth round stated they were "pleased" at the progress made in the fourth round and made no mention of the request for separate negotiations. No mention of separate negotiations was made in Salii's statement of the afternoon session of April 12, 1972, in Ambassador Williams's final statement of April 13 (which was inserted in the record but not read), or in the joint communique of the fourth round. The Marianas letter and statement of position can be found in the United States version of the official records of the fourth round, but not in the Congress of Micronesia's version.

Micronesian disapproval of separate negotiations was to remain an underlying issue between the United States and the Micronesian negotiators. The issue surfaced several times in subsequent negotiations. For example, Senator Salii several times requested materials concerning United States land requirements in the Marianas and pointed out:

> As you are aware, the mandate received by this Committee from the Congress of Micronesia requires that our consideration and negotiations encompass the entire present Trust Territory and not only five out of six districts. The unilateral action of the United States in accepting separate negotiations with the Marianas does not, obviously, relieve this Committee from the obligations with which the Congress has entrusted us.

In the seventh round, the problem came up again when finance was being discussed. The Micronesians, in their report to the Congress of Micronesia, described the situation thus:

> One problem associated with the subject is the refusal of the United States Delegation to accept the Joint Committee's mandate to negotiate a future political status agreement for all of Micronesia, so that each district would

have the opportunity to accept or reject that agreement. The United States position, in refusing to negotiate with respect to one district, would prevent the residents of that district from voting on the Compact. It is not the purpose of this analysis to discuss this situation except insofar as it relates to a further complication in the computation of proposed support payments.

The United States supplied figures of support payments based on five districts, while the Micronesians based their figures on six. The Micronesians, in order to compare the proposals, increased the United States figures by 20 per cent when discussing six districts and decreased Micronesian figures by 16.7 per cent when discussing five districts.

By not openly debating the issue of the separation of the Mariana Islands, the Micronesians appeared to consent to the desires of the Mariana Islanders. Senator Lazarus Salii acknowledged in an interview that the Micronesian negotiations "more or less" gave the Marianas the go-ahead to discuss separate negotiations when they did not specifically disapprove the action of the Marianas representatives at Koror. On the other hand, Salii maintains that disapproval would not have stopped a Marianas request for separate negotiations or United States approval of them.

The Congress of Micronesia never endorsed separate negotiations. In the spring of 1973 it passed a resolution stating that the Micronesian group was the sole authority in the negotiations. Eighteen members of the Congress of Micronesia voted for the resolution, eleven voted against, and twelve abstained. Since in the Congress of Micronesia abstentions are counted as affirmative votes, the resolution passed thirty to eleven. Ambassador Williams explained the vote's significance to members of the United States House of Representatives Territorial Subcommittee in this way: "This vote in both their senate and their house was split. The number of congressmen and senators who voted 'no' added to those who abstained, in both cases were in the majority against the resolution. However, by the rules of the Congress of Micronesia, those who abstained were put in the "yes" column, so the resolution was passed."

United States officials thought the Congress of Micronesia resolution was merely a bargaining chip. According to one State Department official, the Congress of Micronesia, fearing it would not get "as big a pot" without the Marianas, was trying to use its approval or disapproval of separate negotiations as a means of bargaining for a better position. He added that by resisting separate negotiations, the Congress of Micronesia hoped to achieve more concessions, but the United States negotiators didn't feel "the slightest need to buy off the Congress of Micronesia." The United States unofficially took the position that the Congress of Micronesia would not be allowed to exploit the issue and if they got too troublesome or started to raise legal problems, the Secretary of the Interior's order creating the Congress of Micronesia (and stipulating its composition and authority) would simply be rewritten.

Although United States officials are quick to explain the logic of separate negotiations with the Marianas, this logic does not, in their opinion, apply to any of the other five districts. In fact, Washington is gravely concerned about further fragmentation. So concerned, according to one United States government official, that in 1973 United States negotiators considered ordering Palau district administrator Thomas Remengesau to veto legislation which would have established another status group for Palau. Remengesau vetoed the legislation on his own before Washington sent its instructions.

One of the most potentially troublesome problems faced by the United States was the proposed separation of the Marshall Islands, a move that some government officials saw as part of the bargaining with the Congress of Micronesia over revenue sharing. In March, 1974, the Marshall Islands District Legislature adopted a resolution informing the United Nations that it was unwilling to be a part of Micronesia after the termination of the Trusteeship Agreement and that the Marshalls intended to "commence shortly" negotiations with the United States. But the United States expressed its view that the problems of the Marshalls were internal and to be worked out within the Congress of Micronesia. The United States representative to the United Nations Trusteeship Council told the Council that the United States had not received a formal request from the Marshalls. In an interview, Ambassador Williams dodged taking a position on separate negotiations with the Marshalls, again arguing that no formal request had been received from the Marshalls. However, other United States officials stated that United States policy was to reject the bid. Although some Americans refer to the Marshalls movement as "different" from the Marianas, the only difference appears to be the longer history of the movement in the Marianas. Both appear to be motivated primarily by economic factors and secondarily by a fear of being dominated by the more populous (and less prosperous) islands.[3]

By mid-1975, the United States was formally faced with a request from Palau for separate negotiations. The United States rejected the request and urged Palau to work with the other five districts.

The task before the United States was to mount a convincing case against further fragmentation, but its own actions with the Marianas had already set a difficult precedent. The United States would receive neither land nor sovereignty but only administrative headaches from further fragmentation. "Can you imagine the number of people who would have to be involved in Washington and the various offices that would have to be created merely for administrative purposes? It would be a nightmare," mused a State Department official. The same official maintained that further separation would negatively affect what the

---

[3] Still another potential case of fragmentation is the Polynesian island of Nukuoro in the Ponape District, whose people told the 1964 United Nations Visiting Mission that they also wished to separate if the Marianas were allowed to do so.

remaining territory could achieve, composed as it would be of the poorest but most heavily populated and isolated islands.

But certainly the same argument can be used against the separation of the Marianas. What Micronesia could achieve without them is considerably less, since the Marianas district is the most advanced economically and has potential for the two most attractive immediate resources in Micronesia: tourism and military facilities.

Many Micronesians genuinely concerned about the future of the status negotiations and the future of Micronesia as a country are worried and baffled by the separate negotiations. Although all Micronesians will admit to distinct cultural and social differences, there is a belief among many that steps taken toward a united Micronesia have succeeded: English as a common language, the Congress of Micronesia, Air Micronesia, the flag, and the educational system. Many Micronesians, now suspicious of United States motives, ask why the United States did not "keep its word" regarding unity and "sought" to split the islands to the disadvantage of the Micronesians. When more than a year passed between the sixth and seventh rounds of talk, one member of the Micronesian negotiating team surmised that the United States was deliberately delaying the talks – now that Tinian was secured there was no immediate need to conclude talks with the rest of Micronesia. This assessment of United States motives was very different from the earlier Micronesian judgement that the United States had "not been lacking in good will."

Even if no one was surprised that the Marianas requested separate talks, it came as a surprise to many Micronesians that the United States would grant them. Historically opposed to the concept of fragmentation, Washington officials had emphasized that they wanted Micronesian unity. While still a member of the Micronesian negotiating team, Benjamin Manglona, a member of the Marianas Political Status Commission, indirectly approached several top officials at Washington parties. When he explained to them that the negotiations were not accommodating the needs of the Marianas and that the Marianas wished to explore the possibility of separate negotiations, the United States official reply was, "We cannot entertain you at this time." A State Department legal advisor recalled sitting in on three or four meetings before the formal request and hearing even from those American agencies he would have expected to be in favor of a split, presumably the military, that the Marianas could not be separated. In fact, Manglona felt that those in Saipan who advocated "reintegration" with Guam or separation from the Trust Territory were looked down upon by the Trust Territory government. Since the United States had long held a position against separatism, former United States Congressman Nieman Craley, now the high commissioner's liaison with the Congress of Micronesia, remembers that the Micronesians were "dumbfounded" when Pangelinan indicated that the United

States would negotiate separately. Andon Amaraich, Senator from Truk, remarked "We've been had." Carl Heine, then staff director for the Micronesians, had the same reaction.

UNITED STATES JUSTIFICATIONS

United States officials give several reasons for granting separate negotiations, ranging from the concrete — the letter received from the Marianas, the consent of the Micronesians for the Marianas to negotiate separately (although they have since backed away from earlier statements citing Micronesian consent), and the unhappiness of the Mariana Islanders with the Congress of Micronesia — to the theoretical — the argument that there is no such thing as a "Micronesia" because it is an artificial creation. Although criticized for not doing more to promote unity, United States officials contend there was nothing they could have done to have stopped separatist sentiment in the Marianas and that had separate negotiations with the Marianas not been agreed to, the talks with the Micronesians would have been stalled. And Haydn Williams maintained in his reply to the Marianas position statement that to seek a common solution to the status question against the expressed wishes of the Marianas population would be imposing upon them a status which they have said is unacceptable and denying them their right of self-determination.

But as one State Department official put it most appropriately, "We call it pragmatism." Separate negotiations resulted primarily from United States military considerations. The United States always preferred a "commonwealth status" to free association and free association to independence in the belief that the more permanent the set-up, the better United States military interests would be protected. While nothing is really "permanent," the "commonwealth" arrangement would make the Marianas a territory over which the United States has sovereignty. A military base on sovereign United States territory would present fewer problems than a base where the United States does not have sovereignty — such as the other Micronesian districts in free association with the United States. "The looser the relationship the Joint Committee talked about, the more Defense became interested in something closer with the Marianas," recalled a State Department legal advisor in mid-1973. By early 1975, Secretary of Defense Schlesinger was candidly discussing the importance of American sovereignty as a goal in the Micronesian negotiations. Having Micronesia, said Schlesinger, would "give the United States the option of supporting forward-deployed forces when appropriate from *U.S. territory without the political involvement or constraints stemming from bases on foreign soil. Moreover, automatic involvement in another nation's conflicts is avoided by operating from U.S. controlled soil.*" (Emphasis added.)

However, there is no evidence presently available that the Marianas broke away at the *explicit* urging of the Pentagon. State and Defense Department officials maintain there was no plan to negotiate separately with the Marianas in case an agreement could not be reached with the Micronesians. However, although there were no "plans" there had been consideration of Marianas separation as an option. One former official recalls that one of the first policy papers considered by the Nixon administration contained the option of separate negotiations with the Marianas in light of their longstanding desires and in light of the prime location of the Mariana Islands for United States military needs. The fragmentation option had not been selected at that time for fear the United States would be accused of following a "divide and rule" strategy. But clearly, subsequent events, most notably the so-called "summer of discontent" when Marianas opposition to continued unity became violent, made it possible for the United States to entertain separate negotiations at an acceptable political cost.

Pentagon officials deny that Defense base construction plans for Tinian played a role in the Marianas request for separate negotiations. Such suggestions are "misleading," Defense Secretary Schlesinger told the House Defense Appropriations Subcommittee in March, 1975, because Defense land requirements and base plans for the Marianas were not revealed until May, 1973, one year after the Marianas request for separate negotiations. Schlesinger's response is itself misleading, if not inaccurate.[4] Actually, in October, 1971, United States negotiators had outlined defense land requirements for all of Micronesia and had made it clear that the Marianas were the only district where the United States had "definite" plans. In fact, according to the negotiators, the United States hoped to limit land requirements elsewhere by "consolidating" future activities on Tinian. Moreover, it was common knowledge that Defense was interested primarily in the Marianas. Thus, Schlesinger's statement is accurate only insofar as it was not until May, 1973, that the precise acreage and the seven-stage construction plan were revealed.

The Micronesians may have unwittingly helped ease the United States dilemma. Ambassador Williams recalls having been urged by Salii to bite the bullet and lay the separatist issue to rest by coming to the fourth round of talks prepared to take a firm stand on separation. Salii hoped, and in the opinion of Carl Heine, fully expected, that the United States would again reject separation and thus strengthen Salii's hand within his Micronesian delegation. But the United States quickly calculated otherwise and, according to Heine, "took

[4]Schlesinger's response was submitted to the committee for the record and was not "cleared" in advance by relevant agencies concerned with Micronesia. The United States negotiators learned of the Schlesinger testimony only after portions of it were reprinted in the Micronesian *Independent*.

advantage of us." Instead of dashing Marianas hopes[5] and enabling the Micronesians to negotiate from a unified and strengthened position, the United States accepted separate negotiations.

Military needs in the area came to affect not only the substance of the talks but also their very procedure. There would now be two sets of negotiations instead of one. The bargaining positions of the United States, the Joint Committee on Future Status, and the Marianas Political Status Commission would all change. The breakaway of the Marianas left the Micronesians in the least desirable bargaining position. One senior staff member of the Joint Committee on Future Status believes the Micronesians were completely undercut by separate negotiations with the Marianas. The Micronesians still had their so-called strategic location, and they had Kwajalein (though no one knew how long the military would need it), but the Micronesians no longer had Tinian, the prime immediate selling point.

However, two Marianas representatives continued to negotiate with the Micronesians. In theory, at least, the Marianas did not preclude the possibility that they might once again unite with the rest of Micronesia. The chairman of the Marianas Commission even admitted that he personally had misgivings about separation from the rest of the islands. But a reunion with the other five districts appeared highly unlikely, given the detail and extent of United States-Marianas negotiations. United States officials did not believe reunification likely, and in fact sought to accelerate negotiations with the Marianas and gave the Mariana Islands preferential treatment.[6]

THE SETTING FOR NEGOTIATIONS

The setting for the negotiations between the United States delegation and the Marianas was much different from that of the opening round of talks with the Micronesians in 1969. Because the status the Marianas desired was the one the United States also favored, the delegations were able to proceed from that assumption. Already familiar with the provisions of the "commonwealth" proposal, the Marianas and the United States could work out, in their words, "the exact form and substance of that relationship." Preliminary contact had been extensive, so the United States delegation knew what to expect and was well prepared. Time would not be wasted making proposals which would be rejected. Since the Office of Micronesian Status Negotiations had been established in

---

[5] As Australia did with Bougainville and Papua, France is doing with the island of Mayotte in the Comoros and the United Kingdom did, *inter alia*, in the cases of Buganda and the northeast frontier of Kenya. Recently, Portugal has refused to countenance secession of Cabinda from Angola.

[6] For example, the United States gave the Marianas priority treatment in land surveys.

1971, there was one central office which could carefully study the Marianas position, and many of the bureaucratic hassles apparent in the opening rounds with the Micronesians were therefore avoided. In fact, the Department of State dropped out of the second, third and fourth rounds of United States-Marianas negotiations on the grounds that no international issues were involved and that the State Department was "short of personnel." The Marianas could also learn from the mistakes of the Micronesians. Talks with the United States delegation were much more informal, and there was less of an adversary relationship. One United States official commented after the second round of talks with the Marianas that more progress had resulted from three weeks of negotiations with the Marianas than from three years with the Micronesians.

The Marianas Political Status Commission also differed from the early Micronesian Political Status Delegation. The representatives knew what they wanted and because they were negotiating for one district instead of six, they could more easily reach agreement on issues. According to one Micronesian staff member, both Edward Pangelinan (co-chairman) and Herman Guerrero of the Marianas Commission had been primarily concerned with protecting the Marianas interests instead of thinking on a territory-wide basis while they served on the Micronesian delegation. The fifteen member Marianas Commission, drawn from both the public and private sectors and from all the principal islands and municipalities of the district, was described by Ambassador Williams at the first round as "broadly representative of the people of the Marianas." Unlike the Micronesian delegation, where Chairman Lazarus Salii exerted strong authority, each member of the Marianas Commission had equal power.

In the Marianas negotiations, the United States was in a good position to pursue its own objectives of denial and use of land, for unlike the Micronesian Status Commission, the Marianas Political Status Commission did not present the United States with specific minimum requirements for a future relationship, though clearly they had some. United States objectives were not threatened as they had been by the Micronesians' demand for a unilateral termination clause. In fact, Senator Pangelinan did not state what his minimum requirements were. At the first round of the Marianas negotiations, Pangelinan stated that the desire for the close relationship with the United States was "premised upon our conviction that such stability will enhance our capacity to develop our resources and to improve the economic well-being of our citizens." This goal accommodated the objectives of the United States — the United States could pay for permanence.

But even though the signs were auspicious, the Marianas negotiators were to drive a hard bargain and were not to rush into any new relationship. Edward Pangelinan described himself as a politician out to get the best deal out of the circumstances. Before the negotiations began in December, 1972, the Marianas hired several consultants: Howard P. Willens, from the Washington law firm of

Wilmer, Cutler, Pickering; James R. Leonard, an economic consultant from James R. Leonard Associates, Inc., of Washington and a participant in the Robert Nathan economic study of Micronesia; and James E. White, an American, who became executive director of the commission's staff. Joseph F. Screen, an expatriate businessman in Saipan, was also listed as a consultant but seems, in fact, never to have fulfilled that role.

Willens was to serve as counsel to review questions with regard to political status and to make the Marianas presence known to United States congressional leaders and members of the United States executive branch. He was in frequent contact with the Office of Micronesian Status Negotiations. In Micronesian terms both Willens's and Leonard's firms are paid handsomely for their work, although their fees are undoubtedly small in United States terms. The Marianas Political Status Commission devoted the largest part of its budget to the services of these consultants.

THE NEGOTIATIONS

The talks between the United States and the Marianas were, in the words of joint communiques, largely characterized by "free, frank, and searching exchanges" and "mutual trust and common objectives." Appearing frequently in the proceedings of the negotiations and press releases were phrases which described the negotiations as proceeding "efficiently and harmoniously" and "marked by good will and uninterrupted progress." But the joint communiques gave a false impression and masked rather large differences. For example, members of the Marianas group opposed issuance of a joint communique at the close of the December, 1973, talks. According to sources on each side, there was more disagreement than agreement, but United States negotiators insisted on the issuance of a joint communique so it would not appear that the momentum of the negotiations had been stalled. Similarly, the Marianas group for some time cooperated with the United States in omitting from the communique the sharp differences which existed on United States land requests. On one occasion, agreement was reached on a joint press release on economic measures. However, in a separate statement the Marianas publicly denounced the position taken by the United States in the joint release.

Although at the conclusion of negotiations with the Marianas the United States representative would state that the Covenant was openly arrived at, this was hardly the case. Official reports contained largely formal and ceremonial statements. The Marianas had indeed made complete written reports to their legislature after the second round, and these included position papers exchanged by each side. However, the United States strenuously objected to the release of such detailed information and threatened to cease exchanging position papers if the Marianas made further complete reports. The United States position prevailed, and henceforth the Marianas negotiators limited their reports to less complete presentations.

A total of five sessions, all on Saipan, were held before the United States and Marianas negotiators signed a Covenant to Establish a Commonwealth of the Northern Mariana Islands in Political Union with the United States of America. The negotiating sessions were (in chronological order): December 13-14, 1972; May 15-June 4, 1973; December 6-19, 1973; and May 15-31, 1974. The final session was divided into two parts, December 5-19, 1974, and February 4-15, 1975. Formal negotiations were preceded by extensive informal contacts between representatives of each side or through working committees.

THE FIRST ROUND

The first round lasted only two days, December 13-14, 1972. It was generally a ceremonial and exploratory session with the Marianas expressing their desire to become part of the American political family and with the United States, flattered, recalling various ways this desire had been communicated to the United Nations, the United States government, and the Congress of Micronesia. "The coming of the United States in Micronesia ushered in a new era for our people," said Pangelinan:

> For the first time in four centuries we could enjoy the fundamental human rights to which all men are entitled. . . . After a quarter century of American administration, our people have come to know and appreciate the American system of government. The concept of democracy has been very important and significant to us. . . . We desire a close political union with the United States of America — a membership in the United States political family.

Williams's reply spoke of American ideals, goals, and love of country:

> As an American and as the representative of the President of the United States, I cannot help but be moved by these words and the eloquence and sincerity of the statements of your leaders . . . with all of our human imperfections, we cannot be less than enheartened and grateful that the people of the Marianas would have reached the conclusion, voluntarily, to become a permanent part of the American family, that you have chosen to place your faith in the ideals which continue to guide and motivate the American nation as it strives to perfect its own systems and to improve the quality of life of its citizens and people everywhere.
>
> I am reminded of what Adlai Stevenson once said: "When an American says that he loves his country, he means not only that he loves the New England hills, the prairies glistening in the sun, the wide and rising plains, the great mountains and the sea. He means that he loves an inner air, an inner light in which freedom lives and in which a man can draw the breath of self-respect."

But not all was sweetness and light. Pangelinan's identification of the issues ahead was itself an indication of difficult negotiations. Essentially, the United States-Marianas negotiations involved three major issues and one procedural, though substantively important, issue.

1) *The form of political association.* Would the Marianas have a "common-wealth," unincorporated, or other territorial status? More important, what do those various relationships imply in terms of sovereignty and the application of the United States Constitution and laws, citizenship, political and human rights such as voting, internal self-government and participation in foreign affairs? Pangelinan himself noted that the existing precedents might not be sufficient to resolve the issue. It might, he said, be necessary to develop a "totally new" political status for the Marianas. We hope, said Pangelinan, "that the United States will be flexible and responsive to our desire to develop a political status unique to the Marianas. After all, there was no established precedent for the Constitution of the United States in 1789."

2) *Land.* More than 90 per cent of land in the Marianas was controlled by the United States government through the Trust Territory government or the United States military, either as public land or military retention land. The land question has long been hotly debated throughout Micronesia, the people maintaining that land, their scarcest and only asset, had been wrongly taken by both Japanese and Americans and should be returned. The Marianas agreed in principle to provide land for United States military needs but precisely how much, where, and on what terms would be a matter of dispute. As Pangelinan put it, "Land — its use, sale, and development — is probably the most important and difficult problem we face in the future." In addition, they wished to insure that whatever the political relationship with the United States, land could not be purchased by other than Marianas descendants, i.e., land could not be alienated.

3) *Financial and economic arrangements.* In addition to funds received through the lease or sale of land to the United States military and to funds generated as a result of United States military construction and operations, agreement needed to be reached on the level of funds to be provided by the United States for operation of the Marianas government and for capital improvement. Most important, agreement had to be reached on the controls to be maintained on United States funds. For example, could agreement be reached on specific lump sum appropriations so that the Marianas government could not be controlled in internal matters through the United States control of the purse strings?

4) Finally, there were the procedural questions of *transition.* Legally, the Marianas could be administered separately, but only under the provisions of the Trusteeship Agreement. No change in the political status of the Marianas could

take place without amending the Trusteeship Agreement, a step which the United States believed to be politically infeasible since the approval of the United Nations Security Council would be necessary. The Security Council might oppose separate status for the Marianas, especially if such a proposal was presented prior to a resolution of the status of the rest of Micronesia. Thus, politically, it was more desirable to administer the Marianas separately until agreement was reached with the larger Micronesian group and the entire Trusteeship Agreement could be terminated at once. Clearly, the Marianas — and the United States — wanted to implement the provisions of the new status without waiting for a formal and internationally approved change in status.

While each of the above issues would be dealt with separately, no one was misled about their interrelationship. As one American official put it in commenting on the relatively low level of economic support offered the larger Micronesian grouping, "the closer the relationship, the more money." The Marianas were to gain economically from the closeness of their relationship with the United States, just as the larger Micronesian group was to pay for the right to "opt-out."

Following Pangelinan's presentation of the issues, Williams's remarks touched on future status, finance, and land. Guam, American Samoa, and the Virgin Islands, he noted, all enjoyed certain basic rights, benefits, obligations, and guarantees under the United States Constitution. Continuing assistance could be given to the Marianas along the lines of federal grants to match locally collected revenues; budgetary support could be made available until an adequate tax base was developed; and there could be the full range of federal programs and services available to all United States states and territories for public works, health and education, and housing.

Regarding land, the United States expected to transfer to the new government of the Marianas all remaining public lands in the Marianas after the "minimal" needs of the United States government were met. Williams also noted the concern about land alienation and pledged to work to find ways to protect against land alienation or ownership of land by persons who were not of Marianas descent. Military land requirements, he said, would take into account United States military needs as well as the basic interests of the Marianas people, as the United States hoped to achieve its objectives with "maximum harmony and a minimum of trouble to the people." In order to avoid disruption, the United States hoped to consolidate its military activities on the island of Tinian, where a joint service Air Force-Navy airfield logistic facility and rehabilitation of the harbor were planned. Limited facilities, said Williams, such as maintenance, communications, and logistics support facilities might be developed on Saipan at Isley Field and Tanapag Harbor, but these would not constitute major requirements.

But, in Williams's words, the first round of United States-Marianas talks was primarily organizational "to set forth basic procedures for the conduct of talks, and to discuss a timetable for future meetings"; therefore, the United States did not offer any concrete proposals.

THE NATURE OF THE POLITICAL RELATIONSHIP

Following the organizational first round, the delegations could proceed to discuss principles of the future relationship at the second round of negotiations, held six months later, from May 4 to June 15, 1973. Agreement in principle on the nature of the relationship came relatively easily, although spelling out that agreement was to prove difficult.

In their position papers for the second round, the Marianas Political Status Commission concluded that after studying the alternatives "commonwealth status possessed by Puerto Rico is superior to the status of an unincorporated territory" and "this political status affords the most freedom to the people of the Marianas to determine their own destiny within the American family." However, in addition to providing the most freedom, an advantage to the commonwealth status was that the Marianas would also be secure in the relationship, for fundamental provisions of the agreement can only be modified by mutual consent. This would be the first occasion that the United States had explicitly agreed to this provision for a territory. According to a provision of the joint communique at the third round:

> It was agreed that specified fundamental provisions of the Status Agreement, including certain provisions designed to assure maximum self-government to the future Commonwealth of the Marianas, may not be amended or repealed except by mutual consent of the parties. To this extent, United States authority in the Marianas would not be plenary. The Status Agreement would be drafted so as to reflect clearly the intention of the United States and the Marianas Political Status Commission that this undertaking be enforceable in the federal courts. Specific recognition would also be made of the fact that approval of the Status Agreement by the people of the Marianas would constitute a sovereign act of self-determination.

Howard Willens, attorney for the Marianas, believes this language protects the Marianas from United States legislation which might try to "reintegrate" the Marianas with Guam. The question of the constitutionality of the provision arose. Certainly it has been a long held position of the Interior Department that the United States Constitution gives Congress the right to do whatever it wishes regarding territories. Interior held that one Congress can approve mutual consent provisions but a later Congress could legally, if not politically or morally, alter the legislation.

It was precisely because of these possible legal questions that the United States responded in its position paper at the second round that the United States-Marianas relationship would be " 'territorial' as that term is used in the United States Constitution." The United States saw this as an "essential component" of the arrangement but never fully explained the meaning of the word "territorial." The term is not found in the joint communique issued at the end of the round, so this major point was avoided, perhaps because "territorial" in the sense of incorporated or unincorporated status was precisely what the Marianas did not want. However, the United States position paper went on to state that "the Marianas would become a commonwealth with the right to write its own constitution and would have the maximum possible control over its affairs, subject to the supremacy of the United States federal government."

Perhaps the United States had used the term "territorial" to remind the Marianas that they do fall into a category that has limitations on rights. One official from the Office of Micronesian Status Negotiations admitted that the United States government had great difficulty making the Marianas understand they must remain within the territorial structure and not seek "more rights than states."

A more precise statement of the political relationship between the United States and the Northern Marianas came in the tentatively agreed language of the Draft Covenant of December 19, 1974. What had earlier been referred to as an agreement was now called a "covenant," not a "compact," the term used in the United States-Micronesian negotiations and with regard to Puerto Rico. The convenant is described as being entered into in order "to establish a self-governing commonwealth" for the Northern Marianas within the American political system and to "define the future relationship" between the Northern Mariana Islands and the United States. The covenant is to be "mutually binding" when approved by the United States, the Marianas District Legislature and by the people of the Northern Mariana Islands "in a plebiscite, constituting on their part a sovereign act of self-determination."

Among the provisions governing the political relationship are the following:

1) Upon termination of the Trusteeship Agreement, the Marianas would become the "Commonwealth of the Northern Mariana Islands, in political union with and under the sovereignty" of the United States.
2) The covenant, the provisions of the United States Constitution, and treaties and laws of the United States applicable to the Marianas would be the supreme law of the islands.
3) The Marianas would govern their internal affairs in accordance with a constitution of their own adoption.
4) The United States would have complete responsibility for defense and foreign affairs.

5) The United States could enact legislation applicable to the Marianas in accordance with United States constitutional processes, subject to the reservation: "so long as the Northern Mariana Islands is specifically named in any legislation which could not also be made applicable to the states."

6) The fundamental provisions of the covenant (those regarding the political relationship; the constitution of the Marianas; citizenship and nationality; the applicability of some provisions of the United States Constitution, and protection of alienation of land) could not be changed except through *mutual consent.*

Nowhere in the covenant is the Commonwealth of the Northern Mariana Islands spoken of as a territory of the United States. By reserving its position on the "so long as" clause, the United States sought to leave open the extent of Congress's right to legislate for the Marianas.[7] Just as strongly, the Marianas sought to limit explicitly United States congressional legislation to those enactments applicable to all states. At a minimum the Marianas wished Congress to be conscious of those occasions when it was passing legislation which would treat the Marianas as a territory. The United States delegation dropped the "so long as" reservation after consulting some members of Congress.[8]

The intent of irrevocability without mutual consent is even clearer in the covenant than in Puerto Rico's "compact." Such a covenant is generally defined as an agreement or contract between two parties; it could not be expected that provisions regarding sovereignty would be valid and limitations on Congress would be invalid, especially if Congress knowingly approved limitations on its actions. As James Dobbs points out in the article in the *New York Law Forum* (XVIII, No. 1, Summer, 1972), the Supreme Court has yet to accept a case dealing directly with the question of Puerto Rico's constitutional status and the concept of compact. However, lower federal courts, led by the District Court of Puerto Rico and the United States Court of Appeals for the First Circuit, have generally but not always accepted a special commonwealth status for Puerto Rico based upon an irrevocable compact between Congress and the people of Puerto Rico.

With regard to action by one Congress to bind or limit a succeeding Congress by a legislative act, Dobbs conceded that this usually cannot be done. However, he cites a Puerto Rican view that their compact is a "vested right," such as exists with compacts under which territories become states, homestead grants are

---

[7]"The Congress shall have the Power to dispose of and make all needful Rules and Regulations respecting the Territory or other Property belonging to the United States; and nothing in this Constitution shall be so construed as to Prejudice any Claims of the United States, or of any particular state."

[8]Puerto Rico does not have the advantage.

made, war risk insurance is granted, and contracts and bonds are made, redeemable only in gold. Of particular applicability is Dobb's notation of a recent Supreme Court decision that citizenship (which the Marianas people would gain if they wished) could not be divested without the voluntary consent of the citizen.

There is some evidence that the Marianas were always willing in the final analysis to leave the applicability of Article IV, Section 3 vague, relying on the willingness of the Congress to carry out the spirit of the covenant and not legislate on matters internal to the Marianas. But the issue is ultimately of critical importance to the Marianas and their counsel has stated his intention to take the issue to court if and when the need arises.

In two important areas regarding the political nature of the relationship, the Marianas requests "overstepped their bounds": consultation regarding foreign affairs matters and representation in the United States Congress. In their position paper of the second round, the Marianas maintained that the compact should provide for the "fullest possible consultation" regarding foreign matters affecting the Marianas. The United States responded: "Consultation as a matter of right would be inappropriate. No other state, Commonwealth or Territory has that right . . . we would welcome the advice of the Commonwealth of the Marianas with respect to any international agreement the United States might enter into in the future which might affect the Marianas. However, we cannot agree to give the Mariana Islands a veto over such agreements."

In the Draft Covenant, the United States stuck to its original position on consultation regarding foreign affairs matters. The United States agreed to give "sympathetic consideration" to the Marianas government views on "matters directly" related to the Marianas and to provide opportunities for presentation of Marianas views "to no less extent than such opportunities are provided to any other territory or possession under comparable circumstances." In addition the United States agreed to assist and facilitate establishment of an office in the United States and abroad to promote local tourism and economic or cultural interests of the Marianas; and allow the Marianas, on request, to participate in regional and international organizations concerned with social, economic, educational, scientific, technical and cultural matters "when similar participation is authorized for any other United States territory or possession under comparable circumstances."

The Marianas also sought a non-voting delegate in the United States Congress, and the United States delegation originally agreed to support their request. However, in their position paper, the Marianas Commission went even further by stating that their long term aspiration in this area was to have a *voting* representative in Congress, "who will have all the rights and privileges of other members of the United States House of Representatives." However, the United States government and the Trust Territory administration presented a dim view even of a *non*-voting delegate, and the United States position paper of the second round states: "We are not overly optimistic that this can be arranged in the short run. . . . The U.S. Congress would be reluctant to do so because of the limited Marianas population." One State Department official admitted it was unrealistic to think that only 15,000 people would get a special status. In the Draft Covenant of December 19, 1974, the Marianas settled for a "Resident Representative to the United States," who would be entitled to official recognition by all departments and agencies of the United States government. Nothing is said about a representative in the United States Congress.

The Marianas were of the opinion that specific provision should be made in the Compact regarding periodic review of all aspects of the status at five year intervals, if either party so requested. In reply, the United States maintained that, in the "close, sympathetic relationship" being discussed, there should be no explicit need for a review clause because communication would be regular enough that either side could raise matters of mutual interest or concern at any time. Particularly regarding economic questions, the needs of the people of the Marianas would be kept under constant and continuing review "through normal workings of the annual United States budget cycle."

But the Marianas did not alter their original stance, and in the Draft Covenant of December 19. 1974, the United States agreed to the review clause, on the condition that the five year intervals be extended to ten years, or at the request of either government. The two sides also agreed that multi-year financial assistance would be discussed prior to the expiration of each seven year period of assistance.

Perhaps the area of most difficulty regarded citizenship. The Marianas Commission thought each individual should be able to choose United States citizen or United States national status. The commission felt that no governmental entity has the legal authority to make this election on behalf of the citizens of the Marianas and that the people should be able to choose citizen or national status at the time the referendum is placed before them.

Responding, the United States maintained "the acceptance of a citizen-national option would prove to be a serious administrative inconvenience," so it would prefer to omit this option. The United States assumption had been that everyone would have the opportunity to accept or reject United States citizenship, but those who rejected it would become resident aliens in the new commonwealth. However, at the third round of talks six months later, after this matter had been studied by legal advisors, the United States consented to the Marianas wish. As written in the Draft Covenant, Northern Marianas citizens would have six months following the effective date of the Covenant or six months after reaching their eighteenth birthday to decline United States citizenship, in which case they would become United States nationals.

LAND

During the second round of negotiations in Saipan (May 15-June 4, 1973), Ambassador Williams gave the most detailed description to date of United States military land requirements in the Marianas. The Marianas representatives already knew that most military land needs were concentrated in their islands. They had agreed in principle to make land available to the United States; however, there had been no discussion of specific land requirements. On May 29, 1973, the United States delegation presented its position paper on future land requirements to the Marianas delegation and on June 3 gave a detailed oral presentation. On May 30, Ambassador Williams described the United States military requirements to the public through a radio broadcast (translated into Chamorro). Minimum United States military requirements included: 1) Indefinite continued use of Farallon de Medinilla, an uninhabitable and inaccessible island of 229 acres used by the United States military since 1970 for target practice under a "use and occupancy" agreement with the Trust Territory government; 2) Retention of 320 acres in Tanapag Harbor (Saipan) for future contingency purposes. The United States already held 640 acres, 320 of which would be returned for civilian use and development. The United States did not have an immediate need for the area to be retained and was willing to lease tracts within the retained area for civilian development, as long as it would not interfere with any future military use; 3) Joint use of Isley Airfield in Saipan. Currently located on so-called military retention land, the airfield is being developed as a civilian airfield; 4) Retention of 500 acres south of Isley Field for the possible development of a maintenance and logistics area. The United States was willing to lease this area until it might be required; and 5) The entire island of Tinian, the northern two-thirds to be used as a joint services military base, and the southern third to be set aside for civilian use.

Although the joint communique of the second round stated that both sides agreed that it had been possible to develop "meaningful understanding" as to the significant principles involved, the Marianas had responded negatively to the United States requests. The joint communique was worded: "The Marianas Political Status Commission agreed in principle that a small, uninhabited and inaccessible island could be made available as a United States target area, as Farallon de Medinilla is now being used." But use of Farallon de Medinilla itself was not approved. Instead, the Marianas stated their definite preference that the

United States choose a more distant northern island for target practice. However, in the third round, the Marianas agreed to continued United States use of Farallon de Medinilla as a target area and the agreement is incorporated in Section 802(a)(3) of the covenant.

The Marianas Political Status Commission expressed the view that United States needs on Saipan were "unreasonable," that the contingency nature of the United States plans reflected an apparent lack of confidence that the future Commonwealth of the Northern Marianas would honor its responsibilities "as a member of the American political family" should the need arise. The Marianas position papers from the second round also stated that before the commission agreed to requests for land on Saipan, it would have to be persuaded that contingency needs could not be met through use of land and facilities to be developed on Tinian. The commission "strongly" objected to the United States request in Tanapag Harbor, Saipan. Likewise, the commission took "a very strong negative view" of the request for 500 acres south of Isley Field, arguing that that land was "much too important for Saipan's future economic development to be burdened by restrictions arising from hypothetical needs of the United States in the future."

But the greatest reaction came over the United States request to purchase the entire island of Tinian. As early as the third round of Micronesian negotiations in October, 1971, it was announced that the United States wished to concentrate any military facilities it might establish in the Marianas on Tinian. This island was the military choice for a new base because it would disrupt few people (its population is less than 900), the island was of sufficient size, and in addition, there were runways, roads, and harbors there left over from World War II.

Viewed from the United States, Tinian is a small island in the Pacific, one of thousands of islands. But in the Marianas District, it is the second largest island and one of the five largest islands in Micronesia with a land area of about forty square miles. According to initial plans, the United States hoped to build a joint service (Air Force, Navy, Marine) airfield and logistics facility on Tinian and eventually to station there 2,600 military and civilian personnel (not including dependents). The January 29, 1973, issue of *U.S. News and World Report* reported that "according to tentative plans, the Marianas — along with Guam — would become America's main outpost in the Western Pacific."

United States hopes for acquiring Tinian included taking over the port for military supply purposes. Williams advanced several reasons that San Jose Harbor was necessary: it is located at the only site on the island suitable for harbor development; the property is protected from prevailing easterly winds; the piers are within the only protected reef area on the west coast large enough for deep draft ships; and the area is extensive enough to provide adequate anchorage. According to the United States, no other location on the island possessed these characteristics, and a suitable alternative site for a harbor was not available. Williams did not add that acquisition of the repairable harbor would constitute less of a drain on the increasingly hard-pressed Defense budget.

Acquiring the port would require the relocation of San Jose, Tinian's only village. In Ambassador Williams's words, "We have no alternative but to propose that the village of San Jose be moved to some other suitable location in the southern third of the island." But Tinian residents depend on San Jose's location and harbor for their livelihood, and relocation would have meant moving to the worst section of the island, Marpo Valley. This area, although good for farming, is largely swampy and bordered by rocky hills. There is no harbor and the beach is small and rocky. Approximately 170 houses from San Jose, as well as essential community operations such as public utilities, roads, schools, and churches, would have had to have been built in a new location. What Tinian islanders would receive in return would be United States citizenship status, and according to Williams, "a potentially dramatic increase in revenues."

According to the United States position paper, the United States desired to purchase but not use the remaining southern third of Tinian "in order to prevent undesirable conditions and consequences which could possibly result from the presence of a major military base and which would not be in the interests of either the local residents or of the United States military." Williams assured the Marianas Commission that the Tinian people would participate in the planning for the southern one-third of the island.

The Marianas Political Status Commission was clearly taken aback by the magnitude of the United States proposals. The requests made by the United States for land on Tinian were so overwhelming, said the Marianas representative, that they are "difficult to comprehend in only three days." Earlier, the Commission had stated in its position paper their strong belief that the use of land for military purposes should be kept at an absolute minimum, so the commission was not inclined to agree to selling the entire island with a sublease back of one-third for the civilian community. The commission noted it was "especially concerned" by the dislocation and loss of land which would result from the inclusion of San Jose Harbor in the United States request, and understood that other harbor locations were studied but rejected on cost grounds. It asked for information from the United States regarding cost differences between rehabilitation of the present harbor facilities and construction at other locations.

A significant number of people on Tinian actively opposed the amount of land requested by the United States, its purchase, and the need to move San Jose village. Although some were impressed by the new homes and facilities to be made available, they repeatedly pressed their own minimum demands: lease as opposed to sale of one-third as opposed to two-thirds of the island without relocation of San Jose village. At a number of public meetings on Tinian the issue was hotly debated, and during one, where the negotiations were sharply criticized, placards read "Land for Ranchers, not for Bombers." To reassure the Tinian population that they would have a voice in the determination of their future, the two delegates from Tinian on the Marianas Status Commission issued several statements like the following: "Ambassador Williams has said himself that he will go along with what the people decide" (Hocog) and "The commission members will not approve any military project unless the Tinian people give their approval. . . . No decision of any kind will be made without the people's approval" (Manglona).

To insure that they would really have some say about the future of their island, the Tinian Municipal Council considered a draft bill calling for a referendum to be held September 14, 1973, so that the people of Tinian could vote on the following questions:

> Shall the people of Tinian Municipality allow the United States to make use of Tinian Island for military purposes?
> Shall the United States Armed Forces be allowed to relocate the present village site and the people so that the present village may be used for military installations and facilities?

The bill was not passed. However, on February 14, 1974, the council did pass an ordinance calling for a referendum which was scheduled for April 7. The proposed ballot contained two questions:

> Do you agree to the relocation (moving) of the Village of San Jose from its present site to another area of the Island of Tinian?
> In your opinion, how much of the Island of Tinian, in terms of land area, should the United States military be permitted to occupy? None? One-third? Two-thirds? Other (specify).

However, on March 8, the Marianas District administrator, Francisco C. Ada, vetoed the proposed referendum and advanced two reasons for his action: the timing was inappropriate because no concrete proposals for military use had been presented ("such requirements are extremely general in nature, serving as a point of departure for purpose of negotiation"); and it would be an "attempt to undermine" future negotiations. In light of the independent action of the Marianas, Ada's argument was ironic: "To permit one municipality to even attempt to influence the negotiations will, in my opinion, be the beginning of fragmentation that will lead to no appreciable conclusion in our collective efforts to achieve a political status."

According to a high level official in the Trust Territory government and an official from the Office of Micronesian Status Negotiations, the decision was entirely Ada's own. The United States Status Office did not become involved, they said, until after the decision was made. On the other hand, few people doubt that Ada did not know that a referendum was inconsistent with United States policy objectives.

Felipe Q. Atalig, Tinian's representative to the Congress of Micronesia, believed it should give priority to the referendum in a special session in 1974. Earlier, Atalig stated that a referendum was "the only way to officially determine what the people want." But the Office of Micronesian Status Negotiations all along said that there would be no referendum on Tinian. Several reasons were advanced: the Tinian population is not indigenous and really comes from the Carolines; the land belongs to some people who do not live on Tinian; and a small group of less than 900 should not be able to affect the destiny of all the Marianas. This attitude contrasted sharply with statements from both delegations that they were "committed" to undertake full consultation with the people of Tinian before any final decisions or agreements were made regarding the use of land on Tinian for military purposes. When asked if denying the right of a referendum was not inconsistent with the United States position on self-determination, one official said, with a smile, that the United States was being consistent in following its own best interests. Another United States official speculated that the reason the first draft bill was not passed was that Tinian residents were overwhelmingly in favor of the military. Navy officials visiting Tinian in the spring of 1973 were also convinced this was the case. So, the United States official reasoned, to draw attention to this fact even further in a public referendum would only be putting the Marianas in a bad negotiating position. Besides, consultation could be achieved by public meetings. These were less rigid than a referendum.

But the tenacity of Tinian residents was underestimated. On June 5, 1973, just five days after Williams's broadcast, a petition was drawn up by the office of the speaker of the Tinian Municipal government stating that their "expressed willingness to accommodate the needs of the administering authority military has been misinterpreted by representatives of the administering authority as our being willing to [allow] unrestricted and uncontrolled use of Tinian." The petition was sent to all those involved in the decision-making process, from the Marianas District Legislature to the President of the United States. It noted that the United States "has a moral obligation to give due consideration to the wishes of the people concerned." United States military forces, the petition continued, would be welcome only under the following terms and conditions: 1) Existing military retention lands of approximately 9,000 acres on Tinian should be adequate to develop the proposed combined military complex. If justified, perhaps an additional 2,000 to 3,000 acres adjacent to the existing area could be made available, but no more; 2) The existing San Jose village would not be moved under any circumstances; 3) The existing harbor would remain under civilian control but could be used jointly; 4) If an ammunition dock was needed or desired, then a new dock should be constructed in the Unai Babui or Chulu (Marine beach) area on the northwestern shore of Tinian; 5) Government would remain in the hands of the people without any restrictions on growth and development activities within the civilian community; 6) The civilian community would be accorded free use of and access to West Field (the present airfield) to board scheduled approved commercial aircraft; and 7) The current ongoing homestead program would be continued without interruption.

From the beginning, differences over Tinian were underplayed, at least in official communiques. For example, the only mention of Tinian in the joint communique of the second round was: "It was the understanding of both delegations that the Marianas Political Status Commission would be prepared to negotiate with respect to that portion of Tinian required by the United States for military purposes. In this connection, means would have to be found to assure that social and economic conditions evolve in a manner compatible with the mutual interests of both the civilian and military communities."

At the third round the Marianas Political Status Commission responded to the United States land requests:

Farallon de Medinilla: The United States could use the island as a target area, provided the United States military forces filed an environmental impact statement.

Tanapag: The United States would be able to use the harbor jointly under civilian control, but all 640 acres should be returned to the public domain. The 320 acres requested by the United States could be made available later if needed. (The United States continued to want 320 acres immediately and for the first time indicated that it wanted to use most of this portion of Micronesia's scarcest commodity not for strategic purposes, but to develop as an American memorial park for World War II dead.)

Isley Field: This could be available to the United States on a joint use basis. The United States could lease 250 acres but the remaining 250 acres desired by the United States would be made subject to restrictive covenants. (The United States said it continued to need 500 acres.)

Tinian: Negotiations would continue for a lease. (The United States indicated it still needed approximately two-thirds of the land area including the harbor and adjacent safety zone.)

In the joint communique the United States no longer demanded control and ownership of the entire island of Tinian but agreed that the people of Tinian could control and own one-third of the island. In the United States view, the issue remaining was which third of the island would be locally owned and controlled; in other words, would San Jose village have to be relocated? On the other hand, the statement of the Marianas position continued to mention only their willingness to lease land needed by the United States military. Carefully omitted from the communique was the full extent of United States-Marianas disagreement. The people of Tinian insisted through their representatives that at least two-thirds of the island be locally owned and controlled. The issue of one-third or two-thirds was sufficiently contested that one-third, two-thirds became a standing, but substantively serious, joke among the two delegations.

No futher progress was possible without major United States concessions regarding United States land requirements, particularly on Tinian. Some of these concessions came at the fourth round of negotiations held from May 15-31, 1974. This session consisted of several working meetings on Saipan as well as public meetings on Tinian and Rota.

Tanapag: The United States backed down from its desire for 320 acres in Tanapag Harbor and agreed to 197 acres for future contingency use. Most of this land was for the development of an American memorial park and recreation area for the people of the Marianas. Since none of the 197 acres was for immediate use, the United States agreed to allow the Marianas to sublease the remaining land for civilian harbor-related activities.

Isley Field: The United States agreed to approximately 482 acres, although it had requested 500 acres. This land would also be made available for use or lease for industrial or agricultural purposes "compatible with possible future military use."

Tinian: The United States backed away from its proposal of acquiring the entire island to obtaining two-thirds of it (approximately 17,475 acres). The desired acreage was further reduced by approximately 1,200 acres. The United States conceded that San Jose village need not be moved, and a new dock would be built on Tinian, although in the past the United States position was that no other suitable site was available. In addition, the United States agreed to re-evaluate its military needs in order to make as much land as possible available "for agricultural and other purposes compatible with planned military activities." The United States also agreed that land within the proposed base would be made available for agriculture, fishing, recreation, and other purposes. These changes included all except the first point of the Tinian petition of June 5, 1973, and the Tinian Municipal Council later unanimously approved the land arrangements for Tinian. Thus, in the Draft Covenant, agreement was reached on a land package markedly different from the original United States request. Only a portion of Tinian (17,799 acres, excluding a portion of land at San Jose Harbor), approximately 177 acres on Saipan at Tanapag Harbor (much of it for a memorial park), and Farallon de Medinilla Island were made available. Most of the request for land at Tanapag Harbor and all of the land at Isley Field were dropped.

At the second round also the question of *how* the United States would obtain Tinian and other land was raised. The United States position paper presented its argument for *purchasing* Tinian: "The U. S. Government historically purchases, not leases, land when it requires land for the public good and for uses involving substantial investment over a long period of years. . . . The U.S. Congress is reluctant to commit large sums to projects with only the protection of a lease." But the Marianas Commission replied that it would not agree to the sale of land on Tinian for military purposes—land would only be available on a lease basis. "Prevailing practice in the United States," they argued, "has little relevance to the Mariana Islands, where land is scarce and has a special cultural significance to the people." The commission could not possibly justify to the people of the Marianas the permanent sale of so much of the Marianas limited land to the United States for military purposes.

The joint communique of the third round mentioned that regarding lease versus purchase, the Marianas proposed a combination of long term leases for fifty years renewable at the end of that period. The United States continued to favor purchasing.

The question of lease versus purchase of land was settled at the fifth round. At the opening of the round, Pangelinan repeated the Marianas opposition to the "permanent alienation" of so much of the islands' scarce land. The Marianas proposed, and the United States ultimately accepted, a fifty year lease with a fifty year renewal option. Such a lease, said Pangelinan, fully protected United States security interests.

The means for determining the value of land on Tinian was another matter which had to be resolved. The Marianas suggested that standard procedures for determining land values in Micronesia, particularly those previously used by the United States military, would not apply. Land value should take into consideration the future growth potential of the Marianas and the relationship between the amount of developed and undeveloped land. The commission, therefore, suggested use of land values equivalent to those on Guam or Hawaii. But the United States referred to this as "rather unconventional criteria" and stated that "by law and regulation the U. S. cannot employ any other standard than current 'fair market value' to pay for land."

But while advocating use of "fair market value," the United States was also considering steps to freeze the value of land on Tinian. There were strong indications of rapidly rising land values in light of anticipated military acquisition. In 1973 the high commissioner, at the direction of the Office of Micronesian Status Negotiations, announced that no new applications for homesteads on Tinian would be processed. This action, immediately labeled a "moratorium" by the people of the Marianas, was vigorously and vocally opposed as high-handed and unilateral. In an interview, Ambassador Williams, in a play on words, denied that a "moratorium" had been imposed, pointing out that applications continued to be processed. Only when pressed did he acknowledge that no new applications would be accepted or processed. Other United States officials were more candid.

Privately, United States officials accused at least three of the most prominent members of the Marianas Political Status Commission (including Pangelinan) of involvement in speculative land dealings on Tinian. Pangelinan acknowledged the charges about two of his colleagues but denied his own involvement. He could not, he said, be responsible for the actions of his relatives. A high Trust Territory official told of how a member of the Marianas commission from Tinian bought property for $850, had the sale notarized by a fellow commission member, and within ten minutes sold the same parcel for $10,000 to the notarizer. Don Oberdorfer in the *Washington Post* wrote in February, 1975, that photocopies of a hand-written message, purportedly passed by two Marianas negotiators during an official session, were in circulation on Saipan. Oberdorfer continued: "The note concerns the price which might be asked for land which the note passers obtained on Tinian. . . .The authenticity of the handwritten paper could not be established but informed sources confirmed that at least three members of the Marianas Commission purchased Tinian lands in recent months."

Clearly, both the amount of land and its value were sharp points at issue from the beginning. Yet communiques constantly underplayed the differences.

By the opening of the fifth round, no agreement had been reached on the price to be paid for the lease or purchase of land. Conflicting appraisals of land values had been made by experts hired by each side and these had been discussed informally. Once agreement was reached on the *lease* of land, agreement was then reached on *price*. The final agreement called for the following total payment for up to 100 years: 1) Tinian, $17,500,000; 2) Tanapag, $2,000,000; and 3) Farallon de Medinilla, $20,600. In addition, the United States would place $2 million in perpetual trust to be used for development and maintenance of the memorial park at Tanapag Harbor.

Agreement had been reached in principle in the second round of negotiations regarding the limitation of land ownership to people of Marianas ancestry. The United States had agreed to land alienation provisions: Article IV, section 2, clause 1 of the United States Constitution relating to "privileges and immunities" will apply to the Marianas so that "the ability of the future Marianas government to preserve control of the land...in the hands of Marianas citizens will not be compromised." Yet by the fourth round, no progress had been made toward the implementation of this policy. It was then agreed that a joint drafting committee would consider questions regarding alienation of land as well as the development of appropriate safeguards in the area of eminent domain.

The Draft Covenant tentatively approved at the fifth round provided for protection of ownership of land for the people of the Marianas. The Covenant requires that the Northern Marianas "regulate the alienation of permanent and long term interests in real property so as to restrict the acquisition of such interests to persons of Northern Mariana Islands descent" and to "regulate the extent to which a person may own or hold land which is now public land." The provision extends "twenty-five years after termination of the Trusteeship Agreement" and could continue thereafter. In short, the Marianas are given a permanent right to control alienation of land. It was understood that "Marianas descent" included the Carolinian community, but the latter were later to express fears that they might be excluded from land ownership in the future.

The covenant also outlined the procedures the United States government must follow to acquire additional land. The United States agreed to seek only the minimum area necessary, to try to rent or lease land, to look at public property before acquiring private property, and to purchase land only if no other means is satisfactory. Prior written notice must be given to the government of the Marianas before acquisition of land, and the United States agreed to acquire no interest in land "unless duly authorized by the Congress of the United States and appropriations are available therefor." Immediately following a statement of its military requirements, the United States affirmed that it had "no present need for or present intention to acquire any additional property, or any greater interest in the property leased by the United States in accord with the Covenant than that which is granted to it thereby, in order to carry out its defense responsibilities."

In the final analysis, however, the United States reserved for itself the right to "exercise within the Commonwealth the power of eminent domain to the same extent and in the same manner as it has and can exercise the power of eminent domain in a State of the Union."

ECONOMICS AND FINANCE

The area of economics and finance proved as difficult as land negotiations, if not more so. In the land negotiations, the solution lay in scaling down the size of inflated United States land requirements and allowing interim civilian use of land which would be set aside indefinitely for contingent military use. In the area of economics, the question was how much more money than the United States was then spending was it willing to spend and to what extent was it willing to relinquish controls over expenditures. Unlike the Micronesian negotiators the Marianas group had devoted considerable attention to economic questions from the beginning. They had also hired an economic planning consultant to work alongside their principal attorney.

As early as the second round the Marianas group had indicated their immediate and long term economic goals as well as specific dollar figures which might be needed. They would need sufficient economic resources to enable them to facilitate an orderly transition to new political status; build toward an adequate social and economic infrastructure; provide necessary public services and programs; and encourage and promote the future economic development of the Marianas.

The Marianas presented the United States with very specific proposals—complete with charts of capital investment requirements, budget projections for the fiscal years 1973-79, and projections of the Mariana Islands government expenditures and revenue requirements from 1975 to 1981. In great detail, their paper pictured their development in three phases of transition:

Phase one to last a year and requiring $4.5 million.

Phase two to last seven years (1975-81) and requiring $47.7 million, broken down into the following amounts per year:

1975	$19.2 million
1976	$22.4 million
1977	$23.9 million
1978	$28.3 million
1979	$27.5 million
1980	$21.6 million
1981	$19.9 million

Phase three, "extending to the year 2000 and perhaps beyond," for which no projections were made.

The United States response totally ignored the Marianas estimates and provided no budgetary figures of its own. Deputy United States Representative James Wilson replied: "We will need to explore with you further the nature of these requirements," and "we are by no means clear about the basis on which your total figure of $47.7 million was reached." Instead, the United States sought to explore "general principles leading to general understandings rather than concentrating on budgetary details and precise figures and estimates."

Looking at the examples of Guam, the Virgin Islands, and Puerto Rico as prototypes, the United States suggested two forms of annual financial assistance for a period until the Marianas were able to meet their own financial needs: direct financial grants in support of the costs of government operation and capital improvement programs, and the extension and provision of federal programs and services to the Marianas. Williams was careful to add, "I must always caveat my remarks when talking about money by adding the familiar 'subject to the approval of Congress' clause." In an obvious effort to scale down Marianas estimates, the United States pointed out that the impact of military facilities and expenditures in the Marianas must be considered—probably $10-12 million for the years of construction and approximately $15 million per year after that. Summarizing, the United States position paper states: "Statements regarding the mechanics of a financial relationship are not enough nor is an impersonal rundown of current and potential sources of revenue and support. We should add that quite aside from forms and figures we do agree with your goals and aspirations and with your understandable desire to raise the standards of living of your people."

A description of initial discussions of economic issues in the joint communique was replete with phrases such as "agreed in principle," "prepared to agree," "have agreed to explore," "special attention will be paid," and "will require . . . planning." However, the United States did agree to provide start-up costs and planning assistance. Most important, although clearly indicating the United States desire to maintain control of the purse strings, the United States representative agreed to a provision whereby, subject to the approval of the United States Congress, the United States would "provide financial support over an initial period of years at *guaranteed fixed levels.*" (Emphasis added.)

That the Marianas were disappointed is clear. For it was in the area of economics that Pangelinan made his most pointed criticism of the United States. Commenting on the joint press release, Pangelinan said:

> The Commission wants the United States delegation to know that the Commission is of the unanimous view that the commitments made by the United States in the area of economic and financial support in this release are *not* as *specific, definite* or *generous* as the Commission believes appropriate. The Commission intends to press its views on this matter vigorously in the future at every possible occasion until the United States is prepared to make the financial commitments necessary for the future growth and development of the Marianas.

At the third round the United States came with figures, but they fell far short of the Marianas expectations. The United States proposed approximately $14.5 million of direct assistance annually for the first five years, to be broken down as follows: $7.5 million for budgetary support for government operations; $3 million for capital improvement projects; $1 million to a Marianas development loan fund; and an estimated $3 million in federal government programs and services. This did not include payment for the use of land for public purposes, including military uses or an amount estimated after five years to reach $4.5 million annually from customs duties, excise taxes, and federal income taxes which would be generated from within the Marianas. In addition, the United States continued to cite the indirect benefits accruing from the establishment of a United States military base. However, the joint communique of the third round stated: "No attempt was made to reach definitive agreements on United States financial assistance to the future commonwealth government. The Marianas Political Status Commission noted that its own detailed studies to date indicate that a higher level of external assistance than that provided by the U.S. proposals would be required during the first 5 years under the commonwealth arrangement."

The fourth round saw United States land requirements significantly scaled down and a corresponding willingness by the Marianas to agree to new United States proposals of economic assistance. The agreed amount differed from the initial United States offer in three respects. The guaranteed assistance level would cover seven years instead of five years. The package would total $16.5 million instead of $14.5 million (operational up $0.5 million to $8 million: capital improvement increased by $1 million; and approximately $3 million in federal services). Finally, up to $1.5 million would be provided to cover the costs of transition. Other indirect benefits, such as taxes, would remain the same.

One aspect of the agreement on economic and financial issues is indicative of internal Marianas politics. The people of Rota have never been overly enthusiastic about their fate at the hands of Saipan. And some on Tinian have felt that their island provides the major commodity for which the United States is paying. It is thus not surprising that the agreement specifically designates money for each area: $500,000 annually each in development funds for Rota and Tinian "because of the urgent development needs on those islands."[9]

At the fifth round in December, 1974, final agreement was reached on the economic package and for the first time agreement was reached on the amount of money the United States would pay for use of land in the Marianas. Agreement was not reached, however, before the United States officially confirmed what had been whispered around Guam since the earlier visit of Deputy Secretary of Defense Clements. Clements had stated privately that the United States would not proceed immediately with construction of the base on Tinian. His statements were consistent with an earlier warning by the United States House Appropriations Committee that a new base on Tinian could not be justified so long as the United States continued to maintain bases in Japan and the Philippines. Finally, an anticipated United States budget deficit in excess of $40 billion exerted extensive pressure on the funds available to Defense and thus forced the Pentagon to choose its priorities even more carefully. The result was a decision not to proceed immediately with construction of a base which Clements himself had said all along was not needed until the "out" years, meaning fifteen to twenty years hence.

The Marianas were not the only ones surprised by the decision not to proceed immediately with the building of the Tinian facility. Williams had not been informed of the decision even though he had heard rumors. When the talks began, he continued to act as if he still didn't know. Though he surely knew by then of the change, Williams made no hint of it at the opening of the fifth round. The cancellation of the base undercut the United States position in the financial negotiations, for one of the reasons advanced by the United States for a smaller financial package was the economic advantages the Marianas would receive as a direct by-product of immediate military base construction and

---

[9] For similar reasons, Rota and Tinian insisted at the last round that a bicameral legislature, where in one house their representation would be equal to Saipan's, be made a part of the covenant.

operation over a period of seven years. Though they could and did ask for more money as a result of the base cancellation, the Marianas had never fully accepted the United States contention that part of their compensation should be a by-product of the base. Even before the base cancellation, Pangelinan told an interviewer that the Marianas had to protect themselves against the distinct possibility that the base either would not be built or would be delayed.

The joint communique of the fifth round stated that in view of reduced revenues and employment levels as a result of the decision not to proceed with construction of the Tinian base, the United States would increase its compensation by $500,000 for each of the seven years of the initial financial agreement. (Two hundred and fifty thousand dollars would be provided yearly for low-income home construction loans; and $250,000 would be provided for such things as retraining workers, school curriculum development, and training of civil servants.) This would bring the total *direct* United States payment (excluding land) in each of the first seven years to $14 million. Not stated is a previous agreement under which the United States would provide $1.5 million in "transition" expenses. Also not mentioned is the estimated $50 million cost of moving the Micronesian capital from Saipan to somewhere in the other five districts.[10] Thus, the total financial package is as follows:

Land Lease		
Tinian		$ 17,500,000
Farallon de Medinilla		20,600
Tanapag		2,000,000
	Total $	19,520,600
Move of Capital		50,000,000
Transition Expenses		1,500,000
Government Support		57,750,000
Capital Improvements		28,000,000
Economic Development Loan Fund		12,250,000
Federal Programs and Services		21,000,000
Total Cost of Marianas Package		$190,020,600[11]

As indicated earlier, the United States agreed to *guarantee* annual payments.[12] Section 702 of the covenant states that approval of the covenant

---

[10] The capital might have been relocated in any event, but relocation is made necessary by the separation of the Marianas.

[11] In constant United States dollars. The Marianas would also benefit from the five-year development program announced in late 1974. These costs undoubtedly figured in the willingness of the Marianas to accept a smaller financial package.

[12] In these areas, the Marianas got more than the District of Columbia, whose budget and finances are still subject to congressional whims and whose legislation is still subject to disapproval by the Congress.

constitutes "a commitment and a pledge of the full faith and credit of the United States for the payment, as well as an authorization for the appropriation" for guaranteed annual levels of expenditures. Thus, the legislative process for appropriations is shortened. Congress would go through the formality of appropriation, but the authorized amount (subject to dollar fluctuation) is already fixed.

TENSION IN THE MARIANAS

One issue which lay in the background in the Marianas negotiations and which may cause problems later was disagreement among the Mariana islands, i.e., disagreement between Rota, Tinian and Saipan. The people of Tinian objected to the apparent ease with which other Mariana Islanders particularly those on Saipan, were willing to negotiate land on Tinian; Rota, which had continued to be administered by Interior while Saipan was administered by Navy, objected to the dominant role of Saipan. In addition, a group of Carolinians on Saipan objected to the dominant role of the Chamorro majority. Some of these differences manifested themselves in election returns. In 1974, the people of Tinian elected a new mayor who opposed military base plans; and in November, 1974 the people of the Marianas defeated the dominant Popular Party and elected representatives of the Territorial Party. The status negotiations, particularly objections to their secrecy and haste, were a major issue. Included among those defeated was Edward Pangelinan, head of the Marianas negotiating team. Included among the newly elected was Oscar Rasa, an outspoken American-educated Marxist critic of the negotiations.

Some of the differences within the Marianas are smoothed over in the covenant. Specific money is set aside for use on Tinian and Rota. There also seems to be an informal agreement that a percentage of money paid for lease of Tinian land will be controlled by Tinian. By far the major protection for Tinian and Rota is a covenant provision that the Marianas Legislature be bicameral with one house of equal representation. There is no doubt, however, that Rota and Tinian will be locked into the new Northern Marianas political entity. For, according to the negotiating history, the provision which insures that union with Guam is not foisted on the Marianas also serves to insure that there will be no fragmentation of the Marianas.

Not until the eve of the signing of the Marianas Covenant did pressure build up to stop it. The immediate issue was not the status of association with the United States but the terms of the association. Two members of the Marianas Political Status Commission, Oscar Rasa for one, spoke out strongly against the "haste" with which the covenant was being signed. Rasa's newspaper accused the

United States of buying off Marianas representatives by promising $24,000 for work on transition matters. In the end, two members (Rasa and Felix Rebauliman, a Carolinian) of the fifteen-member Marianas Commission refused to sign the covenant, although they were said to have previously approved it.

Another attempt to stop Marianas separation came from the Congress of Micronesia. On February 14, 1975, a Marianas representative (Jose P. Mafnas) asked the High Court of Micronesia, in a class action suit, to temporarily and permanently restrain the Marianas Commission, Legislature and Trust Territory government from proceeding with the signing of the covenant and the subsequent conduct of a plebiscite. The suit was argued by Michael A. White, a staff attorney for the Congress of Micronesia, and, according to Micronesian sources, paid for by the Congress of Micronesia. White argued that under Trust Territory law only the Congress of Micronesia could authorize status negotiations and that the Marianas District Legislature had exceeded its authority since it was limited to local matters.

The Marianas responded, in a brief prepared in cooperation with United State negotiators, that 1) the question was a political matter, 2) that the question was not a last minute one and should have been raised earlier, and 3) that the Congress of Micronesia would, in effect, deny the Marianas their right of self-determination. As to legality, the Marianas suggested that the negotiations had been conducted with the consent and at the direction of the President of the United States, who had final authority in Micronesia, under United States law. Finally, the Marianas suggested that the plaintiff(s) would suffer no irreparable harm since many steps remained before the covenant would go into effect.

At a hearing held just three hours before the scheduled signing of the covenant, Trust Territory Chief Justice Harold Burnett, who is appointed by and removable by the Secretary of the Interior, denied the temporary restraining order. By June 29, 1975, the Chief Justice had taken no action on the request for a permanent injunction. As a matter of law, there were no further actions by the Trust Territory government, The Marianas Legislature, or the Marianas Commission which could have been effectively stoppped after the signing. The Chief actor in the events, the United States government, was not a defendant and could not have been since the matter was in the territorial court.[13]

PLEBISCITE AND TRANSITION

With agreement behind on several major issues, the last round of Marianas negotiations began to look ahead to transitional measures and actual implementa-

---

[13] In any event, the plaintiff, under pressure from family and friends, resigned from the Congress of Micronesia and ceased participating in political matters.

tion of a new government. At the fourth round, a joint committee was appointed to draft a Marianas status agreement for consideration at the next round of negotiations. The Marianas repeated their request for early transition to self-government and separate administration. In what must have been a burst of patriotism, the negotiators set July, 1976, as a possible early date for installation of the new government of the Northern Marianas. At the fifth round, the Marianas again reiterated their desire for separate administration from the remainder of Micronesia as promptly as possible after approval of the convenant. The United States representative responded that he would "strongly recommend" that the Secretary of the Interior "take all necessary action" to meet the Marianas request. In the agreed document on negotiating history and in a press conference held after the signing of the covenant, the United States went further. It stated its intention to administer the Marianas separately as soon as the covenant had been approved in a plebiscite and *before* approval of the covenant by the United States Congress. In fact, the covenant allows for implementation of some of its provisions *prior* to termination of the Trusteeship Agreement.

On April 11, 1975, Secretary of the Interior Rogers Morton issued a proclamation which set June 17, 1975, as the date for a plebiscite in the Marianas. Morton also announced the appointment by the President of Erwin D. Canham, former editor of the *Christian Science Monitor,* as plebiscite commissioner.

As set forth in Secretarial Order 2973, dated April 10, 1975, Canham was to insure the conduct of an impartial plebiscite education program; appoint a plebiscite register; oversee the administrative plans for and supervise the plebiscite; and appoint an executive director responsible for the execution and coodination of the plebiscite. Given the brief time between his appointment and the date of the plebiscite, Canham had to rely heavily on Nieman Craley, a member of the "cabinet" of the high commissioner.

Many of the most crucial questions governing the conduct of the plebiscite were already set before Canham's appointment and would directly influence the outcome of the plebiscite whose fairness he was to certify. Among these was qualifications for voting, a question of major importance in an area which, because of its function as the seat of government, has many long-time residents from other districts. But the two most important issues were the questions to be voted on in the plebiscite and the timing of the vote.

The questions to be voted on were stated in Morton's proclamation.

> YES—I vote for Commonwealth as set forth in the Covenant to Establish Commonwealth of the Northern Mariana Islands in Political Union with the United States of America.
>
> NO— I vote against Commonwealth in political union with the United States as set forth in the covenant, recognizing that, if Commonwealth is rejected, the Northern Mariana Islands, will remain as a

district of the Trust Territory with the right to participate with the other districts in the determination of an alternative future political status.

The wording of the plebiscite ran into immediate criticism. It stated that a negative vote was a vote against commonwealth ("if Commonwealth is rejected") rather than a vote against the covenant. Thus, the wording virtually forced a "yes" vote by those who supported the idea of commonwealth but wished revisions and by those who simply wanted more time to consider the question. The implication was reinforced by wording which, if not read carefully, implied that the alternative to approval of the commonwealth was inclusion in the uncertain political unit being negotiated by the other five districts.[14]

The principal objection came from the Carolinian community. Their position was supported by United States Representative Lloyd Meeds, who wrote the Secretary of the Interior and urged that the plebiscite wording be changed. In the end, however, Acting Secretary of the Interior Kent Frizzell turned down all requests for a change in the ballot, saying that the wording of the plebiscite was agreed on by the various agencies of the United States government only after the most careful consideration of the obligation of the United States under the Trusteeship Agreement. Frizzell did not add that the wording was a compromise: State blamed Williams's office for the unsatisfactory wording and Williams's office said they were responding to the demands of State for language which would indicate that there was a choice of remaining with the other five districts.

Part of the haste in holding the Marianas plebiscite was to pre-empt a July territory-wide referendum called for by the Congress of Micronesia. The referendum proclamation, signed by the high commissioner on May 15, was to "ascertain the wishes of the people of Micronesia with respect to their future political status choice, the unity of Micronesia and the role of the Congress as a negotiating agency on behalf of the Micronesian people." The referendum was set for July 8, 1975.

Between April 10 and June 17, the plebiscite commissioner also had to educate the voters of the Marianas on the choices before them. There had been previous education efforts conducted by the Marianas negotiators and by the Trust Territory government, but neither of those efforts was free of suspicion since both parties had an interest in the outcome of the plebiscite. Given the tendency of local newspapaers to take strong editorial positions even in news

---

[14] Another group may have been influenced to vote in favor of the plebiscite. Within two weeks of the plebiscite the Trust Territory government circulated a report recommending that 525 Marianas residents working for the government be allowed to keep their jobs during transition in the interest of an "orderly and efficient transition." It was a timely assurance for those who may have leaned toward voting against the plebiscite in the interest of job security.

columns, an objective education program under Canham was even more important. Time, however, was against the plebiscite commissioner. Not until two weeks before the vote did the Office of the Plebiscite Commissioner announce completion of booklets, in the three relevant languages, explaining the proposed commonwealth convenant.

In the plebiscite, the commonwealth was approved by a certified vote of 3,945 to 1,060 (or by 78.8 per cent). Delegates of Australia, France and the United Kingdom were sent by the United Nations Trusteeship Council to observe the vote and the political education program.[15] According to the *Micronesian Independent*, Plebiscite Commissioner Canham described the result as "so decisive that this is a clear mandate of public opinion."

As expected, the Marianas District Legislature promptly asked that the Marianas be administered separately, and excluded from the territory-wide referendum and from the constitutional convention, which was convened in July, 1975. Of the requests, the most important to the Marianas leaders was separate administration.

For its part, the Congress of Micronesia had previously expressed opposition to separate administration of the Marianas until the people of the Marianas had had an opportunity to vote on the draft compact. At a special session in mid-1974, a committee of the Congress reported:

> THE UNITED STATES undertook some very important obligations to the people of Micronesia when it entered into the Trusteeship Agreement. We may fairly summarize that spirit of all these obligations quite simply: to do what is right by the people of Micronesia, and to treat them fairly and equally.
> TO DENY any possibility of the unity of Micronesia by the administrative separation of a district prior to the time when its people have had the opportunity to vote on the Compact of Free Association is to deny everything which the Trusteeship system stands for, everything good about democracy which the United States purports [to] represent, and even the slightest pretense that the United States is in Micronesia for any reason higher than its own base and selfish interests.
> WE DO NOT BELIEVE that anyone in Micronesia would have any quarrel with the separation of a district if its people had conclusively voted to reject the Constitution and the Compact. But, by the same token, we regard it as a serious infringement on our own rights and dignity if even the slightest chance for a united Micronesia were destroyed by the actions of the administering authority. If the United States has confidence in the integrity of its relations with that district [the Marianas], it has nothing to lose by testing the faith of the people of that district by permitting them to vote on the question of the future of all of Micronesia . . . .

But more important opposition to separate administration of the Marianas came from some members of the United States Congress who did not wish the

---

[15] The Soviet Union voted against the proposal to send observers from the Trusteeship Council and refused to go to Micronesia when the resolution passed.

executive branch to anticipate or pre-empt the decision of the United States Congress on the covenant. Faced with congressional opposition, the administration decided just after the plebiscite to drop its plans for the immediate separate administration of the Marianas. Instead it pressed the Congress to act on the Marianas convenant by September, 1975. Once again haste was the watchword.

If the projected 1980-81 date for free association of the rest of Micronesia holds, the American bicentennial would see no change in the international status of the Northern Marianas, only their separate administration under the Trusteeship Agreement. The significance of transition prior to termination of the Trusteeship Agreement is substantial and might have been suggested by the United States side even if the Micronesians had not done so. The amount of opposition which fragmentation would face in the United Nations or in the United States Congress would be substantially less if separate units were already functioning.

CONCLUSION

It is premature for a definitive assessment of what the Marianas have achieved now that the covenant has been signed and approved by 78 per cent of the Marianas voters (55 per cent was required.). Before the covenant takes complete effect, it must be approved by the United States Congress and by the President. In the meantime, the Congress of Micronesia might find legal and/or political means to effectively block the Marianas separation. United Nations Security Council approval is needed to terminate the Trusteeship Agreement, although both the United States and counsel for the Marianas have suggested that United Nations approval is not necessary.

There are other factors which might derail the Marianas Commonwealth even after it comes into being. American tradition is that once a part of the United States, always a part of the United States—unless, of course, the United States decides otherwise, as in the case of the Phillipines. But the Civil War which established that principle ended more than a hundred years ago. The United States might react differently in the very different political climate of the seventies, especially where geographical separation and cultural distinction might bolster secession. Certainly, the United States would be faced with problems not dissimilar to those of France in Algeria should significant nationalist sentiment in the Marianas and its people conclude that the commonwealth is not sufficient to fulfill their aspirations.   There may be a tendency to dismiss the possibility of serious dissidence in the Marianas—and surely time and the fulfillment of mutual needs will lessen that possibility. On the other hand, it should not be forgotten that the meaning of some of the language used in the convenant is still subject to dispute. Some ambiguities seem to have been deliberately built-in in the give-and-take of negotiations.

It is worth remembering that at the very outset of negotiations there were problems about the word "permanence." The United States assumed that the word "permanence" could be used freely and openly. After all, when the Marianas leadership asked for separate negotiations, they noted that the desire of the people of the Marianas to become "a permanent part of the United States of America is fundamental and has existed over a number of years." But the formal mandate of the Marianas District Legislature instructed its delegation to negotiate a "close association." The mandate did not mention "permanent." Accordingly, the Marianas Commission noticeably avoided use of the word except in their initial statement at the first session of the negotiations. Since then, "secure," "enduring," and "lasting" are words the Marianas use to describe the relationship they seek.

The Marianas sensitivity to the use of "permanent" is partly in recognition of the temporary nature of *any* arrangement. But it is also possible they could have been thinking seriously of later alteration. At the moment when the Marianas were distancing themselves from any association with the United States that might eventually dissolve under pressure for independence or that, at least, was not close enough for their liking—even at that moment, there was hesitation to use the word "permanent." Who is to say what the aspirations of any people may be in the future?

Knowledge of worldly political developments remains limited in the Marianas. Rhetoric to the contrary, the people and their leaders are now largely motivated by pressing economic objectives which they believe cannot be resolved except by bartering their strategic location. The time may come when economic objectives loom less large—although no one now sees such a time. The people of the Marianas may then wish to re-evaluate their relationship with the United States, perhaps to seek improvements in that relationship within the terms of an association with the United States, or to seek a new relationship with Guam or the other islands of Micronesia, or something totally different. The covenant provides for regular review and thus there is an opportunity to accommodate changed circumstances. If the covenant does not prove sufficiently flexible, American military officials who look upon the Marianas relationship as a permanent solution to their needs for bases in the western Pacific may find themselves faced with a status problem in new and more difficult dimensions.

Whatever the needs—whether real or imagined—of the Pentagon in the western Pacific, the willingness of Washington to deal so generously with non-citizens while denying their fellow Americans equal treatment can only be viewed with suspicion and resentment by the people of Guam.

—A. Won Pat

VII

Implications for Guam and the Other United States Territories

Both Congress and the executive branch have always been aware that negotiating a new status for Micronesia might have implications for other territories of the United States. In the Kennedy and Johnson years, those implications, repeatedly put forth by the Department of the Interior with the strong backing of Congressman Aspinall, had often blocked policy decisions which might have led to an earlier resolution of Micronesia's status. At the same time the territories have looked for precedents in the Micronesian negotiations which they might use to improve their own status.

Guam, particularly, followed the tactic of encouraging the Marianas to hold out for more extensive United States concessions and criticized the United States for offering the Marianas a better status than that enjoyed by Guam. In 1973, Jose Cabranes, then on leave from his position as a Professor of Law at Rutgers University, and serving as administrator of the Office of the Commonwealth of Puerto Rico and counsel to Puerto Rico's governor, saw by analogy new alternatives open to Puerto Rico as a result of the Micronesian negotiations for free association.

Hawaii and Alaska may have been the last United States territories to follow the traditional pattern of progress toward statehood. Compared to the forty-ninth and fiftieth states, the Commonwealth of Puerto Rico and the remaining territories—Guam, American Samoa, and the Virgin Islands—are even more geographically, demographically, culturally and historically distinct. These factors seem to limit their expectations, if not their aspirations. If their people cannot hope to achieve equality within the American system, they seek to determine how close they can come or how much autonomy they can exercise. Some Guamanians have begun to discuss independence, just as some Puerto Ricans have done for decades. The Virgin Islands also seeks changes in its status. On the other hand, the people of American Samoa recently again voted down a proposal to elect their own governor.

The amount of political restlessness varies from one territory to another, but the pursuit of a satisfying status remains the major preoccupation of all territorial politics. Pressures for changes in status, in fact, are sometimes welcomed as indicators of social and economic advancement. Congressmen returning from a trip to Micronesia and American Samoa in 1974 complained to interviewers that the Samoans had not, in their longer association with the United States, developed the political maturity and assertiveness which the Micronesians had.

All United States territories may have some basis for complaint if fewer limitations are placed on new United States territories as the result of negotiations with the United States. Technically, the only new United States territory under consideration is the Northern Mariana Islands which would come under United States sovereignty; a comparison of that territory's prerogatives with the (often rather limited) prerogatives of other territories is most relevant. There are a variety of congressional reactions to objections that the Marianas are going to have more benefits, rights, and power than other United States territories. These reactions range from the feeling that five different and unequal statuses demonstrate "correct flexibility" to the notion that the new status of the Marianas will be an incentive to other territories to press Congress for a better status for themselves.

GUAM

Guam would be included in a discussion of Micronesia's status even if it were not directly affected by precedents which might be established. Guam is geographically and anthropologically, but not politically, a part of Micronesia. Guam is likely to remain an integral part of Micronesia, especially of the Mariana Islands chain, of which Guam is the southern-most island. But the question of Guam's future status would have been important even if the Marianas had not decided to break away from the rest of Micronesia and seek a separate relationship with the United States. However, the separate negotiations and the substance of agreements reached spurred Guam's interest in Micronesian developments and caused Guam to question anew its own relationship with the United States.

Guam and the Marianas Have Common Roots

Guam has similar cultural, ethnic, and linguistic roots with the rest of the Mariana Islands. However, Guam developed separately after it was severed from the other Mariana Islands and ceded to the United States by Spain following the Spanish-American War. The Mariana Islands had been quite densely populated until the Spanish introduced Christianity. Continual native resistance to it, however, culminated in uprisings which the Spanish quelled by moving the entire Chamorro population to Guam and killing off a large percentage of them. In one sense there are no Chamorros. Those who survived intermarried with Filipinos, Spanish, Chinese and others to form the basis of the present population of Guam and of the Northern Marianas.

When Guam was ceded to the United States, the remainder of the Marianas went to Germany. Even at the time of Pearl Harbor, little was known about the rest of Micronesia. The Navy administered Guam but didn't seem to believe it had any strategic value. Before the Japanese invasion, Guam was classified "temporarily dispensable" and all American personnel and dependents were evacuated. It is a sore point with some Guamanians that the United States left Guam to the mercy of the Japanese. On the other hand, probably a larger number of Guamanians are grateful to the United States for recapturing the island.

When Guam was liberated on July 21, 1944, a Guamanian spokesman revealed Guamanians' patriotism: "We have never subscribed to any foreign ideologies or influences; we pledge allegiance to no flag except that of the Stars and Stripes; we have proven our loyalty, have demonstrated our valor, and have sacrificed for a common cause."

Guamanians are proud of their association with the United States — "Where America's Day Begins" reads a newspaper banner. "The people of Guam are without a doubt among the most loyal Americans on the face of the earth," said the president of the Guam Junior Chamber of Commerce before a congressional subcommittee. "Everyone knows," said another observer, "that Guamanians will sing 'God Bless America' at the drop of a hat." Guam remained a military base after the war. The island was placed under strict naval security clearance regulations, which, along with Navy control of large blocks of land and almost all essential services, had a severely adverse affect on economic development. Tourism, for example, could not be developed because of restrictions on entry.

In 1950, with the passage of an organic act, a civilian, Carlton Skinner, was appointed governor, and administration of the island was placed under a civilian agency, the Department of the Interior. Guam first elected its governor in 1971, and in April, 1972, a bill was approved under which Guam would elect a nonvoting delegate to the United States Congress. It was not until Typhoon Karen devastated the island in 1962 that Guam began to come alive economically. Congress passed the Guam Rehabilitation Act and new facilities were built. The island is still largely dependent on the contribution of the military to its economy. However, since 1962, Guam has developed a booming tourist industry which attracts large numbers of Japanese, especially young couples who go to Guam for their honeymoons.

Micronesia is heavily dependent on Guam. Virtually all Trust Territory commerce goes through it. Up to mid-1974, even goods shipped from the United States West Coast and destined for the Marshalls, went first to Guam. Guam once served as the seat of government for Micronesia. And the University of Guam serves as the institution of higher education for Micronesia.

On the other hand, Guam depends on Micronesia for a substantial amount of agricultural products, and its dependence is likely to grow if plans materialize for improved agricultural development on Tinian and Rota. A Guamanian entrepreneur from Texas already has a meat and dairy ranch and a slaughter house on Tinian. Most of his products are shipped to Guam. Similarly, the University of Guam attracts a large number of Micronesian students and would suffer if that number were reduced significantly.

Political Barriers

Thus, in every aspect except political, the relationship between Guam and Micronesia seems to point to unification. This is particularly true of the relationship between Guam and the Northern Marianas. But the political barriers are substantial, perhaps impenetrable.

As early as 1961, the people of the Northern Marianas proposed their "reintegration" with Guam on grounds of ethnic, cultural, and linguistic similarities. And to the extent that Guam is American in its ways, the Northern Marianas are more similar to Guam than they are to any other area of Micronesia. There is undoubtedly an element of truth to the suggestion, prevalent in the early sixties, that the Marianas reintegration movement was initially promoted by the American Navy on Guam; but American citizenship and the higher wages paid by the military on Guam also played a major role in "reintegration" efforts. In any event, repeated overtures by the Marianas were met with solid opposition from the United Nations and from the United States under pressure from the United Nations. In 1969, Guam itself joined the anti-reintegration side when a poorly publicized, low voter turnout referendum on Guam resulted in the rejection, by a narrow margin, of "reintegration" with the Northern Marianas. Guamanians are said to harbor bitter feelings against the Saipanese because many Saipanese were used by the Japanese to guard Guamanians during the Japanese occupation of Guam. Guamanians speak condescendingly of their poor northern neighbors.

Guamanians may, however, be changing their attitudes about political reintegration with the Northern Marianas. In a recent but unscientific poll conducted by Guam's delegate to the United States Congress, Antonio Borja Won Pat, 86.2 per cent voted in favor of reunification with the Northern Marianas. Former Guam Governor Carlos Camacho felt strongly about an eventual union: "The link between Guam and the Northern Marianas . . . was broken only by a quirk of history. We all have so much in common and we should be working in a mutual partnership for the benefit of all the people in the islands." But Won Pat projects that plans to unify the Marianas and Guam will be unrealistic for quite a while — at least fifteen to twenty years, because resources, both human and material, are lacking.

The Marianas were faced with rejection by Guam and became the object of growing antipathy from the rest of Micronesia. Realizing that the United States military was primarily interested in building military facilities on their islands, not on other islands in the rest of Micronesia, the Marianas formed a status group to begin their own negotiations with the United States. Guam did not figure in their new position, which opposes reintegration. The United Nations Visiting Mission of 1973 reported that although there exists a feeling of kinship between Guam and the Northern Marianas, it is less talked about now than it used to be. James Leonard, a United States-based economic consultant to the Marianas, thinks that at this point the Marianas do not feel any great desire for "reintegration." With a population of only 13,381, the Marianas now see themselves overpowered by a permanent Guam population of about 71,000 people and a good many experienced politicians. Moreover, the Marianas group feels that its negotiating position is sufficiently strong that it can drive a hard bargain with the United States and eventually negotiate a status better than that of Guam's. Guamanians agree. Delegate Won Pat states, "Micronesians are better off than Guam because they didn't have to go through the period of military control which Guam did." Governor Camacho agrees that the Marianas are in a better position than Guam was in 1950 (the year the organic act was passed), because Guam was not given the opportunity to negotiate with the United States about its political status.

Domination of the United States Military

One issue of particular concern to Guamanians in the last few years is the extent of the military presence in Guam. The life and economy of Guam have been dominated by the omnipresence of American naval and air force personnel and their dependents, who constitute about 22,000 temporary residents, more than one third of the population. In addition, there are more than 8,000 semi-permanent Philippine residents who were brought in by the military to work on the military bases.

The American way of life has had a profound and far-reaching impact on Guam. Agana, the capital, has American television; it receives news from American sources; and it has adopted the American educational system. Chamorro customs are rapidly going the way of the Chamorro language — they are dying out, with the result that a growing group of Chamorro "nationalists" have started a campaign to reintroduce Chamorro into the schools.

Before World War II, most of the people of Guam earned their living from agriculture. The total value of imports was several times greater than exports, but the balance-of-payments was met by expenditures of the naval station. As a result of postwar developments, land previously used for agriculture was pre-empted in favor of military purposes. The island is approximately 200 square miles in size, and over 33 percent of the land, much of it agricultural, is controlled by the military. Until the recent growth of tourism, Guam's prosperity was to a large extent a by-product of heavy military expenditure on the island. The economy is still affected to a large extent by the build-up or cutback in military expenditures. More than 10,000 Guamanians now do government or government-related work.

Since 1898 (and continuing until about ten years ago), the island had been virtually isolated from social and commercial intercourse with the rest of the world because of the security restrictions imposed by the military, and consequently, it had a stagnating economy that resulted in an almost total dependence upon military activities. It was not until the summer of 1962 that the naval security clearance was abolished by President Kennedy, over the objections of the Navy. When those restrictions were lifted, Guam experienced a massive economic boom—with the assistance of Typhoon Karen.

Military and Land

A serious problem for Guam as well as for the rest of the Marianas is land. Foreign land speculators are rapidly acquiring land, and because of the acutely limited availability of land, prices have skyrocketed. Young couples, unable to afford house lots, are forced to live with parents or relatives. They drive to work on a military base every day and travel across vast acres of federally held land lying completely idle. The military actually uses only 25 per cent of its land holdings. Partially because its economy and land are dominated by the military and persons not of Chamorro descent, Guam is frequently cited by Micronesians as an example of what they wish to avoid.

No one is really against the military presence on Guam, says Delegate Won Pat, but many question the present use of the island and are opposed to further military acquisition. The Naval Air Station is utilized more by civilians (75 per cent of the Naval Air Station area is civilian used) than by the military, yet the Department of Defense will not part with any of the land. The Naval Air Station is directly in the middle of a growing community and former Governor Camacho pointed out, "It has become something of a sore point — to get from Barrigada to Tamuning you have to go all the way around the base instead of going right through. I'm not too happy at the way the military is utilizing the property it is holding. They always say they have future plans, but I have heard that comment for ten and [sic] twenty years." Guamanians, said Camacho, were starting to feel uncomfortable about the military, mostly because of the land issue. "There is a growing resentment because the people have to look through the fences at all of those enclosed areas of the island which the military has," says Camacho. Former Guam Senator Frank Lujan commented, "We know that the military retention of one-third of our limited land area is hampering normal development of the economy. The very presence of the military constitutes a drain upon our human and natural resources."

The Navy has plans for a $100 million ammunition complex and dock to be constructed at Sella Bay, the last "unspoiled" area of Guam and one of the most beautiful — perfect for the development of tourism. Many Guamanians believe the federal government took advantage of the Guamanians' desperate need for a new airport and used the airport as "hostage" or "bait" to soften Guamanian opposition to giving up Sella Bay. The Guamanians had almost no choice but to trade Sella Bay for an international airport, an absolute necessity for growing tourism. In 1974, members of the Guam Legislature and members of the Sierra Club and Friends of the Earth filed a suit in San Francisco's Federal District Court to stop construction of the complex. They charge that the Navy and the Guamanian government engaged in an illegal land transfer and held no public hearings as required by the National Environmental Policy Act. The lawsuit was successful and the transfer has been stopped — at least until proper land transfer procedures are followed.

The scarcity of land, in fact, is a major reason for the new questioning of Guam's political status. As Senator Lujan put it: "We are keenly aware of the fact that the United States military wants to expand and intensify their activities on Guam, which means a Guamanian move toward self-determination is becoming an extremely sensitive issue." In testimony before the 1972 House Subcommittee on Territories hearings, Guam Senator Paul Bordallo noted that the United States was negotiating land questions with the Marianas and apparently was willing to enter into long-term leases. Why, asked Bordallo, didn't the United States negotiate leases with Guam rather than continue ownership? One Guamanian teacher summed up what is perhaps a widespread and growing feeling among islanders: "Many of us want to become American (i.e., want statehood) not because we want to be absorbed into American culture, but so that we can protect ourselves better against the military. This is more important than ever now that the Navy has its eyes set on Sella Bay, the last part of the island we can call our own."

The Guam Status Commission: "We Do Not Intend to Sit Idly By . . ."

Even prior to the separate negotiations with the Northern Mariana Islands, Guamanians had kept a wary eye on the Micronesian status negotiations. Delegate Won Pat expressed dismay that the United States was not encouraging "long overdue reunification." After the Mariana breakaway, Guam's governor signed legislation on April 19, 1973, which established a special commission to review the island's political status. Specifically, the commission was instructed to study the following alternatives: statehood; independence; affiliation with another nation; commonwealth or associated free state[1]; and unincorporated territory. Senator Lujan was the commission's chairman and Paul Bordallo, then a Senator

---

[1] Unlike the Micronesian Status Commission, the Guamanians apparently looked upon "commonwealth" in the same way as Puerto Rico, that is, as a "free associated state." The Spanish language name for the "Commonwealth of Puerto Rico" is *Estado Libre Asociado de Puerto Rico*.

and brother of Guam's current governor, was an outspoken member of the commission.

The United States-Marianas communique of May, 1973, in which United States negotiators agreed to a "commonwealth" status for the Marianas, was a particularly bitter pill for Guamanians to swallow. Then Governor Camacho, a supporter of political reunification, challenged the United States tentative agreement with the Marianas: "We do not intend to sit idly by while ... [the Marianas] negotiates itself a political status better than ours. Our status review is underway and when they present theirs, we will move to insure that Guam is treated equally. Our long loyalty to the United States entitles us to nothing less." A steady stream of statements came from Guam Status Commission members, mostly expressing dismay at the Marianas negotiations and Guam's "inferior" status as an unincorporated territory. Among other things, the chairman of the commission wrote a series of harshly critical articles in the *Pacific Daily News*, describing Guam's territorial status as a "nothing status" and a "political no man's land." According to a reliable congressional source the Navy was sufficiently concerned about political dissent among Guam legislators that it began contingency plans to relocate facilities in Micronesia.

The concern felt by Guamanians on their status was expressed in the report of the Political Status Commission to the Guam legislature in September, 1974. Written with the assistance of Arnold Liebowitz, former counsel with the Puerto Rico Status Commission, the Guam Status Commission report is couched in more restrained language than the Lujan articles in the *Pacific Daily News*. However, the desire to change Guam's political relationship with the United States is unmistakable, particularly when the conclusions are read in the context of the entire report.

In its analysis of legal constitutional factors regarding the status of Guam, the Guam Status Commission cited three general roles given the Department of the Interior by Congress in governing United States territories: a representative role before the Congress and elsewhere in the executive branch; a review function over expenditures in the territory; and a direct administrative and supervisory role in specific areas.

The extent to which the Interior Department fulfills these roles varies. On one end of the spectrum is the "commonwealth" of Puerto Rico where neither the Interior Department nor any other United States government agency exercises a representative, review, administrative, or supervisory role.[2] On the other end of the spectrum is the "unincorporated" and *unorganized* territory of American Samoa, which is governed under a constitution approved by the Secretary

---

[2]Ironically, while the Puerto Ricans worked hard to achieve this status, they now complain that there is no mechanism in the United States government to coordinate Puerto Rican interests. There is a White House staff person responsible for all "territories," including Puerto Rico, but this is not adequate.

of the Interior and by a governor appointed by the President. In the middle — in "no man's land" — are Guam and the Virgin Islands, which are "unincorporated," and *organized* territories, meaning they have been constituted by an organic act of the United States Congress. They can govern themselves only to the extent permitted by Congress. Since 1971, Guam and the Virgin Islands have elected their own governor. According to Deputy Assistant Secretary of the Interior Stanley Carpenter, Interior's current role in Guam and the Virgin Islands is limited to five statutory areas: the audit function of the Federal Comptrollers of each territory; responsibility for submerged lands; the Virgin Islands Conservation Fund; the Virgin Islands Matching Fund; and the Guam Rehabilitation Act.

The Guam Status Commission Report argues that the extent of federal control, i.e., including the role of Congress and other agencies such as Defense, is more pervasive in Guam and the Virgin Islands than Deputy Assistant Secretary Carpenter implies.

The basic instrument of government, the organic act, stems from congressional action and does not even in theory take its powers from the people of Guam; it is "at all times subject to such alterations as Congress may see fit to adopt." In addition, the organic act contains "a number of legal reservations on the exercise of local governmental authority and institutionalizes a review of Federal bureaucratic intrusions within the local structure." For example, Guam and the Virgin Islands are limited in that the governor's authority to appoint and remove all officers and employees of the executive branch of the government can be limited by other acts of Congress and the governor must submit an annual report and any other report requested by Congress to the Secretary of the Interior who in turn submits the reports to Congress. Similarly a government comptroller appointed by the Secretary of the Interior reviews the operations of the government and brings them to the attention of the Secretary of the Interior and the governor. The comptroller may communicate directly with any person or with any departmental officer and he may even summon witnesses and administer oaths. The laws of the Guam Legislature may be annulled by the Congress of the United States. Judges in the District Court of Guam are appointed for a term of years rather than for life as in other District Courts throughout the United States and Puerto Rico. Finally, in Guam particularly, the organic act established "a special sanction for the military presence on the island which may permit an expansion of military authority more readily than elsewhere in the United States."

The report concludes:

1. The relationship between the United States and Guam should be based on self-determination and it is essential that decisions are undertaken with the wishes of the Guamanians in mind.

2. The organic act does not permit the people of Guam to effectively manage their own affairs and is inadequate for Guam's needs. The act does not delimit federal power, so local governing institutions remain weak. Federal law extends more broadly to Guam than to any state or commonwealth because the presumption of the validity of the local statutory acts does not operate.

3. Various status alternatives from commonwealth to independence are within the power of the people of Guam and the Congress to establish under the Constitution.

4. The military has played an unduly large role in Guam in areas not affecting the national security but of critical importance to Guam, particularly in control of land.

5. Participation in such regional Pacific institutions as the Economic Commission for Asia and the Far East (ECAFE) and the Asian Development Bank would be desirable economically and politically to Guam, but the United States government has resisted this participation. The report complains that "instead of the U.S. government appearing . . . to seek out and generously promote opportunities so that its . . . citizens can benefit from participation in the world community, the people of Guam have seen almost the contrary to be the case. . . . Although the people of Micronesia, who are not U.S. citizens, have gained the full endorsement by the State Department for their participation in these institutions, no such endorsement has as yet been forthcoming for Guam."

The report recommends the development by the people of Guam of a constitution for the governing of Guam and a referendum in which the people of Guam could choose between a new constitution or continuation of the organic act. Whatever was chosen would be an interim position similar to the commonwealth status granted Puerto Rico and being discussed for the Northern Marianas. The report noted that "the interim position is not necessarily the longer term status goal. It may be that the Commonwealth would continue to develop and grow, but it could also be that the people of Guam would wish closer association with the United States through statehood or a more distant one similar to that being discussed with Micronesia at the present."

The report also favors the return of land holdings not necessary to the national security interest. It further recommends that, as in the cases of Micronesia and the Marianas, administratively secured documents be made available to Guam planners on present and future military needs so as to aid them in a more effective planning for future developments on the island. Finally, the commission recommended the creation of an ad hoc committee to review fully United States military presence on Guam.

The Guam Commission report, however, had little impact even in Guam itself. Only fifty copies were distributed. Moreover, coming just prior to the 1974 elections, the report was greeted cautiously by politicians. Future action on the report is uncertain, especially given the defeat of the chairman of the Status Commission in the 1974 elections. However, it appears unlikely that Guam will let the status question rest for very long. Within a month after his inauguration, the newly elected governor of Guam (a brother of the defeated Guam Status Commission member) raised Guam's status with Interior officials in Washington.

Opposition of Guam's Congressional Delegate

Although the Guam Status Commission gained little attention in Guam and in Washington, the island's concerns have been brought to the attention of Congress. Guam's delegate to Congress watched relatively silently as the Marianas negotiations progressed. Finally, on February 4, 1974, Guam Delegate Won Pat expressed Guam's outrage on the floor of the United States House of Representatives: "To accord these individuals a political status higher than that now accorded Americans in the United States Virgin Islands or Guam . . . is a grave trespass on the boundaries of the union which exists between territorial Americans and their counterparts in the fifty states." Won Pat went on to say that by promising the residents of the Northern Marianas "a degree of political autonomy far greater than that presently enjoyed by the American citizens of Guam, the United States may well have created an effective impediment to reunification for the foreseeable future."

Won Pat didn't think the Northern Marianas wanted even to discuss reunification with Guam since its level of political autonomy is far below that being offered the Marianas. "It comes as no small shock to our people," said Won Pat, "to see the United States readily, even eagerly, offer our neighbors to the north a host of privileges which we on Guam do not enjoy." He concluded that "whatever the needs—whether real or imagined—of the Pentagon in the western Pacific, the willingness of Washington to deal so generously with non-citizens while denying their fellow Americans equal treatment can only be viewed with suspicion and resentment by the people of Guam."

Guam is particularly disturbed because there was no official response to Guam's status initiatives. Won Pat asked President Nixon to set up a Status Commission for Guam, pointing out the Puerto Rican and Micronesian precedents, and stating that "as citizens of a free democracy, the people of Guam are only asking that their positions within the framework of this great country be reviewed and improved." But the White House took no action. Instead, Department of the Interior officials offered to meet with Guam representatives.

Guamanians remarked bitterly, "The Micronesians got to negotiate with a Personal Representative of the President; all we got was Stan Carpenter [Director of Interior's Office of Territorial Affairs]."[3]

Less outspoken than Delegate Won Pat but making essentially the same point was the delegate from the Virgin Islands who in late 1974 told a hearing of the House Subcommittee on Territories that he too was concerned that the Marianas was getting greater advantages than the United States gave the Virgin Islands.

OTHER TERRITORIES

American negotiators do not believe that the provisions of the Draft Compact with Micronesia set precedents for Puerto Rico. The argument is that the Compact does not apply to a territory over which the United States has sovereignty, and the United States has sovereignty over Puerto Rico. Using this logic, only the Marianas Covenant could have precedential implications for Puerto Rico. On the other hand, Puerto Ricans, who already resent the provisions of some United States laws that Puerto Rico is "a territory of the United States," consider their "free association" status the same as Micronesia's[4] and have cited the Draft Micronesian Compact in their effort to achieve improvements in Puerto Rico's status. Such improvements, they argue, are necessary if Puerto Rico's present status is to remain viable. From the Puerto Rican point of view, at least three changes for Puerto Rico would result from the Micronesia Compact. They are:

---

[3]In a letter dated May 15, 1975, Guam delegate Won Pat made a similar request to President Ford. On May 22, 1975, Won Pat informed his constituents by newsletter that he was drafting legislation to form a Select Committee to recommend "a more relevant Federal Territorial Relations Act" for Guam.

[4]See W. Michael Riesman, *Puerto Rico and the International Process: New Roles in Association* (Washington, D.C.: American Society of International Law, 1975). See also statements by Jose Cabranes before the 1973 annual meeting of the American Society of International Law and the University of Texas Law School, December 4, 1974; and the presentation of Puerto Rican Governor Rafael Hernández-Colón on April 27, 1974, before the Ad Hoc Advisory Group on Puerto Rico.

Told that Puerto Rico was being called a United States "territory" in order to differentiate it from a free associated Micronesia, a leading authority on Puerto Rico wrote the author: "It should be reiterated that the orthodox U.S. and Puerto Rico position concerning the Commonwealth status of the island is that it ceased to be a 'territory' on July 25, 1952. If there are indeed federal officials who continue to claim that Puerto Rico's status is that of a 'territory', they are persons quite unwilling to publicly state their views. If they did, any such statement would be of great interest to me personally, to 3 million Puerto Ricans and to the Committee of 24 of the U.N. General Assembly, where the U.S. has argued for a generation that Puerto Rico is not a 'territory.' It seems quite clear that the unnamed federal officials to which reference is made cannot publicly argue out of both sides of their mouths. They must choose to characterize Puerto Rico as a 'territory' (*i.e.*, an outright colony) or as something else — namely, an 'autonomous political entity' freely associated with the U.S. (General Assembly Resolution 748 (VII) of 1953.)"

1. *Wider latitude in foreign affairs* would include associate membership and, in some cases, full membership in United Nations agencies and other international organizations. It also includes specific consultation and approval of international agreements with major impact on Puerto Rico.
2. *The right to unilaterally alter its relationship with the United States*, even though there is no serious consideration currently being given such an action.
3. *Complete control over internal affairs*, leaving only foreign affairs, defense, and other areas explicitly agreed on to the United States. This is not presently the case. Under Section 9 of the Federal Relations Act, "statutory laws of the United States not locally inapplicable . . . shall have the same force and effect in Puerto Rico as in the United States."

If, on the other hand, one takes the view of United States officials and looks upon Puerto Rico's free association as different from the free association of the Micronesian Compact, then only the Marianas Covenant contains possible precedents for Puerto Rico. It is, for example, most important to amend Section 9 of the Puerto Rico Federal Relations Act so that laws passed by the United States Congress will be applicable to Puerto Rico only if Puerto Rico is specifically mentioned. Similarly, a commission with a Puerto Rican majority should review current United States laws and recommend those which should be applicable to Puerto Rico. Although Puerto Rico allows foreign ownership of land, they may wish to control future alienation of land. Other possible precedents of the Covenant are control over immigration, customs, excise taxes, and the opportunity to negotiate with the federal government, particularly the military, over the amount and cost of land it uses.

The specific precedents for Guam, the Virgin Islands, and American Samoa are similar to those for Puerto Rico when Puerto Rico is looked upon as a territory under United States sovereignty. However, precedents are more far-reaching for these three territories which do not already have the relatively advanced status held by Puerto Rico. Some of the precedents for Guam, the Virgin Islands, and American Samoa are: protection against land alienation; the right to negotiate the nature of their relationship, if any, with the United States; the right to write, adopt, and amend their own constitution and laws; the ability to negotiate land usage; restrictions on the applicability of United States laws; control over such areas as customs, excise taxes, and immigration; the right to establish a supreme court; deletion of the requirement to submit a report to the Secretary of the Interior or to the Congress; deletion of the right of Congress to annul legislation; and long-term authorizations of a specific commitment of funds.

The precedents listed above are a few of the items which governments of United States territories might cite as being provided the Marianas and currently unavailable to already established territories. Not all of the above will be equally important in each territory. But on the whole, the desire for changes for United States territories, in the wake of the Marianas Covenant and the Micronesian Compact, is an indication that the United States has yet to develop a stable, long-term relationship with its offshore possessions.

It is strange that this should be so thirty years after the United States had championed "self-determination" in the United Nations Charter. The simple truth is that the United States has always been reluctant to admit that it, just like Britain, France and Portugal, has colonies. But Britain, France, and now Portugal have largely succeeded in adjusting their relations with the territories over which they ruled. In the long term they may have been fortunate that they recognized a colony as a colony and that those colonized put up resistance to continued foreign rule.

I don't object to spending money over there, but what I object to is the hypocrisy which this country has . . . in its relationship to Micronesia, making these people expect something which they can't have— independence.

—Wayne Aspinall

VIII

Congress and Micronesia

The Trusteeship Agreement had its roots in firmly-held anti-colonialist sentiments in the executive branch, particularly within the White House and the Department of State. President Truman thought the Trusteeship Agreement between the United States and the United Nations Security Council sufficiently important to seek approval in both the House and Senate, instead of in the Senate only, as required by the Constitution in the case of treaties. The agreement was approved on July 18, 1947, but in Congress as in the American military establishment, the American draft plan for trusteeship was viewed as a legitimization for territorial expansion rather than as a new approach to the development of dependent areas. Throughout twenty-five years of involvement with Micronesia, Congress would assert its territorial imperative to Micronesia, would deal with the area as if it had no international significance except strategic, and would assign legislation regarding Micronesia to committees which dealt solely with domestic issues.

Attempts had been made to annex the territory. In 1945, Congressman F. Edward Hébert introduced a resolution declaring it the sense of the Congress that the United States retain "permanent possession" of all islands captured from Japan. Similarly, in an August, 1945 report, the House Subcommittee on Pacific bases of the Committee on Naval Affairs stated that the United States "should take outright the Japanese mandated islands." Others in Congress had more grandiose ideas. Congressman James J. Delaney proposed an "American commonwealth of nations" consisting of the British Caribbean islands, the Galapagos, Baja California (which he felt could be taken from Mexico), and Micronesia. The delegate from the Territory of Hawaii, Joseph Farrington, whose elderly widow would become director of Interior's Office of Territories in 1969, suggested that "the territorial formula which had proved so successful in the development of our country through more than 150 years can . . . be readily adapted to the vast new areas of the Pacific." The views of Congress were consistent with public expressions at the time: in 1944 with the island-to-island battles fresh in their minds, 60 per cent of Americans surveyed told the Gallup organization that the United States should retain possession of Micronesia.

When the Trusteeship Agreement was presented to Congress for approval, little was said about the United States capability to assist Micronesian social, economic, and political development. Little was said which would lead any congressman to think that the agreement gave the United States less than unquestioned control of the islands. Such was congressional opposition to any status short of outright control that emphasis on United States obligations was non-existent. Senator Byrd of Virginia, for example, said that it would be absurd to consider placing the Pacific bases under trusteeship when the Soviet Union was extending its sovereignty over the Kurile Islands. In trying to win approval of the Trusteeship Agreement, even congressmen sympathetic to the developmental goals of trusteeship went out of their way to assert that the plan guaranteed unquestioned American control of Micronesia. Congressman Fulton, floor chairman of the bill, stated that the Trusteeship Agreement would "establish United States control on a regular basis." Congressman Mike Mansfield, who had visited the area in 1946, encouraged approval of the agreement on the grounds that it would "give us the kind of title to the new Territory of the Pacific that we should have and which we have earned." The American veto power over any change in Micronesia's status, along with provisions allowing military use of the islands and the right to restrict access, were seen as guarantors of American ownership.

The United Nations had little choice but to approve any United States decision on disposition of the islands. An investigative report submitted by Mike Mansfield to the *Congressional Record* quoted John Foster Dulles informing the United Nations Trusteeship Council that even if the American draft Trusteeship Agreement was rejected by the United Nations, the islands would remain under United States control. In less polite terms, it was a "take it or leave it" situation. Amidst these circumstances the Trusteeship Agreement was approved by the Congress—and then only after Admiral Nimitz and General Eisenhower had testified that the agreement fully protected American defense interests.

Even prior to approval of the Trusteeship Agreement, some in the executive branch questioned the emphasis on United States security interests. This took the form of a bureaucratic struggle between State and Defense over whether Micronesia should be annexed or placed under the proposed Trusteeship system; and between the Interior Department and the Navy over which agency should administer the islands. On September 28, 1945, Acting Secretary of the Interior Abe Fortas wrote to President Truman outlining Interior's argument for civilian administration of all United States territories, including Micronesia:

> By maintaining naval administration of Samoa and Guam, the United States has had the dubious distinction of being the only Pacific power which governs an inhabited colonial area as a mere appurtenance of a military base. This is not, I believe, a distinction which the American people will justify at a time when enlightened opinion, at home and abroad, demands expert attention to the progress of dependent people.

In May of 1947, Secretary of Interior J. A. Krug returned from a trip to Micronesia and recommended to President Truman that at the conclusion of the Trusteeship Agreement then under consideration, the United States should ask Congress to "define the civil rights and political status of the islanders in their new relationship to the United States. . . . It is vital that by act of Congress we guarantee these people the maximum degree practical of the civil liberties and basic freedoms enjoyed by United States citizens." In response to Krug's recommendation, Truman asked the Department of State to draw up an organic act for the Trust Territory.

Legislation to define the political status of Micronesia reached Congress on May 21, 1948, (S.J. Res. 221) and was referred to the Senate Committee on Interior and Insular Affairs and the House Subcommittee on Territorial Affairs, then a part of the House Public Lands Committee. On the same day, a special joint committee to study organic legislation for United States territories was proposed. But while that special joint committee was established and proceeded to consider organic legislation for Guam and American Samoa, the proposed organic legislation for Micronesia was left to the interior committees, which gave it no consideration. This was a foretaste of the course which Congress would pursue on all legislation regarding Micronesia's status for the following twenty-five years.

"Congress," in the Micronesian situation, would come to mean the Interior Committees. The House and Senate Interior Committees are domestically-oriented, and since they deal with issues such as natural resources, parks, grazing lands and recreational areas, they traditionally attract a predominantly western membership. Energy and environmental problems of the seventies have resulted in some membership changes; however, earlier Interior Committee members tended to represent areas which obtained statehood in the western expansion of the United States and were inclined toward annexation as a solution to territorial problems. Increasingly, Micronesia became the special interest of westerners. (Micronesia is also an opportunity for western patronage. The last two high commissioners, Norwood and Johnston, are Hawaiians.) These western representatives often have at least a minimum amount of economic concern since West Coast companies have some chance of winning government contracts in Micronesia, Guam and American Samoa. Finally, many members of the Interior Committees share a general distrust of, perhaps distaste for, the United Nations, especially now that the United States votes constantly on the losing side on many issues.

EXIT FOREIGN AFFAIRS

The direct involvement of the Senate Committee on Foreign Relations and the House Committee on Foreign Affairs in Micronesian matters terminated with the approval of the Trusteeship Agreement and the subsequent decision to assign civilian responsibility for Micronesia to the Department of Interior. The Senate Committee on Foreign Relations exercised responsibility only for the approval of American representatives to the United Nations Trusteeship Council. In fact, the involvement of the Senate Committee on Foreign Relations has been so minimal that during the confirmation hearing for Eugenie Anderson as ambassador to the United Nations Trusteeship Council in 1964, Senator Fulbright, long-time chairman of the committee, asked whether the United States had a full time administrator in one of those trust territories. Still later, the Senate Committee on Foreign Relations passed up the opportunity to consider the Micronesian War Claims Agreement between the United States and Japan, leaving that task to the Senate Interior Committee. On the House side, the Committee on Foreign Affairs showed similar lack of interest, although that committee did consider the war claims measure. The action of the House committee responsible for foreign affairs, however, was probably more attributable to the active interest of Congressman Donald Fraser, chairman of the Subcommittee on International Organizations, than to a conscious effort by the full committee to consider Micronesia as a foreign affairs rather than a domestic question.

It is an irony of history that in its foreign policy on dependent territories, the United States was one of the foremost advocates of decolonization and international oversight, except for the small dependent island areas of its own responsibility. Moreover, the selection of the Interior Department to administer Micronesia was meant to emphasize the broad civilian, as opposed to the military aspects, of the American presence. Yet, the conclusion of the Trusteeship Agreement and the change from military to civilian administration actually resulted in decreased concern for international oversight and decreased involvement by those responsible for international affairs: the Department of State and the legislative committees on foreign affairs.

There was little evidence of congressional concern over the poor development in Micronesia. During the fifties, Congress appropriated less than $6 million annually for administration and capital improvement in the far-flung territory. In Micronesia's schools, pencils had to be chopped in half to increase the supply, and during the entire decade the many unqualified Micronesian teachers were backed up by only one qualified American teacher. Yet one former congressman, even now, is inclined to think that the fifties were a golden age of American administration in Micronesia. "Del Nucker," said Congressman Wayne Aspinall, "was the best High Commissioner we ever had . . . he ran a better ship with four or five million dollars than we've done since."

In the absence of pressure from the executive branch, from the American public, from the international community or from the Micronesians themselves, Congress took no initiative for action in Micronesia. However, other territories over which the United States had sovereignty did receive attention, particularly in regard to their political status. Hawaii and Alaska attained statehood; Puerto Rico became a commonwealth; and Guam and the Virgin Islands were organized into largely autonomous political units.

As noted earlier, "considerable dissatisfaction and discontent" among the Micronesians, reported by a highly critical United Nations Visiting Mission in 1961, along with the acceleration of decolonization, shook the executive branch and the Congress from self-assured apathy. President Kennedy responded by requesting an appropriation of $17.5 million in 1963 for the Trust Territory. In 1963, Wayne Aspinall, representative from Colorado, who had become House Interior Committee chairman in 1959, introduced a bill calling for increased appropriations for the "economic and social development of the Trust Territory of the Pacific Islands." Michigan Congressman Gerald Ford opposed Aspinall's presentation, saying, "The initiation of such a program at a relatively small amount per year is only the kick-off for an ever-expanding, never-ending program." But the bill passed, since, as with most Micronesian bills referred by the committee, no significant floor opposition was encountered. Congress soon authorized $15 million, eventually increasing to $60 million in 1972.

The next United Nations Visiting Mission, in 1964, prodded the United States government and Congress, in particular, toward further action. Senator Bartlett of the Senate Territorial and Insular Affairs Subcommittee submitted the report of the chairman of the Visiting Mission to the Senate. "The territory is now moving and the hum of activity can be heard throughout Micronesia." Visiting Mission chairman Frank Corner of New Zealand said, "The territory is reaching the point of political breakthrough; and this makes it possible to face up to the question of the self-determination of Micronesia as a real rather than a hypothetical issue." The United Nations team had observed political restlessness among the Micronesians and perhaps realized that the United States had no internal mechanism for the consideration of Micronesia's political status. The United Nations report went on to apply pressure directly to the Congress which, it said, "has immense power for good or ill over the evolution of Micronesia in the period immediately ahead." Congress had treated the question of the self-determination of Micronesia as a hypothetical rather than a real issue; now it was being warned to consider the issue in real terms.

But Congress did not respond to the United Nations Visiting Mission suggestion, just as in 1963 it had not responded to the second major initiative of the Kennedy administration, the appointment of the Solomon Committee. More specifically, Interior Committee chairman Aspinall looked upon the United Nations reports as meddling and saw the Solomon group as the first of a series of efforts to by-pass—and criticize if it could not by-pass—the Interior Department and his committee. The Solomon Report showed little concern for congressional sensitivities; it did not deal with the practical problems likely to confront Congress. Aspinall, for example, had his own ideas about the evolutionary advancement of American territories, and the self-governing political status thought to have been recommended by Solomon did not set well with Aspinall. To Aspinall, status was determined by a long evolutionary process; Micronesia might be "ready" in fifty years. According to a State Department official, in a hearing on Micronesia closed to the public, Wayne Aspinall told State: "As far as status goes, the Trust Territory is on the bottom, American Samoa is next, Guam and the Virgin Islands are above it, and Puerto Rico is on top. What you guys at State want to do is take the bottom one on the list and put it on top." Solomon, said Aspinall, "messed up things because he set up certain unapproachable goals and this has caused some difficulty." Interior's cautious reaction to Solomon's recommendations was largely a reflection of congressional views, particularly those of Aspinall and other senior members of his committee. Aspinall believed that neither his committee nor Interior needed to be told how to run Micronesia. Aspinall voiced his views over the years at hearings of the House subcommittee. Unfortunately, the full story may never be told; subcommittee hearings at which Micronesia's future was discussed were closed to the public.

CONGRESSIONAL PROPOSALS

The movement of Congress from a period in which Micronesia was left unattended to a period in which questions about Micronesia were to be confronted was not an easy process. The process took from 1963 to 1970, seven very important years in the political development of Micronesia. Wayne Aspinall presided over those years, with virtually complete control over his Congress, but very little control over the forces at work in Micronesia.

Some in Congress noticed uneasiness in Micronesia, particularly those members from the new Pacific state, Hawaii. In 1965, Senator Hiram Fong of Hawaii proposed that Micronesia be incorporated into the state of Hawaii. He mentioned the dream of Kalakaua, a Hawaiian monarch who ruled from 1874-1891, of a confederation including most of the islands in the Pacific. It was time, said Fong, for the United States to consider Micronesia's status since there had been significant progress toward "political maturity and development toward the goal of self-government." Fong warned, "If the United States fails to take the initiative in helping to determine the permanent political status of the Trust Territory of the Pacific Islands, the increasingly rapid liquidation of colonialism will heighten the mood of intolerance in the United Nations toward the remnants of anything even faintly resembling that practice." "It would be ironic," the Senator ventured, "in view of our self-proclaimed anti-colonial tradition, that as this final chapter is written on the era of colonialism, our own policies should come under the harsh criticism of world opinion."

Statehood for such a scattered and small population was untenable, Fong thought, but in union with the state of Hawaii, the interests of the Micronesians, he said, "would be fully protected. They would be first-class American citizens, with all the rights, privileges, and immunities conferred upon them by the Constitution and the laws of the United States." Hawaii, Senator Fong added, "shares many of the cultural, ethnic, and historical traditions of the Micronesia territory." Fong's bill failed in committee, but he is said to believe that it was successful in calling the attention of Congress to the issue of Micronesian status at a time when no one was sufficiently concerned.

Senator Fong soon realized that the subcommittee which handled territories, particularly in the House, helped to prevent congressional action on Micronesia's future status. Thus, on April 27, 1967, the Hawaii Senator presented a resolution to establish a bipartisan Joint Committee of the Congress on Overseas Insular Areas to "make a full and complete study and investigation of the relationship, present and future, of island areas with the United States, and to report to Congress its findings and recommendations." The proposed committee, composed of six members of each house, was to consider political status questions in the American territories of Guam, American Samoa, the Virgin Islands, the Commonwealth of Puerto Rico, and the Trust Territory of the Pacific Islands. But Fong's proposal died a predictable death: it was referred to the Interior and Insular Affairs Committees.

After a 1968 visit to Micronesia, Congresswoman Patsy Mink of Hawaii introduced legislation providing for an organic act for Micronesia. Convinced of the islands' strategic importance, Mink thought a plebiscite as early as 1972, as proposed by President Johnson, was too soon and would be a "serious error." The enactment of an organic act, she felt, would "assure that the determination of political status will be viewed with favor and will result overwhelmingly for a permanent association with the United States." No action was taken on Mink's legislation either in 1968 or in 1969 when she reintroduced it.

In 1969, a number of congressmen expressed concern over the political status of Micronesia by supporting a bill drafted by the Johnson administration. On March 25, Congressman Clement J. Zablocki of Wisconsin told Congress that the Congress of Micronesia had passed and sent to the United Nations one resolution condemning United States stewardship of the islands and another asking the Soviet Union to "present" its form of government to the people of Micronesia. These resolutions, Zablocki asserted, "were intended to shock the United States into taking definite action on the status of the Pacific Islands." Introducing President Johnson's bill to establish a study commission on status, Zablocki said, "The people of that area are demanding to be heard. They wish to be released from the political limbo in which they now find themselves. If given a choice, I have no doubt that the great majority of Micronesians will choose close association with the United States."

Also in 1969, Congressman Jonathan Bingham of New York, whose interest in Micronesia stemmed from his term as United States ambassador to the United Nations Trusteeship Council from 1960-62, reintroduced the administration bill he had first proposed in 1967 to set up a commission of Americans and Micronesians to give the Micronesians a chance to express their preferences on the status question. The bill was supported by a companion bill in the Senate introduced by Senator Quentin Burdick, chairman of the Senate Interior and Insular Affairs Subcommittee on Territories. In 1967 Bingham had said that there could be no guarantee that the islanders would reject independence in a plebiscite, but the urgency of the status question required taking such a risk. Now, Bingham looked back on two years of inaction on the status question and asserted that passage of his 1967 legislation "might have precluded the build-up of pressures." Bingham thought there was still a chance of establishing a close and permanent relationship between Micronesia and the United States and that the risks of a full range of choice on a plebiscite were worth taking. "Complete independence," said Bingham, "is not likely to be an appealing prospect for the Micronesians." An organic act, as proposed by Congresswoman Patsy Mink, would help Micronesia, Bingham acknowledged, but it was not enough by itself. The United States had to investigate the question of Micronesia's permanent political status.

On September 30, 1969, the House received a bill, introduced by Congressman Lloyd Meeds, which offered both a federal relations (organic) act and a method for the self-determination of Micronesia. This legislation would have established a constitutional convention whose members were elected by Micronesians. Until the proposed convention produced a constitution acceptable to the Micronesian people, Micronesia would be an unincorporated territory of the United States, with a bill of rights, an elected bicameral legislature, and a chief executive appointed by the President. In introducing the bill, Congressman Meeds stated, "Micronesians do not want to be studied for another twenty-five years. They want and need action now."

We have already traced elsewhere the bureaucratic struggle which preceded President Johnson's 1967 request for a commission to consider Micronesia's future status so that a plebiscite could be held no later than June 30, 1972. Interior had attached particular importance to involving Congress in any status recommendations, but Interior's efforts to involve the Congress were frustrated by the Congress itself. According to a former Interior official, the Johnson commission proposal had been discussed with Congressman Aspinall prior to its submission and, although he had no love for commissions, Aspinall had agreed that a joint legislative-executive commission would be an appropriate way to approach the status question. But, when the bill finally reached Capitol Hill, the official complained, Aspinall acted as if he had never heard of it and it never received a committee hearing in the House.

Aspinall, who chaired the full Interior and Insular Affairs Committee, felt that no changes should be made in Micronesia's status and that to promise the Micronesians a status other than something like that of Guam or, more probably, the lesser status of American Samoa, was foolhardy. He had blocked all previous legislation on Micronesia's future political status and was not about to let this one pass, even though it was endorsed by President Johnson. Johnson's endorsement, Aspinall told an interviewer four years later, did not amount to much. "He didn't know anything about the Micronesian situation. He was just advised by some of his advisors that this would be a way to sweep it under the rug for a while." No action was taken on the legislation in 1967, and when Johnson sent the same legislation to Congress in 1968, the wily old Colorado representative argued that Lyndon Johnson was a lame duck and a new President should be given the opportunity to decide his own policy. In fact, however, Aspinall was unalterably opposed to the legislation.

Interior officials believed the bill would have passed on the floor of the House. But the House structure and its beneficiary, Aspinall, blocked the House from considering the bill, and any bill like it. Throughout his chairmanship, Aspinall firmly held that the status question should never be considered, and in late 1973 he still felt that neither the Johnson administration nor the Nixon administration ever really intended that the status of the Micronesians should be worked out. "Johnson," Aspinall said, "understood that the decision couldn't be made. Therefore, the way to postpone it was ... to study it. Nobody has ever done anything except study and survey."

Exactly what Patsy Mink in 1968 and Lloyd Meeds in 1969 feared might happen was that the question of status would be merely studied. They hoped, in presenting proposals for organic acts and constitutional conventions that positive action would be taken and decisions would be made. Aspinall told an interviewer that Lloyd Meeds's Federal Relations Act was justifiably ignored, since Meeds was "a new congressman.... He'd only been in there two years, maybe." Actually, Meeds and Mink had been in Congress for five years. Aspinall's power dramatizes the perils of a seniority system that allows one man to determine that so many proposals be forfeited. The views of members of his own committee—Mink, Meeds, and Bingham—were lost and belittled as "premature."

Similarly, Aspinall's negative attitude toward foreign affairs was in itself a barrier to congressional consideration of Micronesia's international significance. He was always unimpressed with the State Department and their concern for the United Nations. "I don't care about the State Department," he told an interviewer. "If I know the State Department, they don't give a damn either [about Micronesia].... There's more double talk that goes on in the State Department than anywhere else in government." On one occasion just prior to a hearing, he went up to the United States representative to the Trusteeship Council and warned against alleged State Department efforts to "interfere" with Interior's administration of Micronesia. United Nations Visiting Missions did not move him either. "I've seen the way the opposition gangs up on us ... they take a team through there to look and see what we're doing. Then it always ends up that we do whatever we think is best. We always listen to their advice. But we always do whatever we think is best for those islands."

WHAT WAYNE ASPINALL THOUGHT BEST

Actually, what *was* done was what Wayne Aspinall thought best. Until his leadership was thwarted—in the committee in 1970 and in his district in 1972—he determined a foreign policy that was no less than colonial.

Aspinall had arrived in Congress immediately after the Trusteeship Agreement was passed and had watched Micronesia longer (1948-1972) than any member of the subcommittee, always insisting that the United States had to retain control over the islands. "I came to the conclusion," he told an interviewer, "that what is left open to them is the same status that we have had throughout all our history as far as areas such as that are concerned, and that's a territory—an unincorporated territory." "There is no such thing as independence unless you can support it," he said, and "we've got to have those islands."

He was aware of the United States obligation under the Trusteeship Agreement to promote political development but was concerned that United States actions toward that end produced political thinking which did not adhere to his plan: "There was too much emphasis placed on politics," he said. "People grew up with the idea that they must participate in politics." His attitude toward the Congress of Micronesia followed this reasoning: "I offered no objection at all [to the establishment of the Micronesian legislature], but I didn't expect it to go into the operations it's going into. Since it was established it has produced the political ambitions of leaders who are playing with another nation's money." Aspinall never saw the trusteeship as an experiment in funding a backward area while allowing it free expression of its political desires. Rather, he saw Micronesia as a territory won by the United States and never to be accorded sovereignty because it was economically backward. Aspinall felt that United Nations obligations were secondary; when others in government made commitments to such obligations he felt that they were hypocritical. "I don't object to spending money over there, but what I object to is the hypocrisy which this country has ... in its relationship to Micronesia, making these people expect something which they can't have—independence."

When the executive branch began negotiations with Micronesia, Congress was still unable to make the distinctions that understanding Micronesia's unique status required. To Wayne Aspinall, who felt that everyone "strong" recognized Micronesia's inability for self-government, various status proposals were merely efforts to pacify the Micronesians. When asked by an interviewer whether he favored a free association proposal, Aspinall replied: "I don't know. This is what we've been doing under different nomenclature—and why? Why are we doing it? We haven't got the guts to come to a decision as to what we want to do, and why we can't let go." If the United States had guts, in Aspinall's view, it would realize the inevitability and necessity of a territorial status for Micronesia.

The Interior Department had taken over administration of the islands because it was felt a civilian agency would look out for the rights of the Micronesian people and make basic improvements unhampered by military intentions for the use of the islands. In the interior committees, it might have been thought that the rights and advantages of the Micronesian people would be the prime objective also, but observation reveals that at least on political status, primary concern for the islands in the committee was based on an interest in protecting the strategic value of the area. We cannot lead the Micronesians to believe that they can be self-governing, according to Aspinall, because "we've got to have these islands—for military purposes." During Aspinall's chairmanship, the Interior Committee adhered, as did the Department of the Interior, to the advice of the Defense Department, at least on the status question. Aspinall himself echoed the Defense Department's fall-back theory. When asked if South Korea, Thailand, Taiwan, and the Philippines could not support United States defense commitments, Aspinall replied, "If we're honest, we'll leave those other places." Asked why Micronesia should carry the weight of United States needs, he replied, "Because *it's ours*." (His emphasis.) Micronesia, in his view, is ours because of our strategic interest, and strategic because it's ours.

"We're just not about to give them up," he said. "You don't continue to keep on fooling them—give one excuse or another, when, in the background—and they're smart enough to figure it—if there's a war on or otherwise, they're the buffer zone." In no other government figure did the conflict between our strategic interests and the stated goal of self-determination for the Micronesians manifest itself as clearly as in the chairman of the House Interior and Insular Affairs Committee.

Ironically, though Wayne Aspinall wanted a territorial relationship between the Trust Territory and the United States, he did much to make such a relationship impossible. He ignored the small but growing independence movement in Micronesia, the increasingly hostile, anti-colonial attitudes in the United Nations, the growing political sophistication of Micronesian leaders, the development of concern in the State Department, and the pressing desire for responsiveness among members of his committee. He positioned himself in such a way as to bring all these forces to an impasse, never understanding that the only way the United States could protect its strategic interests was to deal with these forces rather than to discount them.

Aspinall remained in Congress long enough to see his colleagues proved correct, although he continued to think all present proposals were also "premature." Nevertheless, by the time the United States got around to offering Micronesia a status similar to Guam (mislabeled, however, a "commonwealth"), the Micronesians had already moved on to seek "free association." By 1972, the Congress of Micronesia passed a resolution to pursue independence. Barring an unforeseen change, the chance for a legitimate plebiscite, satisfactory to the United Nations, which might have resulted in a close relationship with the United States, had been lost.

Despite the very severe mistakes and setbacks caused by Chairman Aspinall's power, something must be said for the interest and commitment which he gave Micronesia. He had a staffman, John Taylor, who was knowledgeable about and sympathetic to Micronesia. Aspinall devoted more of his personal concern to the area than any other Interior Committee chairman, more than most subcommittee chairmen. Even after he lost his grip on the committee, he received, read and made lengthy notes on the negotiations within a day after the negotiators returned to Washington. This type of intense interest won the respect of officials at Interior and Defense. It is badly needed on Capitol Hill where few subcommittee members even find the time to attend their hearings on Micronesia. Few disputed or condemned Aspinall's interest, even though they regretted his power and complete control over Micronesia in that period. Congressman Lloyd Meeds put it most succinctly: "Wayne Aspinall is a man who is delightful in many respects—tough, honest, and hard; but I blame him as much as any person for the problems we've encountered in Micronesia."

THE DOWNFALL OF WAYNE ASPINALL

Aspinall had always maintained complete control of his subcommittees. Subcommittee chairmen could not schedule meetings which Chairman Aspinall could not attend. If the subcommittee chairman wanted to hold a meeting to discuss something which Aspinall opposed, Aspinall would say that he could not attend, and the meeting would be postponed or cancelled. Aspinall sat next to the subcommittee chairman and was dominant when he attended the meetings. One subcommittee chairman was recently asked if he enjoyed his position, and he replied, "At least now there isn't a full committee chairman sitting right next to you." Aspinall also picked the committee and subcommittee staffs himself and maintained control over staff work. Finally, Aspinall selected conferees for meetings to iron out differences in House and Senate legislation. Once, Lloyd Meeds fought for a "North Cascades bill" which he considered the biggest thing in his career at that point. It passed the House, and when it returned from the Senate, Aspinall did not choose Meeds as a conferee; people with relatively little or no concern for the bill decided its final text. On another occasion, Philip

Burton excused himself from a hearing to go to the rest room. While he was gone, Aspinall deleted Burton's amendments from a bill. Such punches made bruises, and members of the House Subcommittee on Territories began to consider rules changes which would reduce the powers of the committee chairman.

The revolt was led by Meeds, Burton, Mink, and O'Hara in 1970. Meeds, Mink, and O'Hara were veterans of another successful revolt, the one against House Education and Labor Committee Chairman Adam Clayton Powell over travel funds. They were also successful in the Interior Committee revolt. By the narrow margin of one vote, subcommittees were released from having to satisfy the chairman's schedule as long as subcommittee chairmen agreed to try to prevent conflicts with the schedule of other subcommittee meetings; subcommittee chairmen were permitted to control their budgets and to choose their own staffs (the full committee budget is now an amalgam of the subcommittee budgets); and conferees were chosen by party caucus.

These rules changes marked a turning point in the history of United States relations with Micronesia. With Aspinall's decline, a group of congressmen who had been attracted to the subcommittee in the 1960's, who had developed an interest in and understanding of the special significance of the Pacific trust, and who had spoken out on legislation responsive to Micronesians, assumed a larger role in Micronesian affairs. Some remnants of Aspinall's ideas would remain, but the House subcommittee's involvement in Micronesia was significantly changed under the leadership of Philip Burton of California, a leader of the liberal Democratic Study Group.

Wayne Aspinall was no more successful in working with the urban voters suddenly included in his previously rural legislative district, and he went down to defeat at the polls in 1972. The new chairman of the House Committee on Interior and Insular Affairs, James Haley of Florida, was less autocratic. He kept informed on the progress of United States-Micronesia negotiations, but left most matters to subcommittee chairman Philip Burton, who in turn allowed greater latitude to members of his subcommittee.

In the Senate, Henry Jackson of Washington is chairman of the Interior and Insular Affairs Committee. Jackson has been a major figure on Puerto Rican status questions, and, given his interests in defense matters, can be expected to have a decisive voice on Micronesian status. There is no evidence that Jackson was deeply involved in Micronesian status questions during the first four years of negotiations. The Chief United States Negotiator, Hadyn Williams, is known to have repeatedly sought consultation meetings with Jackson. For two years, most of these efforts were unsuccessful. When Williams was successful in getting a meeting, he received but a few moments of the senator's divided attention.

Like Aspinall, Jackson hires the professional staff for the committee. It is to the staff of the full Senate Interior and Insular Affairs Committee which subcommittee chairman J. Bennett Johnston turns to for information regarding Micronesia. Generally senators like J. Bennett Johnston himself, put Micronesia low on their list of priorities and very quickly move to committee assignments which have no responsibility for Micronesia. House predominance on the Micronesian scene is possibly a result of numbers. With 435 members, assignments and chairmanships on committees and subcommittees are scarce and therefore more desired than in the Senate where there are only 100 members and freshmen senators may instantly become chairmen of subcommittees.

THE HOUSE SUBCOMMITTEE ON TERRITORIES

Some of the members of the House Subcommittee on Territories have maintained an interest in Micronesia for the greater part of their careers. In fact, no other group of individuals in government has sustained such a long-term interest in the Trust Territory. State, Interior and Defense officials advance or move out, the concern of the United Nations fluctuates, and Senate subcommittee members switch to other committees, but the House subcommittee has maintained a relatively permanent watch. It is an advantage that there is one institution which has the potential for long-range involvement. It takes time and experience to understand the complexities of the Micronesia situation. Long-range involvement, of course, can have disadvantages, but, especially now when the negotiations require expert congressional scrutiny, the interest and experience of the House subcommittee members is greatly needed.

The present interest developed under Wayne Aspinall, often out of frustration with Aspinall's policy. It developed among representatives of states which have a potential interest in good relations with the Pacific Islands: Washington, California, and Hawaii—namely, Congressmen Lloyd Meeds, Thomas Foley and Philip Burton and Congresswoman Patsy Mink. In numerous interviews with congressmen, these four were mentioned most often as being "Micronesia experts." They have a keen interest in the area which manifests itself in their proposals for legislation and their willingness to travel to Micronesia and to meet with Micronesians in Washington.

The House also has the benefit of the advice of two territorial delegates. House members mention Antonio B. Won Pat of Guam as a "Micronesia expert" because of Guam's "proximity" to Micronesia. Indeed, Won Pat often refers to his "fellow Micronesians." Both Won Pat and Ron de Lugo of the Virgin Islands have expressed concern about the effect of the negotiations on political destinies of their older, more populous territories. The United States-territorial relationship is discussed fully elsewhere, but it is important to note here that the territorial delegates who vote on matters before the committee are not without influence in the House subcommittee, although they are peculiarly subject to influence by other members. Their impact in the Senate is at best minimal.

CONGRESSIONAL INTERESTS AND ATTITUDES

Interest in Micronesia is not widespread in Congress. In most cases, interest has developed only through rather unique personal circumstances. Hawaiians are expected to have an interest in Micronesia because of the popular congressional conception that Hawaiians are the same "racial and cultural type" as the Micronesians. A common congressional misconception is that Micronesians and Hawaiians are next door neighbors. A southern congressman once asked Hawaii Representative Spark Matsunaga about Micronesia: "It is out around near you, isn't it?" Matsunaga reportedly replied, "It's only 4,000 miles away." (Actually, the Marshall Islands are 2,070 miles from Honolulu.)

Some congressmen developed an interest during the war. Senator Henry Bellmon served on Saipan and Tinian; Congressman William Ketchum served on Guam; and Congressman Don Fraser served in the Marshalls. Congressmen Sid Yates and Jonathan Bingham became interested during their experience as United States representatives on the United Nations Trusteeship Council. Additionally, Jonathan Bingham's grandparents were among the first American missionaries in the Pacific. With an issue like Micronesia, which does not attract widespread concern, obscure coincidences can make a congressman an expert on Micronesia. Such coincidences do not occur often and Micronesia attracts little attention. Even on the House Subcommittee on Territories, there are members who consider Micronesian questions unimportant. One subcommittee member, when asked by an interviewer how important Micronesia was to him, said that it was at the bottom of his list. The islands, he went on, "are merely specks in the Pacific." His involvement with the subcommittee is so peripheral that he did not even know his colleagues: "Patsy Mink isn't on that subcommittee, is she?" he asked.

The positions of Republicans are difficult to discern. During negotiations there was a tendency to wait and see the results before making any public comment. It is quite natural for the Republicans to avoid confrontations with a Republican administration, but it is not natural for them to avoid, as they do, advocacy of administration proposals. According to United States officials, the ranking minority member of the House Subcommittee on Territories in fact said nothing in consultation sessions. Administration officials dubbed them "head-nodding sessions."

The effect of the attitude of Republicans meant that Ambassador Williams had to deal largely with a liberal congressional voice and consequently was encouraged to negotiate liberal benefits for the Micronesians. The danger is that the whole process will backfire if conservatives conclude, when a new status for Micronesia is up for congressional approval, that the administration has gone beyond what they assumed its limitations would be.

Those few who have devoted time to Micronesia expect to be listened to when the time comes to approve the final agreements. In fact, one of the most prominent United States congressmen on Micronesian affairs initially planned to rely on Congress's general apathy to facilitate approval of the agreements and the large sums of money needed for them. The clear implication was that an open and detailed debate in Congress might very well result in rejection of current proposals. Assuming no large scale and detailed debate, the views of those who are concerned about Micronesia are thus acutely important.

STATUS PROPOSALS

Some congressmen have been quicker to discuss status options than administrative or policy problems. Given the wide range of feelings on Micronesian status, it would appear that congressional debate could be lengthy and thorough when the proposals reach Capitol Hill, especially in the Senate. The administration, supported by key congressmen, may seek to avoid such debate, but views on the issues seem to taking a definite shape.

Independence

As a status proposal to be advocated, independence was taboo on Capitol Hill for a long time. But the first person to break the taboo did so with eloquence: "What greater demonstration of our worth could there be," questioned Congresswoman Patsy Mink in the January, 1971, issue of the *Texas International Law Forum*, "than an unconditional release of these people to pursue their own destiny." The question was whether to give the Micronesians the option of independence. Senator Lee Metcalf advocated it "to get the question out of the way." Patsy Mink advocated it hoping for close United States-Micronesian relations. "Such a meritorious step," she maintained, "would be the single thing most likely to inspire the Micronesians to choose partnership with our country."

Congress does not want to find itself in the position of limiting the free expression of Micronesian aspirations. In a June, 1969, speech, Senator Inouye said, "It is imperative that all discussion begin with the principal question: What do the Micronesians want? Do they want to be completely independent? If so, we should exert all efforts to ensure that they achieve independence with all speed." Chairman Burton of the House Territories Subcommittee emphasizes that the final status must be "whatever they want, whether wise or stupid."

While it is doubtful that Congress would now oppose, as it did when Aspinall was interior committee chairman, the offer of an independence *option* to Micronesia, there are many congressmen who oppose the thought of actual independence. "I think there are a number of liberals who automatically assume that independence is a good thing." Congressman Thomas S. Foley told an interviewer, "but independence is always sought with enthusiasm and high expectations which are lost in normal, practical, governmental functioning. The United States has a a responsibility to the people of Micronesia; we must not forget that."

Congressman Foley's concern goes beyond economic considerations, but there are many on Capitol Hill who argue against independence on economic grounds alone. "I can't see how they could be self-governing," Congressman Joseph Vigorito said in an interview. "If we withdrew our money, they would have to go back to subsistence, to living off the beaches." In a hearing before the House Appropriations Subcommittee on the Interior, then chairwoman Julia Butler Hansen and Congressman H. Gunn McKay warned Interior officials of the importance of finances in establishing a new type of government in the Trust Territory. "I don't care what way they go," said chairwoman Hansen, "as long as they don't get disillusioned by the fiscal problems." And Congressman McKay added something which is often heard on Capitol Hill: "It would be pretty hard to be politically independent if you're not fiscally independent." Interestingly enough, an inversion of the economic argument is used by one Republican on the subcommittee who opposes a close relationship with the islands. "There is no particular advantage to a closer relationship with the islands," he says. "Puerto Rico has failed to accomplish much except put more people on welfare in New York City; and I don't see much indication of Puerto Rican love for the relationship."

Free Association

Rather than supporting independence, Congress would more likely support free association—an arrangement whereby Micronesians exercise self-government with some United States involvement. Congress would probably have proposed something akin to "free association" even if the United States delegation had not developed the concept in negotiations with the Micronesians. For example, in looking back at his 1969 Micronesian-Federal Relations Act, Congressman Lloyd Meeds told an interviewer, "They were to have total self-government. The United States would handle foreign affairs and defense: otherwise, they were like a state." Senator Inouye's suggestion was similar. "A fair arrangement would be to give them control of all internal affairs, let them use American currency, assist them in providing security and diplomatic relations," he told interviewers. "All of these things would be done, realizing it would be too costly for the Micronesians to do them."

Arrangements like these satisfy most hesitancies about independence. Lloyd Meeds, probably the foremost advocate of free association, has always concentrated on the development of an economic infrastructure and political maturity in Micronesia. In an early interview, he charged that the Interior Department had "done a very poor job of educating middle level management, doctors, and mechanics." Later, after a trip to Micronesia in 1974, he noticed that some success had been achieved in these areas. He had talked to many Micronesians who held positions which were once filled only by Americans and who were justifiably proud of their effectiveness. Meeds also saw "vast improvements" in public works: airfields, colleges, hospitals, electric generators, sewers, water catchments, ports, and highways. He feels we must encourage Micronesian participation in all aspects of life as we maintain a committed presence in Micronesia. In the period of free association, he says that the United States should make a major effort to assist the Micronesians. That help could come in the form of direct financial support, research into methods of developing capital and clarification of Micronesia's ocean boundaries.

While there are a significant number of congressmen who believe that through the development of "ocean agriculture" Micronesia could become "the biggest pastureland in the world," many are not optimistic about Micronesia's potential for economic development. In a late 1974 hearing Congresswoman Mink reminded Interior Department officials that proposed capital improvement projects were the same ones she had heard about ten years before. Little had been done. Others think that American money has been an unfortunate intrusion in Micronesia, and that Micronesians' aspirations have increaaed in a way that makes close association with the United States mandatory. Senator James A. McClure observed that when he visited the Inter-Islands High School in Truk in 1969 "every student had a transistor radio attached to his ear. These kids long for the outside world and are very dissatisfied with life in the Trust Territory. They volunteer for the United States military service just to get away." McClure concluded, "Until there is a dollar economy, the Micronesians will not be able to absorb dollars."

There are other problems with "free association." Congressman Thomas S. Foley's primary concern is that the United States might be making permanent the hierarchy of Micronesians who are presently in power. Traditional chiefs have retained a great deal of power in modern Micronesia. Senator McClure, traveling with Foley in 1969, tells of asking a senator of the Congress of Micronesia whether he would run for re-election. The Micronesian replied that he did not know; he had not yet asked the Chief. "Traditional culture," says Foley, "violates almost every principle the American people have ever known. There is a small, able elite which would find themselves in control. Maybe they are not well-motivated to serve the interests of their people." While many congressmen are hesitant to try to enforce democratic government in Micronesia, there is the problem of the proper use of American money. "As long as the United States maintains responsibility for the islands," Foley says, "we must guarantee civil rights and the administration of justice, the protection of American citizens, and the proper conduct of their foreign affairs." Other congressmen object to free association for they think it does not protect United States strategic interests.

The chairman of the Senate Subcommittee on Territories, J. Bennett Johnston, was startled when interviewers pointed out that the negotiations included an independence option. In his view, the area was too important strategically to allow Micronesian independence. Though there had been no objections at poorly attended senate hearings, senators later expressed strong concern.

In the Senate Interior Committee, there is little faith in continued Micronesian friendship. Senators Johnston, Buckley, Bartlett, and McClure are all on record as opposing the administration's method of insuring United States strategic interests after possible Micronesian independence. The Draft Compact calls for a mutual security pact to be negotiated when the Micronesians move toward independence. The senators objected to leaving the pact undefined; they want it negotiated before the administration seeks approval of the negotiations on Capitol Hill.

DEFENSE

Congress is left guessing about specific defense needs. In the subcommittees on territories, general base plans are well-known and are accepted "if the Micronesians want the bases." In the Senate subcommittee, at least among the present, largely conservative membership, it is assumed that base construction is justified strategically. The Defense Department is supposed to have consulted the Armed Services Committees about new Micronesian bases. However, in late 1974, Congressman F. Edward Hébert, then chairman of the House Armed Services Committee told interviewers that neither he nor any member of his committee had been consulted regarding plans for the multi-million dollar base on Tinian, a major part of the negotiations with the Mariana Islands. In 1974 the Defense Subcommittee of the House Appropriations Committee made an attempt to uncover military plans for Tinian and, even though it had not been asked for funds, reported: "The Committee wishes to advise the Department of Defense that its actions in this connection are being closely watched and that the Committee doubts that construction of a new base complex can be justified so long as the United States retains access to Japanese and Korean bases."

In the two territorial subcommittees, the base on Tinian has been discussed as a fait accompli. Members assume that base development would bring badly needed economic advantages; there was a general feeling that the Marianas want the base on Tinian so they can develop "like Guam." However, there are significant misgivings. Senator Daniel K. Inouye has watched Micronesian attitudes toward the military very closely. In 1969, he noticed that Micronesians were beginning to feel that if they were an independent nation, the United States would have to pay larger sums for the lease of military bases. "That the Micronesians seem to feel it is easier to get money from Congress for defense needs than for Department of the Interior projects," Senator Inouye concluded, "is a very sad commentary on our administration of the islands." "Military development," said Senator Lee Metcalf, former chairman of the Senate Subcommittee on Territories, "is an artificial thing that is forced on people. A Chamber of Commerce can make a choice between a fishing cannery, or watch factories, or things like that, but with military installations there is no choice whatsover."

Even with some objections to military development and skepticism regarding defense needs in the Pacific, most congressmen in the Interior Committees think the base will be approved. The chairman of the Senate Subcommittee on Territories put it this way: "I don't know the figures for the Tinian base but getting Congressional approval for it is not going to be that big a problem. The Tinian base is important." Aides to Senator Henry Jackson, chairman of the full Interior Committee in the Senate, say that the "military is his primary concern in Micronesia." The picture that develops is one in which the Senate Interior Committee places a high value on the strategic importance of Micronesia and feels that it could approve or win approval of bases there while the House Committee emphasizes the Micronesians' economic interest in bases but leaves strategic questions to the defense committees which, in turn, were not consulted about Micronesian bases and are highly skeptical of their worth.

THE MARIANAS "COMMONWEALTH"

"Commonwealth" status might be approved for the Marianas, if only because, in Patsy Mink's words, "a group of people wanting to be Americans is an exciting phenomenon nowadays." However, there is a strong belief that the Marianas and Guam should form a single political entity and a hope that unification will eventually take place. Chairman Burton repeatedly emphasized union with Guam in his discussions with chief Marianas negotiator Edward Pangelinan. Patsy

Mink told an interviewer that Guam's interest in statehood would be aided by union with other islands. At the same time, there is realization that the Marianas do not presently want union with Guam. "That would make them the tail of the dog," Congressman Manual Lujan pictured, "and they are going to have a hard time wagging that dog."

One item which Congress would definitely not give the Marianas is a non-voting delegate to Congress. Several sources have said that in talks with Marianas negotiators, House subcommittee chairman Burton came down against a non-voting delegate for the Marianas (population 13,500) "like a ton of bricks" and such sentiment undoubtedly led to elimination of a nonvoting delegate as an issue in the Marianas negotiations. It is a simple matter of demography. Non-voting delegates may vote in committee. Thus, a delegate representing 50,000 people votes with the same power as a congressman representing 450,000 or a Puerto Rico commissioner representing three million. "Perhaps a representative should be sent to Washington to appear before the agencies," a member of the House subcommittee told an interviewer, "but already there are on the subcommittee one delegate from the Virgin Islands and one from Guam—both of whom are very nice people—but I couldn't afford to have these people narrowing the significance of my vote."

The Marianas can expect sympathy for their desire to restrict land ownership to people of Marianas ancestry. Most subcommittee members share the views of Congressman Philip Ruppe of Michigan. "Some kind of land alienation measure is essential. People with little knowledge of business affairs will sell too quickly out of need. These are the people who scream later. We could do two things: prevent the sale of land to non-Americans or prevent the sale of land to anyone, but the people should not be unprotected from speculation." At the same time, congressmen unfamiliar with the special role of land in territorial areas may object to giving American citizens (if indeed the people of the Marianas become citizens) privileges not shared by the people on the mainland. A precedent for such congressional objections exists: At the time of passage of an organic act for Guam, Congress deleted a provision which would have limited land ownership to Guamanians. On the other hand, protection of land has precedents in American Indian, Hawaiian, and Alaskan law. Thus, the question may be political and not legal.

The divisive aspirations of the people of the Trust Territory have resulted in United States plans to assist in the separate development of the Marianas "commonwealth" and "free associated" Micronesia. When it is discussed, the division of the Trust Territory evokes, with amazing repetitiveness, the work "regrettable." Every congressman interviewed regrets the fragmentation, using the word "regret" in numerous ways. Fragmentation is regretted because a different policy could possibly have brought all of Micronesia into a relationship more conducive to United States strategic interests, and because as a policy it may encourage the separatist tendencies of other island groups in Micronesia. Congressional support of a separate status will put the United States Congress in direct conflict with the territory-wide Congress of Micronesia which has opposed the separate negotiations. Thus, at this point, Congress looks back on, looks at, and looks ahead to the implementation of a policy which it is uncomfortable with, but which it may feel it has little power to change.

The strategy of both United States and Marianas negotiators has been to make Congress (and the Micronesians and the United Nations) impotent on the fragmentation issue. Even before the Marianas proposal was submitted for congressional approval, Congress was asked for $1.5 million in transition funds to bring the Marianas Commonwealth into being. In addition, the administration has agreed to separate the Marianas from the rest of Micronesia for purposes of administration as soon as the covenant is approved in a Marianas plebiscite, but before approval by the United States Congress.

Congressmen generally see their role as protective of the interests of the people of Micronesia and think that they alone are free from bureaucratic bias. To some congressmen, it appears that the State Department asserts its concern as if "diplomacy were the sport of princes." Interior is viewed as being bureaucratically inept and as having sent its "unfireables" to the Trust Territory. The Defense Department, it is felt, is concerned only with protecting its "negative" interests. The United Nations, most members think, is of no real concern and its expressions are seen as "gamesmanship." Members of the Subcommittees on Territorial Affairs are confident that they will be able to prevail with their perception of what status the Micronesians should have. Unfortunately, Congress itself is not in a position to view Micronesia without prejudice. Congress is trapped by former commitments, by a predisposition toward a formula used in the past to annex territories, and by an inadequate structure to handle the Micronesian situation.

CONGRESS AND THE CONDUCT OF THE NEGOTIATIONS

Congress, though largely uninformed about Micronesia, has a significant membership which is deeply concerned about Micronesia and uncomfortable and frustrated by United States policy toward it. In the past, congressional discomfort was taken out on the Department of the Interior. One congressman returned from a trip to Micronesia and told an interviewer of his recommendations to an official in the Trust Territory government. Asked how the official responded, the congressman said, "Bureaucrats nod in agreement, but then you leave and they go back to their offices and nothing gets done." The feeling is widespread that American money produces insignificant results in Micronesia, largely because transportation and administration costs are high and there is a lot of waste. According to a recent Senate Interior Committee report, a sewage treatment plant construction project begun on Ebeye at the cost of $350,000 was terminated in 1974 with only 13 per cent of the project completed and the funds virtually exhausted.

In recent years, the negotiations as well as administrative problems have frustrated congressmen concerned with Micronesia. Orders for the Office of Micronesian Status Negotiations supposedly came from the White House; they definitely did not come from Congress. Most congressmen remained in the dark about the substance of the negotiations; when there were subcommittee meetings with the negotiators present, discussion of the negotiations was avoided because Congress did not want to "meddle" in the business of the executive branch and because comments on ongoing negotiations were felt to be inappropriate. But when congressmen finally learn the specifics of the negotiations, as in the closed hearing before the Senate Interior Committee on September 12, 1974, they react with, "The United States should have limited the options in the very beginning so that we wouldn't have to take an agreement which goes beyond what we want to do."

Initially, Aspinall tried to outline the limits of United States "flexibility." As he modestly put it, "They [United States negotiators Harrison Loesch, a Colorado neighbor and friend of Aspinall, and Haydn Williams] reported in: we talked it over; I told them what I thought would have to be acknowledged and recognized before they could get anything out of it." However, early in the negotiations, Aspinall's ability to influence the course of negotiations was diminished. In his own words: "Well, of course, the next thing I knew Phil Burton became chairman of the subcommittee. Next thing after that happened was that Phil Burton then decided that everything had to be cleared through him, and he still feels that way about it."

One of the complications is the relationship between the principal actors. The Senate, once again, leaves the House in charge of overseeing the negotiations. Until late in the negotiations, Senate subcommittee chairman J. Bennett Johnston had not seen Chief United States Negotiator Haydn Williams for a one-to-one briefing. The Office of Micronesian Status Negotiations had tried to set up such meetings, but Johnston was never able to fit them into his schedule. One indication of the problems faced by United States negotiators was Johnston's startlingly negative reaction to information that the draft agreement contained an opportunity for the Micronesians to unilaterally declare their independence. The independence option had been so crucial to the Micronesians that it had caused the breakaway of the Marianas, and it had been mentioned in every hearing before the Senate subcommittee. But Johnston first focused on the issue in an interview later on.

House Territories Subcommittee chairman Burton and Ambassador Haydn Williams had their differences, and these differences had an indirect effect on the negotiations with the Micronesians. Ambassador Williams is a quiet, reticent individual who was once described as having "one major fault—a complete inability to relate to human beings." On the other hand, "burly, beefy Philip Burton," to use a Ralph Nader congressional profile description, "has a voice like a sonic boom, the charge of a bull in a congressional committee room, and an emphasis on the one-to-one relationship." The two Californians come from very different backgrounds: Philip Burton considers himself a spokesman for San Francisco's poor; Ambassador Williams is a resident of the rich San Francisco suburb of Hillsborough. Burton hopes that the Micronesians see him as a friend and thinks that the subcommittee is comprised of people "sensitive to social justice."

For many months the contrasting personalities and ideologies of Burton and the head of the United States negotiating team appeared to be a major obstacle in the negotiations. The contrast came into sharp focus at a State Department reception for Micronesian negotiators, November 12, 1973. According to several sources, Burton called Williams a "fascist" and "colonialist." He told Lazarus Salii, chairman of the Micronesian negotiators, that Williams "would lead him down the garden path," but that "Congress will take care of [him]." Williams was shocked by the congressman's actions, and relations between the two were strained for the following two months.

During those months, congressmen often expressed resentment that the Office of Micronesian Status Negotiations was not keeping them fully informed; it was as if communications between Congress and the Office of Micronesian Status Negotiations had broken down completely. In late December, 1973, however, Ambassador Williams made a special effort to meet with Congressman Burton—Williams had just flown in from talks in Hawaii and Burton was going to leave that night for a trip to Micronesia—and relations between the two improved markedly. Two weeks later, in Micronesia, Congressman Foley expressed the often-heard view that Williams was not keeping Congress informed. Burton came to Williams's defense and said that he may have been to blame himself because he had done a poor job of passing information on to the subcommittee. Burton was even quoted as saying, "I have deep respect for the Ambassador."

Senator McClure complained that he and Congressman Foley had tried for three and a half years to get someone from the executive branch to come up and talk to them about Micronesia; no one had. State Department officials repeatedly expressed concern that congressional consultations were infrequent, limited to the Interior and perhaps the Armed Services Committees and excluded the Foreign Affairs Committees. Among the committee members, consultation has largely been limited to committee and subcommittee chairmen and ranking members, although the then head of the House Armed Services Committee told interviewers he knew nothing of Tinian base plans.

Congress is not without blame for inadequate consultations. Communiques from the negotiations are regularly sent to Congress, and the Office of Micronesian Status Negotiations offered to send its public affairs officers to Capitol Hill to provide briefings and to set up interviews with principal officials of the Office in a genuine attempt to open information channels.

But the results of efforts to keep Congress informed were, unfortunately, predictable. Staff members forgot or neglected to attend briefings and thus continued to complain that the Office of Micronesian Status Negotiations had made no attempts to talk with them. Others complained that briefings were inadequate and did not go beyond information which was already public.

A former director of the Office of Micronesian Status Negotiations noted that congressmen would often talk *only* to the chief United States negotiator. Such rank-consciousness complicated consultations with Congress since the chief United States negotiator, San Francisco-based Haydn Williams, had a full-time position as head of the Asia Foundation and thus was in Washington infrequently.[1] Moreover, jurisdictional jealousies and seniority within Congress itself are partially responsible for limiting briefings to senior members of committees concerned with Interior and Defense. Thus, it may be that observance of congressional sensitivities resulted in the injunction that the State Department not consult with foreign affairs committees and that defense committees be left to the Defense Department.

An uninformed Congress presents numerous problems in negotiations. Members of the interior subcommittees travelled officially to Micronesia on inspection tours, and congressional assertions there sometimes undermined or embarrassed the United States negotiating position. Meetings with Micronesians in Washington presented the same possibilities.

One example concerned the Mariana Islands. In conceding to the United States demand for a base on Tinian, the Marianas wished to attain and retain control of their internal affairs and their tax system. United States negotiators

---

[1] Williams's availability changed sharply just before and just after the signing of the Marianas Covenant. In a public hearing before the House Interior Subcommittee, all past difficulties were forgotten and Williams was lauded by Burton for excellent congressional briefings and model negotiations.

had no reason to discourage the Marianas from thinking that they might win these concessions. But during a visit to Micronesia, subcommittee chairman Burton made it clear that tax questions and some status matters might have difficulty in Congress, whether or not the Marianas permitted the development of the base at Tinian. Since Congress will make its judgment on the merit of the *final* proposals, it can have the luxury of being unconcerned about winning concessions from the Micronesians.

Another example occurred in the seventh round of negotiations (November 13-21, 1973). The Micronesians had requested $100 million annually for the duration of a "free association" status. The United States representative rejected this proposal on the ground that it would be unreasonable to give more money to the area after trusteeship than was given during trusteeship. The Micronesians were willing to decrease the amount requested in return for a looser association agreement. But a number of congressmen, including subcommittee chairman Burton, let it be known that they were willing to meet the $100 million request.

On one occasion the United States negotiating position was completely undermined by significant congressional sentiment. In the second round of negotiations with the Marianas, the United States representative presented plans for the *purchase* of Tinian on the grounds that "the United States Congress is reluctant to commit large sums to projects with only the protection of a lease." In 1974, in a three hour meeting on Saipan, several members of the House Subcommittee on Territories suggested to Marianas negotiators that they *lease* rather than sell land to the federal government. Defense, they said, would require a long-term lease, perhaps as long as ninety-nine years, but leasing itself was not objectionable to Congress.

But most important, concerned congressmen did not show great faith in the negotiators, and assumed that negotiated agreements would be changed. The Office of Micronesian Status Negotiations chose to tolerate Congress's uninformed lethargy until the final stages of the negotiations. With increased congressional briefings in 1974, the folly of this approach became clear, and senators who were years behind in their understanding of the negotiations balked at the status proposals.

Over and over, congressmen stated that they had no views but would wait for executive proposals. But a wait-and-see attitude is impractical and may be a continuation of the refusal by Congress to fulfill its responsibilities. In the first place, it is late in the day for Congress to suddenly discover that it is in disagreement with agreements tortuously negotiated and partially implemented in good faith by both the Micronesians and by the executive branch. Second, the very content of the United States negotiating position depends upon the extent to which Congress is willing to follow-up with funds, legislative restraints, etc.

CONGRESSIONAL APPROVAL OF
FINAL STATUS ARRANGEMENTS

Congress has assumed that, at some point, it would receive from the executive branch firm proposals which it could debate and either approve or reject, as a whole or in parts. It has been only twenty years since Congress dealt with the Constitution of the Commonwealth of Puerto Rico in this manner.

But this approval procedure was not to be followed in Congress. Rather, in September, 1974, the executive branch asked Congress to raise the ceiling for authorizations to Micronesia specifically in order to begin implementation of status proposals which would later be submitted to Congress for approval (Senate bill S-3996 and House bills HR-16731 and HR-16793). Authorizations were requested for capital improvements and for "transition" of the Marianas to a commonwealth status.

Mr. Fred Radewagen, speaking for Interior's Office of Territorial Affairs, stated:

> Since 1969, the United States and Micronesia have been negotiating the future political status of the Territory's six districts and termination of the trusteeship.
>
> Public Law 93-111 currently authorizes the appropriation of $60 million for fiscal year 1975, a level which has been maintained since 1971.
>
> The Administration's proposal would authorize a total annual appropriation of $75 million for fiscal year 1975 and the 1975 constant dollar equivalent of $80 million for 1976.
>
> Additionally, in section two, we are asking for a separate authorization of $1.5 million for a special program to aid transition of the Mariana Islands District to a new commonwealth status as a territory of the United States.
>
> These proposals are a direct result of the future political status negotiations.

The money for the Marianas was particularly connected to its future political status, the merits and drawbacks of which Congress had neither formally considered nor debated up to that point. But even the badly needed capital improvement funds called for in the other sections of the bill were connected to future political status by administration officials: "tentative agreement as to levels of accelerated capital improvement program funding was reached in the Carmel talks in March of this year between Ambassador Franklin Haydn Williams, the President's Personal Representative for Micronesian Status Negotiations, and Senator Lazarus Salii, Chairman of the Joint Committee on Future Status of the Congress of Micronesia." Deputy Chief Negotiator Wilson, however, pointed out that the provisions for Micronesia's future political status "are subject to the approval of the United States Congress in the process of approving the compact."

The Marianas transition to commonwealth status would, the administration candidly admitted, go into effect as soon as the Marianas and United States negotiators signed the final agreement. However, Marianas Commonwealth proposals are hardly uncontroversial; they contain perplexing problems that deserve debate. Also, approval of the Marianas transition funds would put the United States Congress in direct conflict with the Congress of Micronesia which had opposed separate negotiations with the Marianas. To make matters more complicated, before Congress had acted on the bills, the people of the Marianas voted their negotiators out of office, replacing them with representatives who advocated a slower pace in the negotiations and, in one instance, opposed the negotiations completely. Thus congressional approval might also go against the implied wishes of the Marianas people themselves.

In spite of all the implications of the finance bills, the executive branch officials vehemently denied that they were intentionally forcing Congress's hand on Micronesia and argued that they were trying to facilitate implementation of proposals if the proposals received congressional approval. There is little doubt that capital improvement funds were badly needed. But thorough consideration and public debate of the status proposals was needed as much, if not more.

Inclusion of aspects of the status negotiations in a bill which needed only to deal with acknowledged fiscal needs in Micronesia was perplexing to many people on Capitol Hill. Senator Johnston commented, "This funding seems a little inconsistent to me. Here you have the Micronesians negotiating for the whole of Micronesia and getting a budget for the whole of Micronesia and the Marianas wanting a million and a half to make the transition to a separate status. Is that inconsistency not rather plain and why do we have to have that?" Senator Johnston, who was insufficiently informed on the negotiations to begin with, received this response from Deputy Chief Negotiator Wilson: "I think there may be some confusion here due to the fact, Mr. Chairman, that we are faced with the proposition, almost, of trying to paint a moving train. We do have the problem of having to fund current administration, the current administration of all six districts at once under the present system while we are, at the same time, trying to devise a new system." Unfortunately, no congressman asked the administration spokesman why a new system had to be funded before it was congressionally approved.

Open hearings on the authorization proposals were held September 25, 1974, in the Senate and in the House on October 1, 1974. Before the hearings, James W. Wilson, United States deputy representative for Micronesian status negotiations, conducted a closed briefing with the Senate Interior and Insular Affairs Committee. At that briefing, Senate misgivings about the status proposals became clear. In the words of staff members of the Office of Micronesian Status

Negotiations, "Senator McClure wanted to rewrite the whole Draft Compact." McClure, Buckley, and Johnston reportedly objected to the entire direction of the negotiations. Interviewed soon after the briefing, Senator McClure said that Congress should have stated guidelines prior to the negotiations.

At the September 25, 1974, open hearing of the Senate Subcommittee on Territories, chairman J. Bennett Johnston began by warning: "I think there is a substantial chance that at least some provisions of the tentative agreements will be recommended against by the committee." Johnston added that he hoped his warning was sufficiently timely to allow Ambassador Williams to take the committee's opinions into account in negotiations. Chairman Johnston stated the basic problem this way:

> Our one real gut interest in Micronesia is a strategic interest. Here we are going to enter into a compact that would say, unilaterally, you can rescind that agreement. I think that is just insane.
>
> It seems to me that we had better get some more sentiment from the committee and I will try to do that for you. In the meantime, I just doubt the wisdom of increasing the budget, really, as more or less of a *quid pro quo* to enter those negotiations—I mean, to enter that compact before we have an acceptable compact.

Senator Bartlett followed up on the chairman's comments and expressed the views of many Senate subcommittee members (Senator Abourezk is a notable exception):

> Mr. Wilson, I share the concern that has been expressed by Senator Buckley and Senator Johnston and perhaps others on the termination by mutual consent of the compact in the first 15 years.
>
> I attended the last hearing [the closed briefing held September 12, 1974] but I was unable to stay long enough to express myself.
>
> In addition, I have concern about the provision that, thereafter, it would be terminated by unilateral action on two years' notice but only after a satisfactory security agreement has been concluded embodying the United States' base right and denying the area to third parties.
>
> It would seem to me that, rather than leaving that final condition up in the air for negotiation at that time, the satisfactory security agreements embodying the United States' base rights and the denial of the area to third parties should be clearly understood prior to the negotiation of the contract.
>
> Having that up in the air, which would be the most important thing, should be clearly worked out in advance so that there are no doubts.

Faced with problems in both Houses, the administration developed strategies which would lessen their plight. To a House subcommittee concerned with the Marianas Commonwealth, but largely content with Micronesian plans, the administration presented the Micronesian plans first. To the Senate subcommittee eager for closer military ties, the administration began with the Marianas proposals. The official explanation was that it was done for "variety," but one staffman agreed that the "variety" was not without political intention.

More important, however, officials at the Department of Interior began to discuss alternative processes for congressional approval of the agreements. The director of the Office of Territorial Affairs as well as the director of the Office of Micronesian Status Negotiations openly discussed whether the interior committees, as opposed to committees responsible for foreign affairs, should deal with the "international agreement" which would be made with the Micronesians. Under this approach, the Draft Compact, which the Senate Interior Committee seemed to want to block, would go to the more liberal Senate Foreign Relations Committee. The interior committees, according to the administration officials, had real jurisdiction only over a Marianas Commonwealth. Whether the intent was to cut out Congress or not, according to this plan Congress would never have been able to deal with the question of fragmentation of the Trust Territory, one of the most controversial political issues.

In the final analysis the Congress refused to go along with the administration's approach. Both houses approved authorization of $1.5 million for "transition" of the Marianas, but explicitly disapproved of any expenditures before Congress acted on the Marianas Compact. The debate on this measure in the Senate provided the first large scale test of congressional sentiment on the administration's plans for Micronesia's future status. Senator Gary Hart of Colorado introduced an amendment on the Senate floor which called for deletion of any mention of funds for the Marianas, arguing that there would be plenty of time to authorize funds for the Marianas transition after the idea was approved by Congress. Hart was particularly opposed to plans for the construction of a military base in the Marianas. The chief critic, in addition to Hart, was Senator Harry Byrd of Virginia, who had served in Micronesia during World War II. Byrd sharply questioned the strategic importance of Micronesia, beyond denial to others. The Hart amendment was defeated by a forty-seven to thirty-nine vote in favor of including the Marianas authorization, but with its restrictive provision. The vote was close despite heavy lobbying by the Marianas and by the administration. However, it is clear from the debate that the majority of the Senate decided to reserve for later debate the question of Micronesia's status.

Despite the clear sentiment expressed by the Senate action limiting funds for the Marianas transition, the administration made no change in its announced plans to administer the Marianas separately immediately after a favorable plebiscite but before congressional action, and it went ahead to spend funds on the plebiscite despite the fact that funds for that purpose had been among those subject to the restricted authorization. Thus, despite a clear expression of its intent to do otherwise, the Congress was still being presented with proposals whose implementation had already reached an advanced stage.

CONCLUSION

One of the problems in the development of Congress's relationship with Micronesia is that Micronesia sends no official representative to Washington.[2] No representatives or senators have a Micronesian constituency. Hawaiian congressmen and lately the territorial delegates, have championed Micronesian problems, but they must be guided by the same conscience which motivates other congressmen on the interior committees to go out of their way to investigate the Micronesian situation.

Working for Micronesia as a member of Congress offers few rewards. Membership on the full Interior Committee is often sought in hopes that it will provide the opportunity for congressmen to influence legislation important to constituents (the Interior Committee authorizes water conservation programs, dams, parks, and recreational areas.) But no bills referred to the Subcommittee on Territories offer any benefits for congressmen's home districts. The singular and minor exception, of course, is in the potential for benefits for states in the Pacific area.

Moreover, since territorial affairs do not often raise issues which catch the public's eye, an assignment on a subcommittee responsible for territories is not very popular. Assignments generally go to freshmen congressmen. This has had an adverse effect on the conduct of territorial affairs, not so much because freshmen congressmen are incapable, but because the subcommittee assignment gives them little political advantage. An assignment on a subcommittee responsible for territories does not help at election time. Thus, Micronesia's interests suffer from a high turnover rate, new members constantly needing to be educated concerning Micronesian affairs.

In the Senate, the situation is particularly bad. Former staff consultant to the Senate Interior and Insular Affairs Committee James Gamble put it this way: "With each new Congress there is a turnover of chairmen. If a new committee is reduced in size and senior members are promoted elsewhere, a newly elected senator without any experience becomes chairman. It is this inexperienced person who is looked to for guidance." The Senate Territorial Subcommittee gets a new chairman most frequently. Freshman Senator J. Bennett Johnston became chairman in January, 1973, and in the first hearing held on territorial matters revealed that he had no idea what the Trust Territory was. "Do I understand that American Samoa is not included as a trust territory?" Johnston asked Interior Director of the Office of Territorial Affairs, Stanley Carpenter. The

---

[2]The firm of Wilmer, Cutler and Pickering has registered as a lobbyist for the Mariana Islands. The firm's contacts have been limited largely to the status negotiations. The firm of Clifford, Warnke and Glass represents the Congress of Micronesia.

senator's bewilderment is understandable, but it is indicative of a structural flaw in the government of the country responsible for Micronesia.

Freshmen who are genuinely interested in territorial issues often must be careful about carrying out their subcommittee duties. A trip to Micronesia is worthwhile, essential for an understanding of the Trust Territory. Congressman William Ketchum, in a hearing on submerged lands, urged that members of the committee visit Micronesia in order to fully understand the issue, but freshmen congressmen must particularly consider the impression a Pacific trip leaves back home. During the 1968 trip, a cartoon in Lloyd Meeds's district portrayed him lying in a hammock watching a hula dancer. In 1974, editorials denounced "junkets" to Micronesia.

But trips to Micronesia are not luxurious or unnecessary. Conditions in the Trust Territory are often arduous and more exotic than luxurious. One congressman complained that to be diplomatic he had to partake of a feast which featured rancid lobster and roast pig which had been sitting in the weather; this is an unusual view, and perhaps is itself a comment on the ethnocentrism of the congressman, since Micronesians are famous for their roast pig banquets. But more objectively, the local political situation is always ready to present a few surprises: In 1968, the congressmen were attacked because of their appearance in business suits on one island and when they decided to change, they were chided for their sloppy attire on the next island. The trips are exhausting and often unpleasant, but freshman Congressman Ralph Regula told an interviewer, "I doubt that argument would be convincing in my district in Ohio."

A very dramatic case of a freshman congressman's dilemma is that of former Pennsylvania Congressman Neiman Craley. Elected in the Johnson landslide of 1964, Craley found the House Subcommittee on Territories intellectually stimulating, if not politically strengthening, and devoted a great deal of time to the issue. Craley lost his bid for re-election in Pennsylvania. Afterwards, he followed his interests and moved to Micronesia where he has served as legislative liaison officer for the Trust Territory administration. Many members of the present subcommittee hold him in high regard.

Perhaps more important than the people charged with Micronesia, however, is the method by which Congress deals with multifaceted issues. Micronesia should probably have been dealt with by a special committee organized to investigate the peculiarities of this special place. The "problem" of Micronesia involves substantial foreign affairs issues and international agreements, multi-million dollar defense investments, and annual appropriations for the development of an impoverished area, as well as the civil administration of an Interior Department ward. The problems could have been handled by the Foreign Relations, Armed Services, Appropriations, or Interior Committees equally ineffectively. But they should have been dealt with by all of them. It is a flaw of Congress that issues and jurisdiction are particularized rather than coordinated.

The assignment of jurisdiction to the interior committees may not have been worse than assignment to any other particular committee. But it had its faults. Outside of the Armed Services Committee, no other committee welcomed trusteeship instead of annexation less than the interior committees. The interior committees had a predisposition toward territorial annexation. Throughout the nineteenth century, western expansion and population growth made the annexation of territories easy, if not just. The pattern of acquisition and development, territory-to-state, seemed natural. Interior committee members thought that the same pattern could be repeated in the Pacific.

But Congress has had difficulty producing satisfactory relationships with any of the United States possessions since the statehood of Hawaii and Alaska. Revisions of the pattern have brought Guam and the Virgin Islands to some degree of satisfaction, but the Trust Territory of the Pacific Islands, Puerto Rico, and American Samoa are caught in a no man's land between independence and statehood. The problems raised by territories are perplexing in an anticolonialist world. Congressman Thomas Foley expressed the sentiments of many members of Congress when he said, "It's too bad the United States ever got involved in the colonial-territorial business in the late nineteenth century; it is a constant source of problems."

The Trusteeship Agreement involved a strong commitment to economic, social and political development toward the goal of self-determination. From the beginning, the United States had committed itself to a more altruistic involvement in Micronesia than it had in the other territories. From the beginning, the Trust Territory had a better status because its sovereignty was reserved. Assuming that somehow Micronesia's status could be handled in the traditional pattern by the traditional subcommittees has proved to be unrealistic, and one can still ask if the United States has truly met its high commitment to Micronesia.

IX

Conclusions and Recommendations

This study concludes with a favorable plebiscite vote in the Marianas and the immediate request by President Ford that the Congress approve the Marianas Covenant. The President's request was dated July 1, 1975. Appropriate legislation was introduced July 15, 1975, in the Senate and hearings were scheduled for the 24th. In the House of Representatives, hearings were announced on July 2 to begin July 14. Plans called for House approval, presumably under a suspension of the rules, by the first of August when Congress began its summer recess. In other words, the House of Representatives felt it could deal adequately with the question of the first acquisition of territory in sixty-eight years—could consider an agreement which grew out of six years of negotiations—in a little more than a month. At administration urging, appropriate Senate leaders also promised similarly prompt action—though after the conclusion of the filibuster on the disputed New Hampshire Senate seat.

In part the hurried consideration by the United States Congress can be traced to the original, imprudent (but legal) plan of the administration to administer the Marianas separately immediately after a favorable plebiscite and before approval of the covenant by the United States Congress. The leaders of the Marianas were understandably disappointed with the changed United States approach. Equally imprudently some Marianas leaders threatened to renege on the covenant unless the Marianas were administered separately by September, 1975.

A single change in the covenant by the United States Congress would mean that the Marianas would have to approve the covenant all over again, whether by the people or by their elected representatives remains unclear. However, assuming approval without change, most of the provisions in the covenant, particularly the provision for self-government, will take effect as soon as the covenant and the Marianas Constitution are approved by the Marianas and by the United States Congress. Nevertheless, legally, the Marianas will remain a part of the Trust Territory of the Pacific Islands until a decision is taken on the future political status of the other five districts. Negotiations on a United States-Micronesian Compact have long since succumbed to the priority emphasis placed by the United States on the Marianas negotiations. In any event, the Micronesian negotiations are at an impasse over (among other things) finances, United States land policies, and the extent of United States control over foreign affairs. The Micronesians have announced that free association is no longer a valid basis of negotiations. In the meantime there are increased pressures for further fragmentation. Even if the impasse in the negotiations is broken and the compact is concluded at an early date, the United States does not plan to seek United Nations Security Council approval of termination of the Trusteeship Agreement until 1980 or 1981.

For the Marianas the delay is political rather than legal. The United States could seek United Nations Security Council approval of an amendment to the

Trusteeship Agreement whereby trusteeship would no longer apply to the Marianas but would continue to apply to the remainder of Micronesia. However, to do so would raise in their most acute form some of the major criticisms of American policy, and the proposal might therefore fail to achieve Security Council approval. The delay for the remainder of Micronesia is also primarily political, but the political problem largely revolves around United States domestic rather than international political considerations. The administration does not believe it can persuade Congress to approve a larger financial package for Micronesia. Thus, a decision was made to complete needed capital improvement programs under the aegis of the United States rather than to provide funds for the Micronesians themselves to make the same capital improvements. The irony is that United States administration of past and current capital improvement programs in Micronesia was recently sharply criticized in the United States Congress.

The delay and the uncertainty of future developments make it difficult to reach conclusions on the advantages and disadvantages of either the Marianas Covenant or the Micronesian Compact. Even after termination of the Trusteeship Agreement, it will be some time before hard conclusions can be drawn. Perspective will make it possible to differentiate between those issues in the negotiations which were truly important and have enduring implications and those issues which, while they profoundly influenced immediate decisions and particularly the atmosphere of the negotiations, have no significant long-term effect. More important, perspective and experience will tell whether the unique relationships which the United States seeks to build with both the Marianas and Micronesians are sufficiently strong and flexible to accommodate changing needs and aspirations. Such changes are likely in developed countries; they are inevitable in a developing area such as Micronesia. Just as Micronesia outgrew the rigidities of a status as a non-self-governing territory of the United States (even before it was offered), it may be expected to outgrow some of the provisions of its new status, if not the status itself. Thus despite the effort of the United States to develop a permanent relationship with Micronesia and Micronesian efforts to be able to freely change the relationship, the length as well as the warmth of the new relationship—even with the Marianas where the United States achieved its objectives—can only be determined by the extent to which it is and remains mutually beneficial.

Despite the uncertainties ahead, it is important to make some judgment on the attitudes and assumptions upon which the present proposals were founded and to draw conclusions regarding the development and implementation of United States policy at this turning point in the continuing relationship between the United States and the islands of Micronesia.

1) *The basic assumption of United States policy—that Micronesia is "essential to the United States for security reasons"—is highly questionable.* Such a

judgment cannot be made outside political, economic, technical, and above all, human considerations. Considered against these trade-offs, initial United States military plans for land acquisition and military base construction in Micronesia not only were clearly extravagant but also affected Micronesian life and aspirations. The military should never have been permitted to proceed so far with preparations for a military base without a firm decision that the area was of such strategic importance that the Pentagon's budget would include the necessary financial support.

There is no doubt that Micronesia is useful from a military point of view. Nor is there any doubt that it is to the advantage of the United States, Micronesia and the international community to insure that the area is never again used for aggressive purposes. But a judgment that Micronesia is useful and must be denied to potential enemies raises very different policy questions from a conclusion that the area is "essential." A more realistic assessment of Micronesia's strategic importance might have resulted in more rapid and less contentious negotiations, if not more serious consideration of such options as international neutralization, a bilateral treaty, and/or long-term base agreements. The last two options, particularly, could have accommodated United States military interests without unnecessarily restricting Micronesian options.

2) *Resolution of Micronesia's status was needlessly delayed by the failure of the executive branch to reconcile conflicts between Interior, State, and Defense.* In the Johnson administration, continued bureaucratic infighting made it possible for a single congressman to exercise almost complete control over United States policy objectives. Even when a coordinated approach was initiated by the Nixon administration, attainment of policy objectives was jeopardized by the administration's dismissal of the experiences of its predecessor, by its initial refusal to restrain military demands and by its insensitivity to Micronesian rights and aspirations.

3) *The Micronesians have not been presented with a free choice on their future status. Rather, they have a free choice within the limited range of options made available to them.* The choice was limited by two factors: The primary factor was United States military strategic policy which precluded independence and allowed internal autonomy only if the United States continued to control defense and foreign affairs. A second limiting factor was economic. United States economic development of Micronesia was a dismal failure. Political, social and educational programs bore no relationship to economic realities and potential. The result is a Micronesia which is considerably beyond a subsistence economy but which is unable to advance further or even to maintain current standards without considerable outside assistance. No pledge of continued United States economic assistance at sufficient levels was made for an independent Micronesia. On the contary, the United States made it clear that the closeness of

the relationship and not Micronesian needs would determine the level of United States economic assistance.

The military and economic factors which limited Micronesian choice were not unconnected. Theoretically Micronesia could have auctioned off its strategic location, but because of firmly established United States military interests, in actuality it was not in a position to do so. A more economically independent Micronesia, particularly a Micronesia not dependent solely on military attractiveness, would have been able to attract domestic and international political support for a wider range of status options.

It is also worth mentioning that as a participant in the status negotiations and as a party whose interests are directly and indirectly affected by the results, the United States may have brought into question its ability to objectively conduct either a political education program or needed plebiscites. At a minimum, the conduct of plebiscites should not be the responsibility of the United States but the responsibility of a neutral and impartial body or individual. Similarly and perhaps alternatively, United Nations participation should be expanded beyond mere observation.

4) *Although it professed to be following a policy of territorial unity, real United States economic and military policies reinforced existing cultural, geographic and other causes for disunity in Micronesia.*The initial Navy separation of the Marianas from the rest of Micronesia in 1951, location of the capital in Saipan far away from the geographic center of the territory, and clear economic and educational advantages for the Marianas reinforced and encouraged separatist tendencies there. These tendencies were also encouraged every time the military expressed a desire for bases in the Marianas. The final decision to negotiate with the Marianas appears to have been made primarily for military reasons.

5) A Commonwealth of the Marianas will neither be integrated into the United States (like a state) nor have a free associated status (like Micronesia). Their status will be new in United Nations terms and may be subject to criticism there. However, it must be recognized that the Marianas will have virtually complete control over their internal affairs and they knowingly and voluntarily entered into the arrangement. *If current plans for the Marianas are projected successfully the Marianas will increasingly want either greater participation in United States affairs or greater independence*, despite the fact that they say they are satisfied with the current arrangements. If the United States fails to accommodate such desires or uses its authority in the Marianas insensitively, the United States can expect the Marianas to seek a change in the relationship.

6) *Given political and economic realities, free association with the United States may best serve Micronesian interests*. Free association status would give the Micronesians maximun internal autonomy, assured economic assistance, protection against third country encroachment, and the responsibility for preserving

significant aspects of Micronesian culture. The Micronesians would also have the option to unilaterally declare their independence at some future date when the political and economic realities which limit current alternatives may have changed significantly.

However, for free association to survive its initially fixed period or beyond, it must indeed be free. Ideally, such an association could be based on traditional American generosity, and on the continuing feeling of responsibility and the bond of friendship which ought to result from the relationship between trustee and ward. Pragmatically, however, free association must be based on mutual interests, on accommodation, rather than subordination, of perceived United States security interests with Micronesia's right to determine its own future and to govern itself. Thus far, subordination has characterized American policy, and it remains one of the major obstacles to arriving at a mutually satisfactory settlement. It may be too much to expect that the United States, which had to be brought screaming and kicking to an arrangement which it could have and should have offered and negotiated graciously years earlier, can make still further concessions.

7) *The threat that other islands will follow the Marianas separatist route and Micronesia's continuing overwhelming dependence on United States grants suggest that the remaining five districts will have immediately before them two tasks at which the United States failed dismally: designing a government so that it provides strength through unity and yet is sufficiently flexible to meet diverse needs which exist among the islands; and developing an economy and way of life less dependent on public appropriations and uncertain military expenditures.* Ideally, the United States also has a continuing responsibility to promote unity and to develop a reasonably satisfactory economy. But the American track record on economic development is appalling, and American credibility on unity may be lost irretrievably. Micronesia cannot escape the shortcomings of previous American mistakes, but it will have the opportunity and responsibility for corrective actions.

8) *Congress is poorly organized to handle questions relating to issues like Micronesia.* The rigidity of the committee system, excesses of the seniority system, dictatorial powers of committee chairmen, and general congressional disinterest has resulted in inadequate attention given to the interrelationship of the international, political, economic and military factors involved in fulfillment of United States trusteeship obligations. Some of these shortcomings have, of course, been changed in recent years. However, such continuing problems as the antiquated committee structure, will continue to adversely affect United States policy in Micronesia and the Marianas even after they gain their new status.

9) *The Nixon and Ford administrations took advantage of congressional shortcomings.* Congress was not encouraged to address in a coherent manner the

policy questions involved in termination of Micronesia's trusteeship status. Instead, the administration took steps which at best would have resulted in piecemeal consideration and at worst narrowed the scope of congressional action. Authorization of funds for transition of the Marianas to commonwealth status was requested before the Marianas Covenant was completed or submitted for congressional approval, before Congress had a chance to look at the implications for or hear the views of the rest of Micronesia and to consider the implication of military plans. In addition, the administration announced plans to hold a plebiscite and, if approved, to begin separate administration of the Marianas prior to congressional approval of a separate status for the Marianas.

The administration can rightly argue that it took these steps openly, after consultation with a few key members of Congress. In fact, it reversed its position on these procedures after congressional opposition developed. Of course, Congress ultimately always had the opportunity to stop all action on Micronesia until it was satisfied with the status question. But Congress doesn't work that way and the executive knows it. Besides risking more distrust of the executive by Congress, the administration's procedure jeopardizes the agreements themselves. Marianas disappointment at not obtaining separate administration immediately after the plebiscite will be nothing compared to how Micronesians will feel if Congress later discovers that it cannot live with agreements whose partial implementation it has already approved.

10) It is too late to give Micronesia's future political status the kind of systematic planning it deserves. *However, Congress, the Micronesians and the United Nations should consider both the Marianas question and Micronesia at the same time.* This would undoubtedly result in a delay for the Marianas, but assuming the Marianas approach is valid, the delay would cause no permanent damage. In fact, to the extent that its validity was established, the delay could have positive advantages. In any event, as a practical matter, the Marianas question cannot be decided without also deciding major aspects of the incomplete United States-Micronesian negotiations. Given the impasse in the latter, it may be that the only way of forcing a resolution of those negotiations would be through detailed consideration of the Marianas question.

However, there is no reason to expect that Congress will suddenly begin to take seriously its responsibilities toward Micronesia. Phillip Burton, the chairman of the House Sub-committee on Territories, and Henry Jackson, chairman of the Senate Interior Committee, are willing and powerful allies of administration efforts to push the Marianas aspect of the Micronesia question through Congress swiftly. The administration, of course, reneged on its commitment to begin implementation of the Marianas agreement before congressional approval. But it is a change without a difference. Faced with threats from the Marianas because the administration commitment was not fulfilled, congressional leaders agreed to give the Marianas agreement pro forma approval without the significant debate and painstaking examination the issues deserve. The way the Marianas proposal has moved through Congress, the way the representatives of other United States territories have been quieted and their objections ignored, as well as the way an uninformed Congress acts should serve as a warning to the Marianas of their future vulnerability to the whims of Congress. Congress, which is frequently criticized for acting with deliberation and no speed, is now acting with speed and little deliberation.

11) *The Marianas Commonwealth and the Free Associated State of Micronesia will bring to five the kinds of territories associated with the United States: Guam and the Virgin Islands; American Samoa; and the Commonwealth of Puerto Rico. The United States should immediately move to insure that the statuses of the other territories are similarly improved.* There is virtue in a flexible approach which tailors political status to the particular requirements of each area. The objective is not to create a rigid formula for all territories or to withhold Micronesia's privileges until other territories achieve a similar status. Rather, it is to recognize that other territories have legitimate concerns which were present even before the Micronesia negotiations. They should not be handicapped because, unlike Micronesia, they came under American sovereignty in another era and thus have not renegotiated their evolving status in the American political family.

12) *Up to the signing of the Marianas Covenant, the United States demonstrated little or no concern for the role of the United Nations.* This is seen in the initial United States proposal for commonwealth, the movement of Micronesian matters from the State Department's Bureau of International Organization Affairs, the discontinuation of State Department participation in the Marianas negotiations and the failure to consult the foreign affairs committees of Congress. Reference to the role of the United Nations is not included in either the covenant or the compact or any communique or in the United States itemized list of the ten steps remaining before finalization of the covenant. Only at annual sessions of the United Nations was that organization involved in Micronesian status questions. Even the United Nations participation as observers of the plebiscite was requested rather late.

On the other hand the United Nations has not performed particularly well at the most important stage of its responsibilities for Micronesia. Consideration of Micronesia, so far, is effectively isolated in the Trusteeship Council, away from the sometimes overly critical eye of the newly independent Afro-Asian and Latin American countries. Only the Soviet Union, among Trusteeship Council members, offers more than perfunctory criticism of United States administration and even Soviet criticism reflects the artificial restraint of détente. Micronesia is the victim of the structure and politics of the organization which is supposed to be its ultimate protector.

* * * *

Two points stand out more than any others after an examination of the twelve years which have elapsed since the United States first began to give serious attention to a resolution of Micronesia's future political status. The first is how extraordinarily complicated the issues are for such a small place, and how much time is required for an adequate, fair and informed treatment of the question. The second point is that no one comes out of this phase of Micronesia's history looking good, not the Congress, not the executive, not the United Nations, not even the Micronesians who too frequently seem to be concerned more about money than about the principles involved. Each has grappled with the problems of that small place and each inadequately. Each will have to continue to do so for the forseeable future, for the dilemma which the United States postponed in 1945 has in reality once again been postponed.

Appendix I

EXCERPTS FROM THE SOLOMON REPORT FROM THE YOUNG MICRONESIANS

(As Reprinted from *The Young Micronesia* in the
July 10, 1971, *Micronitor*)

The Setting

1. The Trust Territory of the Pacific Islands—or Micronesia—comprises the former Japanese mandated Caroline, Marshall and Mariana Islands. Scattered over an area as large as the mainland of the US, those 2100 islands, less than 100 of which are inhabited by the territory's 81,000 people, came under United States control first by conquest and then, in 1947, under a trusteeship agreement with the Security Council of the UN. The islands vary from low coral atolls to higher islands of volcanic origin, the largest land masses being Babelthuap in the Palau district with 153 square miles, Ponape with 129 square miles and Saipan with 46 square miles. Population distribution ranges from islands with a few families to Saipan with 7,800; Ponape with 11,500; and Truk with 15,000.

With a variety of racial mixtures, languages and cultures, essentially a series of individual island communities rather than a unified society, a lack of human and natural resources, tremendously difficult communications and transportation, the area has presented very serious administrative and developmental problems to the US. Historically, life has centered around the village, the extended family, or clan, and its lands, The traditional systems of communal, rather than individual land ownership, of inheritance through matrilineal lines and of the selection of native chiefs continue side-by-side with the forms of democratic institutions introduced by the U.S.

For a variety of reasons, in the almost twenty years of US control, physical facilities have further deteriorated in many areas, the economy has remained relatively dormant and in many ways retrogressed while progress toward social development has been slow. The people remain largely illiterate and inadequately prepared to participate in political, commercial and other activities of more than a rudimentary character. The great majority depend largely upon subsistence agriculture—fruit and nut gathering—and fishing. As a result, criticism of the trusteeship has been growing in the UN and the US press—and in certain ways, among Micronesians.

2. Despite a lack of serious concern for the area until quite recently, Micronesia is said to be essential to the US for security reasons. We cannot give the area up, yet time is running out for the US in the sense that we will soon be the only nation left administering a trust territory. The time could come, and shortly, when the pressures in the UN for a settlement of the status of Micronesia could become more than embarrassing.

In recognition of the problem, the President, on April 18, 1962, approved NASM No. 145 which set forth as US policy the movement of Micronesia into permanent relationship with the US within our political framework. In keeping with that goal, the memorandum called for accelerated development of the area to bring its political, economic and social standards into line with an eventual permanent association.

The memorandum also established a Task Force to consider what action might be taken to accomplish our goal and to provide policy and program advice to the Secretary of the Interior who is responsible for the administration of the Trust Territory. The Task Force, consisting of representatives of the Departments of the Interior, Defense, State, and Health, Education and Welfare, and observers from the NSC and Bureau of the Budget, had considered and recommended several steps for greater aid to the area, both through the increase appropriation ceiling (from $7 to 17.5 millions) and in legislation (H.R. 3198) now pending in the Congress. It also proposed the sending of a survey mission to the Trust Territory to conduct a more thorough study of the area's major problems.

3. The Mission's formal instructions from the President (through NASM No. 243 of May 9, 1963) were to survey the political, economic and social problems of the people of the Trust Territory and to make recommendations leading to the formulation of programs and policies for an accelerated rate of development so that the people may make an informed and free choice as to their future in accordance with US responsibilities under the trusteeship agreement.

4. The Mission consisted of nine men, both Government and non-Government, selected by its chairman and serving for differing periods of time up to six weeks in the Trust Territory during July and August 1963. The Mission visited six district centers in the territory and representative sample of the outlying islands containing in all a majority of the area's population. Discussions were held throughout the area with seven assemblies of local people, eight legislative committees, seven municipal councils and three women's associations; about twenty-five interviews with American missionaries and over forty-five interviews with Micronesians were held. There were also briefings by Headquarters personnel of the Trust Territory government and the six district administrators and their staffs. Wherever possible, roads, communications, transportation facilities, agricultural developments, schools and other facilities and enterprises were examined and evaluated. Several additional weeks were spent in the US preparing the final report of the Mission.

Major Objectives and Considerations

1. Working within its broad frame of reference, the Mission's major findings relate to three key sets of questions that it attempted to answer:

   a. What are the elements to consider in the preparation for organization, timing and favorable outcome of a plebiscite in Micronesia and how will this action affect the long-run problem that Micronesia, after affiliation, will pose for the US?

b. What should be the content and cost of the minimum capital investment and operating program needed to insure a favorable vote in the plebiscite, and what should be the content and cost of the maximum program that could be effectively mounted to develop the Trust Territory most rapidly?

c. What actions need to be taken to improve the relationships between the current Trust Territory government and Washington and to insure that it can implement any necessary political strategy land development program with reasonable efficiency and effectiveness.

2. The Mission's findings and recommendations on these three sets of questions correspond to Parts I, II and III of its report. Those recommendations sum up to an integrated master plan which, if accepted, would provide guidelines for Federal action through fiscal year 1968 to secure the objectives of:

a. Winning the plebiscite and making Micronesia United States territory under circumstances which will: (1) satisfy somewhat conflicting interests of the Micronesians, the UN and the US along lines satisfactory to the Congress; (2) be appropriate to the present political and other capabilities of the Micronesians; and (3) provide sufficient flexibility in government structure to accommodate whatever measure of local self-government the Congress might grant to Micronesia in later years.

b. Achieving rapidly minimum but satisfactory social standards in education, public health, etc.

c. Raising cash incomes through the development of the current, largely crop-gathering subsistence economy.

3. There are, however, unique elements in the delicate problem of Micronesia and the attainment of our objectives that urgently require the agreement now of the President and the Congress as to the guidelines of US action over the next few years. First, the US will be moving counter to the anti-colonial movement that has just about completed sweeping the world and will be breaching its own policy since World War I of not acquiring new territorial possessions if it seeks to make Micronesia a US territory. Second, of all eleven UN trusteeships, this will be the only one not to terminate in independence or merger with a contiguous country, but in a territorial affiliation with the administering power. Third, as the only "strategic trusteeship," the Security Council will have jurisdiction over the formal termination of the trusteeship agreement, and if such a termination is vetoed there, the US might have to decide to proceed with a series of actions that would make the trusteeship agreement a dead issue, at least from the Micronesian viewpoint. Fourth, the 2,100 islands of Micronesia are, and will remain in the now foreseeable future, a deficit area to be subsidized by the US. Fifth, granted that this subsidy can be justified as a "strategic rental," it will amount to more than $300 annually per Micronesian through 1968 and any reductions thereafter will require long-range programming along the lines of a master development plan as proposed in the Mission report. Finally, this hoped for long-range reduction in the level of subsidization and the implementation of the political strategy and capital investment programs through fiscal year 1968 require a modern and more efficient concept of overseas territorial administra-

tion than is evident in the prevailing approach of the quasi-colonial bureaucracy in the present Trust Territory government.

Part 1. Political Development of Micronesia

1. The Washington policy, adopted last year, of having the Trust Territory affiliate permanently with the US, has not had an observable impact on the Trust Territory government. American and Micronesian officials in the area appear still to be thinking in terms of independence for Micronesia as an eventual, distant goal and there appears to have been little attempt to direct Micronesia toward thinking about eventual affiliation with the US. In the absence of further action, the Mission believes that the momentum of previous attitudes and policies which did not involve the concept of affiliation will be hard to overcome.

2. It can be stated quite unequivocally that the masses of Micronesians are not only not concerned with the political future but also are not even aware of it as a question. They simply live in the present reality of the "American time" that has replaced the "Japanese time." The earlier German and Spanish times are dimly, if at all remembered.

3. The situation is not quite the same among the political elite. Political power among the Micronesians is in a triumvirate of the traditional clan chiefs, the educated younger bureaucracy working in the Trust Territory government and the small but powerful group of businessmen operating trading companies. These groups are aware that their political future is still to be resolved, but even they generally shy away from actively concerning themselves with it. The reason lies in their belief that: (a) they cannot stand alone now and that independence, even if they want it, is so far distant that meaingful consideration is not practical; (b) there has been no indication from the US of an alternative to independence—they do not know that the US may desire affiliation; and (c) even if affiliation were possible, the prospect creates feelings of uncertainty and insecurity that they would rather not face.

4. These insecurities arise from general ignorance as to what affiliation means and what it would do to their lives as they know them today. The more important of the traditional chiefs are especially concerned whether "coming under US laws" would invalidate the present restrictions against non-Micronesians owning land and whether it would affect their complicated communal land-tenure systems on which their social organization and customs and the chiefs' powers are based. The merchant businessmen, even though they want more economic development, react against the prospect of a flood of American businessmen with whom they believe they cannot compete. The Micronesians in the government bureaucracy are less fearful of permanent affiliation, but they also share in the general concern among the political elite[−] they don't want to be swamped by Americans and lose their status "as the Hawaiians did."

5. On the other hand, there is a sophisticated awareness among a goodly number of the Micronesian elite that their own interests are not best served by the UN trusteeship simply because, as a provisional non-permanent arrangement, it perpetuates the excessively dependent psychology and habits of a people who have been handed around among four major powers in the last 65 years. There

also appears to be an unexpressed but fairly widespread and awakeable emotional feeling among these more sophisticated Micronesians that they want an "identity" and a permanence of status that is not compatible with the implied impermanence of the trusteeship.

6. Another disadvantage of the trusteeship is its protective and custodian nature, a carryover from the philosophy of the League of Nations mandates, which is not fully compatible with the more recent emphasis on modernization and more rapid development of peoples under trusteeship. Most policies which try to be both development-minded and protective do not seem to do a good job of either. However, a conflict between development objectives and protective attitudes characterized the current administration of the Trust Territory. Although it has become fashionable for American officials connected with the Trust Territory to disclaim any desire to maintain an "anthropological zoo," in reality protective and custodial policies are very prevalent. This conflict within official thinking faithfully mirrors the dilemma of the Micronesians themselves. They desire urgent economic development, but want to retain, at the same time, restrictions on non Micronesians immigrating, occupying land and starting businesses. The Mission believes that, if for no other reason than that of the impending plebiscite, the Micronesians need reassurances on the continuance of those restrictions but, at the same time, we are recommending certain modifications which will initiate long-run liberalization of those restrictions.

7. Another factor of importance affecting the plebiscite is the economic stagnation and deterioration of public facilities that has characterized the US administration of the Trust Territory in contrast to that of the Japanese. The rapid growth under the Japanese was due not only to their large capital investment and subsidy program, but to Japanese government-directed colonization by Japanese and Okinawans. The fact that it was the Japanese rather than the Micronesians who supplied the labor for the then-flourishing sugar cane and commercial fishing industries and who benefited most from the Japanese government's subsidization of the area does not alter the fact that per capita Micronesian cash incomes were almost three times as high before the war as they are now and that the Micronesians freely used the Japanese-subsidized extensive public facilities. For the outcome of the plebiscite to be favorable, the Mission believes there must be an effective capital investment program before the plebiscite to give the Micronesians a sense of progress to replace the deadly feeling of economic dormancy.

8. While more than 95 per cent of the budget of the Trust Territory government is financed by the US and the importance of those funds in influencing a favorable plebiscite result is obvious, the impact of US funds has been lessened by: (a) considerable feeling among Micronesian bureaucrats that a large part (actually, over $2 million) is spent on high salaries for US personnel in Micronesia; (b) numerous complaints about, and dissatisfaction with, the competence of the Trust Territory government (one district congress advised the Mission that, despite area needs, they did not want more US funds if they were not "properly administered by real experts who should be brought in"); and (c) some belief that US aid results only from UN action and that Micronesia might not do as well as a US territory.

9. The Trust Territory government gets good marks from the Micronesians, however, for its genuine fostering of democratic civil liberties and increasing the

participation of Micronesians in various levels of local government (as territorial advisory council, six district legislatures and a multitude of municipal governments). However, Micronesia is still a long way in terms of experience and funds from being able to mount a viable local government. The very multiplicity of local governmental levels is beginning to cause problems, particularly at the municipal level where there is much dissatisfaction because of the realization that, in a large majority of cases, the "U. S. imposed" municipal taxes produce only enough revenue to pay salaries to municipal officials and councilmen for making decisions that the village elders previously made free as a public service. This is a clear case of too much government.

10. The great distances, cultural and linguistic barriers separating the six districts of Micronesia also have special implications for a plebiscite. The Mission found little consciousness among the people of the Trust Territory of themselves as "Micronesians" and no emotional nationalistic feelings. There are no traditions of unity but rather a history of individual island cultures. There is almost universal ignorance in each district as to who are the leaders, political [and] otherwise, of the other five districts, and there is little inclination to compromise on a district's special interest in favor of the territory's advancement as a whole. This regional separation is strengthened by the existence of separate district legislatures, and to date only minor progress has been made toward a centralized indigenous government. The district legislatures function reasonably well given the small revenues they can command, but they represent conservative bastions for the maintenance of traditional policies, and land and social customs. Within some districts, especially Yap and Ponape, there is the additional complication of the outlying island groupings resenting the domination of the islands nearer to the district centers. This situation requires the most carefully impartial handling by the US in the period before the plebiscite and the avoidance in the plebiscite of questions of special interest to particular districts, such as "union with Guam," which is an issue in the Marianas. It also creates the need for the right mix of political compromises in the organization of the territorial legislature. (The Mission's report, in Part I, identifies for each district the particular issues, political groupings and key people of importance in that district.)

11. The Mission has no difficulty in concluding that there is little desire for independence in the Trust Territory. It would go so far as to say that even if a plebiscite were held today without preparation, the total vote for independence would probably be only from 2 to 5 per cent. The Mission also concluded that there is no hard core of feeling against permanent affiliation with the US but, as described earlier, an inchoate insecurity among a substantial number of the elite that can be allayed only through certain actions recommended below:

12. The Mission recommends that the plebiscite be held in 1967 or 1968 because:

a. Our timetable calls for creation of the true territory-wide legislature in the fall of 1964 and having its members serve out an initial three-year term before the plebiscite, during which the members from the different districts can develop more political experience working together than was possible in the present territory-wide advisory council.

b. The maximum impact of the recommended capital investment program will not be felt until late 1967 on the one hand, nor will it be felt as strongly after 1968, since the Mission does not expect the development process in the private sector of the Micronesian economy to be strong enough to offset the anticipated cutback in the capital investment program after fiscal year 1968 (by which time the higher priority capital needs of education, public health and public works will have been met).

c. The early definitive resolution of the political future of Micronesia as a US territory will make it easier for the US, if it so decides, to permit Japanese businessmen, technicians and fishing vessels into non-sensitive areas of the Trust Territory, which would supply a very great stimulus to economic development at no cost to the US and thereby permit reductions in the US subsidization of the territory.

If necessary, the plebiscite could be advanced to as early as 1966 by compressing the schedule for the development of the legislature. The legislature could be created by the spring of 1964 if the High Commissioner were instructed to do so. However, such an advance in the plebiscite timing would be at the expense of giving the legislature less experience and not waiting for the capital investment program to have its full impact.

13. The questions offered in the plebiscite to the Micronesians should be confined to two in number with some such general wording as follows:

(a) Are you in favor of becoming an independent nation?

(b) Are you in favor of a permanent affiliation with the US of America?

There will be some nations in the UN which, sensing our objective, will claim that the plebiscite should be confined to the single option of independence since the basic idea of trusteeships is that they should terminate in independence. There may also be some nations which will claim that, in its 1967-68 state of development and dependence, Micronesia connot realistically chose independence and is therefore not being given [a] real alternative. To some extent, this latter argument could be nullified by including a third plebiscite option—namely, continuation for the time being of the status quo of the trusteeship with the US as the administering power. From our viewpoint, this would reduce the vote for permanent affiliation from 95 per cent of those voting to a substantially smaller percentage, although still a majority.

14. The Mission recommends the following steps as part of the overall program to achieve our plebiscite objective and at the same time promote the longer run political development and general advancement of the Micronesians:

a. A qualified American should be appointed in each of the six districts to develop and maintain continuous liaison with the various leaders of the three politically critical groups. His main job would be to develop, in a gradual way, interest among those people in his district in favor of permanent affiliation by supplying the information needed to eliminate their ignorance and allay their fears as to what the affiliation would entail, as well as its advantages. He would also administer useful adult education and US and world information programs, as well as the local radio programming now handled by the district director of education. These six information officers, in whose recruitment US Information Service should cooperate, would also perform through their supervisor at Headquarters the regular political reporting function so acutely lacking at present.

b. Washington should facilitate the general development of Micronesia interest in, and loyalties to, the US by various actions, three of which are:

(1) Sponsorship by the Department of State of Micronesian leader visits to the US.

(2) Introduction in the school system of US-oriented curriculum changes and patriotic rituals recommended in the section of the Mission's report dealing with education.

(3) Increasing the number of college scholarships offered to Micronesians, a highly sensitive issue in the TT.

c. The Community Action Program by the 60 Peace Corps Volunteers recommended in the Mission report should be begun because it is of critical importance to both the plebiscite attitudes and the overall advancement of the majority of Micronesians living on islands outside the district centers. The program as recommended (which includes use of Peace Corps Volunteers as teachers in the school system) and the realities of Micronesian needs contain all the probabilities of a spectacular success for the Peace Corps.

d. Preparation should be taken to offer Micronesian government employees and other wage earners two specific inducements to seek affiliation with the US. First, after such an affiliation Micronesian and US personnel basic pay scales would be equalized. Since the inequality exists only in the professional and higher administrative echelons, the cost would not be excessive. Second, rather than introduce a retirement program for Micronesian government employees, the Social Security system should be extended to all wage and salary earners in Micronesia (most of whom are government employees) with possible consideration of a more general inclusion simultaneously or at a later time.

15. The final factor of importance to the outcome of the plebiscite will be the Micronesian leaders' insistence on knowing the proposed organization of Micronesia's post-plebiscite territorial government. The Micronesian leaders are intelligent and in many cases quite sophisticated, and they have been led to expect eventual independence; their willingness to produce a large popular vote for permanent affiliation will partially depend on the measure of self-government to be given them within the structure of territorial affiliation. This will also be of critical importance in the UN since the trusteeship agreement requires "independence or self-government" as the terminal objective. On the other hand, consideration must be given to the need for continued adequate control by the US and the traditional attitude of the Congress toward the organization of territorial government. Also, there are clear limitations on the present-day ability of the Micronesians to govern themselves.

As the practical solution of this many-pronged dilemma, the Mission recommends a government organization for the Territory of Micronesia that gives, on the one hand, a reasonable appearance of self-government through an elected Micronesian legislature and a Micronesian Chief Executive nominated by and having the confidence of the legislature, but on the other hand retains adequate control through the continuation of an appointed US High Commissioner. (This arrangement is similar to that now operating in the administration of the Ryukyu Islands.) The powers of the High Commissioner could range from:

(a) The minimum of being able to withhold all or any part of the US funds going to the Micronesian government and the authority to declare martial law and assume all legislative and executive powers when the security of the US so requires; to

(b) the maximum additional power of vetoing all laws, confirming the Chief Executive's appointments of key department directors and dismissing the Chief Executive and dissolving the legislature at any time.

16. The Mission also recommends that, after the plebiscite, the Congress recognize the expressed desire of the people of Micronesia to affiliate by granting them the status of US nationals but that action on an organic act be deferred until Congress judges that the development of the territory has sufficiently advanced, and the territorial legislature has had a chance to take action on the local customs and laws which now protect the lands and businesses of Micronesians. Once the people of Micronesia have expressed their desire to affiliate, it is highly advisable that they feel the question of their political future has been definitely resolved by having the Congress grant them without delay the status of US nationals even though there may be subsequently protracted debate in the Security Council over the termination of the trusteeship agreement. It is worth pointing out that the extension of the status of US nationals appears to the Mission, although questioned by State, to be legally possible under the trusteeship agreement which permits the extension of all the administering authority's laws to the Trust Territory, and that this could be the first in a series of steps that could make the trusteeship agreement an academic issue, even if the Security Council were not willing to terminate the trusteeship agreement.

17. Looking beyond the plebiscite and the subsequent achievement of territorial status for Micronesia, what seems to be the possible long-run political future for the area? First and most essential consideration might be given to the union of the two territories of Micronesia and Guam which would produce (a) economics of overhead in regular governmental administration, transportation and other facilities, (b) a more economically viable area along with a new stimulus to its economic development, frontier in the Pacific. Such a union would involve a very delicate problem of negotiation and would require consistent pressure. However, the payoff would be a substantial reduction in the need for appropriations as these deficit areas came to stand more and more on their own feet. (Part II of the Mission report includes recommendations for immediate action to develop the economic interrelationship between Guam and the Trust Territory.)

The even more distant problem of what ultimately, if anything, could or should be done with the unified territory of Guam and Micronesia is at present too much in the realm of clouded crystal ball gazing. Incorporation as a country in the State of Hawaii has been suggested in various places, and the Governor of Hawaii apparently feels that [it] is very much a possibility, but the Guamanian and Micronesian leaders' long-run political speculations definitely do not contemplate this degree of absorption and loss of political independence. Futhermore, the ultimate status of this territory may very well not be decided separately but as part of a general solution devised by the US for all our remaining territories.

Appendix II

SUMMARY OF
UNITED STATES-MICRONESIAN
NEGOTIATIONS

Round I: Washington, October, 1969.

This was an exploratory round at which the Micronesians outlined eleven principles which should govern a future political relationship. The United States disagreed with two Micronesian principles: whether the Micronesians could control land and whether the Micronesians could unilaterally terminate the relationship.

Round II: Washington, May 4-8, 1970.

The United States presented and the Micronesians rejected a plan under which Micronesia would become a permanent territory (called a "commonwealth") of the United States.

Round III: Hana, Maui, Hawaii, October 4-12, 1971.

The first round in which Williams participated, round three was highly successful, providing a new atmosphere and a new approach to the negotiations, i.e., a discussion of issues as opposed to a specific plan.

The United States agreed with the Micronesian suggestion that future relations could be governed by a Compact of Association. According to the Compact, the Micronesians could draft, adopt and amend their own constitution; and enact, amend or repeal their own legislation. The United States would have no authority either to amend the constitution or enact legislation.

The United States would not exercise eminent domain. All land would be returned to Micronesian control *after* the Micronesians agreed to limited United States military land needs which would be specified in the Compact. In addition, the Micronesians would be asked to agree to procedures whereby the United States would have temporary access to land in the event of an emergency. The United States would pay full and fair compensation. The Micronesians welcomed United States statements but insisted that present United States land holdings would terminate at the termination of the Trusteeship Agreement, that leases be negotiated and that any United States land holdings would revert back to the Micronesians if and when the Compact was dissolved. In addition, the Micronesians required consent for the storage of some types of weapons and a set time limit on emergency use of land.

Micronesians would have full authority in all internal affairs, with the United States controlling foreign affairs and defense. The powers necessary for the United States to fulfill its responsibilities for foreign affairs and defense would be spelled out in the Compact.

The Compact would outline procedures for Micronesian use, if desired, of federal programs in health, education, public works, etc., and of services such as the postal service, banking and currency, etc.

The scope of United States economic assistance depended on the "form, substance and continuity" of a future relationship. Micronesians would be responsible for determining their own economic development priorities. The Micronesians thought detailed discussion premature but said some assurance of the level of finances was necessary.

Termination was a major point of disagreement. The United States proposed that amendment or termination after an agreed number of years be subject to mutual consent. The Micronesians insisted on the right of either party to unilaterally revoke the compact.

Round IV: Koror, Palau, April 2-13, 1972.

Both sides found the talks "highly useful." Basic agreement was reached on a number of issues including Micronesia's right to unilaterally terminate the agreement. Outside the formal talks, the United States announced its decision to negotiate separately with the Mariana Islands.

Agreement was reached that a Compact of Free Association would govern the relationship, with Micronesia completely responsible for internal affairs. The United States would be responsible for defense and foreign affairs, but both would consult on international matters affecting the interest of the other. Micronesians could join appropriate regional organizations and enter contracts not involving intergovernmental obligations. There continued to be sharp differences over the extent of United States authority in both defense and foreign affairs.

The parties reaffirmed agreements reached at Hana concerning Micronesia's right to write, adopt, and amend its own constitution and legislation. United States law would apply only to the extent mutually agreed.

Any land needed by the United States would be negotiated in the Compact. Any additional land acquisition would be subject to Micronesian laws. The United States would permanently relinquish the power of eminent domain at the time the Compact took effect. United States options and leases of land would continue for a predetermined period and not terminate automatically with termination of the Compact. A mutual security pact agreed to prior to signing the Compact would continue in the event of termination.

The parties agreed that either side would be able to terminate the Compact after an agreed period and after due notice. Agreement was not reached on the precise period necessary before termination was possible. The United States proposed fifteen years, the Micronesians five years.

The area of sharpest difference was over the amount of United States financial assistance. The Micronesians proposed $100 million annually. Also, the

United States decision to negotiate separately with the Marianas was made known at Koror and led to additional differences.

Round V: Washington, July 12-August 1, 1972.

Tentative agreement was reached on the Preamble and three titles—Internal Affairs, Foreign Affairs, and Defense—of a Draft Compact of Free Association. Still to be negotiated were provisions on finance, trade and commerce, immigration and travel. The Micronesians suggested that the next talks focus on the United States response to Micronesian proposals on the level of United States financial assistance as well as on transitional arrangements. The United States agreed. Both sides agreed that the language was "tentative and preliminary," pending final agreement on the Compact as a whole.

Major provisions of the Draft Compact included:

1) Micronesians would have the right to adopt their own constitution, which could be changed or amended at any time so long as it was consistent with the Draft Compact.
2) The government of Micronesia would have full responsibility for and authority over internal affairs.
3) In the event the Compact were terminated, the people of Micronesia "in the exercise of their right of self-determination may freely choose their own political status."
4) The government of the United States would have full responsibility for and authority over all matters which related to the foreign affairs of Micronesia.
5) The United States would avoid to the greatest extent possible any interference in Micronesia's internal affairs pursuant to its foreign affairs authority.
6) The government of the United States would have full responsibility for and authority over all matters which related to defense in Micronesia.
7) The government of the United States would have the exclusive right to establish, maintain and use military areas and facilities in Micronesia.
8) If the United States government required additional land, requests would be made of the government of Micronesia to satisfy these requirements.

In Annex B, the United States also listed its land requirements:

1) *Marshall Islands*

   a) Within the *Kwajalein* Atoll, continuing rights for the use of those lands and waters associated with and currently controlled as part of the Kwajalein Missile Range, the land portion of which encompasses approximately 1,320 acres.
   b) In the *Bikini* Atoll, continuing rights for use of 1.91 acres of Ourukaen and Eniman Islets, and to use the pier, airfield, and boat landing on Eneu Island.
   c) In the *Eniwetok* Atoll, retention of such use rights as may be negotiated upon return of the atoll.

2) *Palau Islands*

   a) Access and anchorage rights in Malakal Harbor and adjacent waters, together with rights to acquire forty acres for use within the Malakal

Harbor area, composed of submerged land to be filled and adjacent fast land.

b) Rights for the joint use of an airfield capable of supporting military jet aircraft (the proposed airfield at Garreru Island reef, or Babelthuap airfield/Airai site), the right to improve that airfield to meet military requirements and specifications, and the right to develop an exclusive use area for aircraft parking, maintenance and operational facilities.

c) On the island of Babelthuap the right to acquire 2,000 acres for exclusive use, along with the right for non-exclusive use of an adjacent area encompassing 30,000 acres, for intermittent ground force training and maneuvers.

3) Continuing rights to occasional or emergency use of all harbors, waters and airfields throughout Micronesia.

4) Continuing rights to use of existing Coast Guard facilities.

Round VI: Barbers Point, Oahu, Hawaii, September 28-October 6, 1972.

The talks broke down over the issue of independence. In their report to the Congress of Micronesia after Round V, the Micronesian negotiators had recommended approval of the agreed portions of the Draft Compact and asked the Micronesian Congress for additional guidelines. The Draft Compact had met with sharp criticism, partially because, on the basis of the parts completed, it looked as if the Micronesians were giving a great deal and getting little. The Micronesian Congress had passed a resolution renewing the mandate of their negotiators to negotiate a status of Free Association but added the directive that independence also be negotiated at the same time.

The United States began the negotiations by asking for a clarification of the Micronesian position, particularly with regard to previously agreed principles and the tentatively agreed but still incomplete Draft Compact. In response the Micronesians indicated a desire to continue discussion of remaining portions of the Draft Compact. However, they noted that there were new instructions to negotiate independence as a result of opposition to provisions of the Draft Compact and growing sentiment for independence. The Congress had decided that a plebiscite must include a *choice* and independence was an alternative which had considerable and growing support.

The United States asked what was meant by independence and said it was not prepared to discuss financial assistance or termination procedures until it had considered "the new framework" in which negotiations were proceeding. The United States implied that independence was out of the question because of Micronesia's strategic importance. The Micronesians pointedly reminded the United States that they were negotiating for six districts and did not accept separate United States negotiations with the Marianas.

Round VII: Washington, November 14-21, 1973.

More than a year passed between the sixth and seventh rounds. In addition to disagreement on negotiations on independence, three other issues had accounted for delay: United States negotiations with the Marianas, disputes over the return of land, and a dispute over the content of the political education program.

Prior to the meeting, agreement was reached on a political education program. The United States announced a new land policy just prior to the meetings. But the negotiations broke down over the amount of United States financial assistance, and one of the reasons for the difference was Micronesian insistence on negotiating for six districts (i.e., including the Marianas) and the United States insistence that only five districts were under discussion.

Subsequent Meetings: 1974 to Present.

After the breakdown of the seventh round, the United States and Micronesia began to emphasize informal private discussions between the leaders of the Micronesians and two or three representatives of the United States.

Some progress was made. Agreement was reached on a financial package of $690 million over fifteen years, provided the United States completed a $146 million capital improvement program *prior* to termination of the Trusteeship Agreement in 1981. However, at its regular 1975 session, the Congress of Micronesia rejected the financial provisions of the agreement and expressed concern about the degree of United States control over foreign affairs.

In November, 1974, the land issue which had earlier caused a one-year delay in negotiations led to another abrupt break in informal negotiations. The Congress of Micronesia had twice passed and the High Commissioner had twice vetoed land legislation on the grounds that it did not conform to the eight conditions set by the United States at the seventh round. Among other things, the United States wanted land returned directly to the Districts and not to the Congress of Micronesia. In addition, the United States wished individual owners to agree in advance to "accommodate" United States land requirements. Neither of these conditions or others were acceptable to the Congress of Micronesia. Told at Honolulu that the United States intended to resolve the matter by Executive Order, the Micronesians walked out of the meeting.

In early 1975, the Micronesians indicated by letter to the United States representative that they were prepared to resume negotiations. At the same time, legislation which would have precluded further negotiations was introduced in the Congress of Micronesia and later withdrawn.

In May 1975, a Micronesian representative informed the United Nations Trusteeship Council that free association was no longer a basis on which agreement could be negotiated with the United States.

Bibliographical Notes

I. Interviews

Much of this study is based on interviews. More than 200 people in the United States, Micronesia, Guam and Japan were interviewed. Most interviews were off-the-record because the individual requested it or because we believed that an off-the-record discussion encouraged candor. Accordingly, an effort has been made to protect the identity of most interviewees.

II. Official Documents

These included the records and publications of the Congress of Micronesia; the annual reports on Micronesia submitted by the Secretary of the Interior; the annual report submitted by the United States Department of State to the United Nations Trusteeship Council; the triennial reports of United Nations Visiting Missions to Micronesia; the official summary and provisional verbatim records of meetings of the United Nations Trusteeship Council; and the annual reports of the United Nations Trusteeship Council to the United Nations Security Council.

Each of the participating groups in the status negotiations issued regular reports after each round of negotiations. The American reports were largely formal and frequently included only the opening and closing statements and joint communiques. The report of the Marianas on the second round was the most helpful of the reports issued by the Marianas group because it contained some of the papers exchanged between the United States and the Marianas. However, following United States objections, this practice was stopped and subsequent reports were less helpful. Reports by the Micronesian negotiators to their Congress were more helpful, for they were frequently supplemented with analytical material which revealed differences in the negotiations.

Briefings and hearings before the Senate and House Interior Committees and statements in the *Congressional Record* were occasionally useful for ascertaining congressional attitudes, but some of the most important briefings were not open to the public.

III. Current Information

Information on daily events in Micronesia is sketchy at best. Occasionally articles appear in the *New York Times,* the *Christian Science Monitor,* and the *Washington Post.* The *Post* has carried several long articles by Don Oberdorfer, the *Post* correspondent in Tokyo. As might be expected, coverage in the *Guam Daily News* and Honolulu newspapers is more frequent and detailed.

Several weekly newspapers are published in the Marianas, Palau and the Marshalls. The *Micronesia Independent* (nee *Micronitor*) comes closest to being a territory-wide paper. The now defunct *Young Micronesian,* published by students in Hawaii, is useful because it expressed the views of young educated Micronesians in the early seventies.

Most news on Micronesia comes through Trust Territory government information services. These are generally accurate, though not unbiased in presentation. The most frequent and most useful is the Micronesian News Service whose reports frequently are the basis for articles in Micronesia, Guam and Hawaii newspapers. The Micronesia *Reporter* is an excellent quarterly magazine, and the weekly Micronesian *Week in Review* and *Highlights* are quite useful.

During the early negotiations, the organization Friends of Micronesia published a monthly newsletter which was also a useful but not unbiased source of information.

IV. Additional Selected Bibliography

Adam, Thomas R. *Western Interests in the Pacific Realm.* New York: Random House, 1967.

Armstrong, Elizabeth and William I. Cargo. "The Inauguration of the Trusteeship System of the United Nations." *Department of State Bulletin* 16 (March 23, 1947): 511-523.

Arnold, Edwin G. "Self-Government in U.S. Territories." *Foreign Affairs* 25 (July 1947): 655-666.

Baldwin, Hanson. *Strategy for Tomorrow.* New York: Harper & Row, Publishers, 1970.

Bast, Benjamin F., ed. *The Political Future of Guam and Micronesia.* Agana: University of Guam Press, 1974.

Blair, Patricia Wohlgemuth. *The Ministate Dilemma.* New York: Carnegie Endowment for International Peace, 1967.

Blakeslee, George Hubbard. "Japan's Mandated Islands." *Department of State Bulletin* 11 (December 17, 1944): 764-768.

Blaz, Vincente T. and Samuel S. H. Lee. "The Cross of Micronesia." *Naval War College Review* 23 (June 1971): 59-90.

Bunche, Ralph S. "Trusteeship and Non-Self-Governing Territories in the Charter of the United Nations." *Department of State Bulletin* 13 (December 30, 1945): 1037-1044.

Clarkson, Robert and Sylvan Kling. "Should We Retain Our Pacific Bases?" *Forum* 106 (January 1947): 48-57.

Cleveland, Harlan. "Reflections on the Pacific Community." *Department of State Bulletin* 48 (April 22, 1963): 613-616.

deSmith, Stanley A. "Micronesia's Dilemma: U. S. Strategy vs. Self-Determination." *War/Peace Reports,* 11 (January 1971): 14-16.

———. *Microstates and Micronesia, Problems of America's Pacific Islands and Other Minute Territories.* New York: New York University Press, 1970.

———. "Options for Micronesia: A Potential Crisis for America's Pacific Trust Territory." Center for International Studies: New York University. *Policy Papers* 3, No. 3 (1969).

Dobbs, James C. "A Macrostudy of Micronesia: The Ending of a Trusteeship." *New York Law Forum* 18 (1972): 139-215.

Emerson, Ruppert. *From Empire to Nation: The Rise to Self-Assertion of Asian and African Peoples.* Cambridge: Harvard University Press, 1960.

———. "Puerto Rico and American Policy Toward Dependent Areas," *Annals of the American Academy of Political and Social Science* 285 (January 1953): 9-15.

———. "Self-Determination." *American Journal of International Law* 65 (July 1971): 459-475.

———. *Self-Determination Revisited in the Era of Decolonization.* Cambridge: Harvard University Press, 1964.

Fite, Jerry. "Colonizing Paradise." *Washington Monthly,* December, 1970, pp. 50-58.

Gilchrist, Huntington. "The Japanese Islands: Annexation or Trusteeship?" *Foreign Affairs* 22 (July 1944): 635-642.

Goodrich, Leland and Edward Hambro. *Charter of the United Nations: Commentary and Documents,* 2nd ed. Boston: World Peace Foundation, 1949.

Gruening, Ernest. "Statehood for Micronesia." *The Nation* 209 (December 15, 1969): 664-665.

Heine, Carl. *Micronesia at the Crossroads.* Honolulu: University of Hawaii Press, 1974.

Heneman, Harlow J. "The Administration of Japan's Pacific Mandate." *American Political Science Review* 25 (November 1931): 1029-1044.

Hickel, Walter J. *Who Owns America?* Englewood Cliffs, New Jersey: Prentice-Hall, Inc., 1971.

Higgins, Rosalyn. *The Development of International Law Through the Political Organs of the United Nations.* New York: Oxford University Press, 1963.

Hughes, Daniel T. and Sherwood G. Lingenfelter. *Political Development in Micronesia*. Columbus: Ohio University Press, 1974.

Jacobson, Harold K. "Our 'Colonial' Problem in the Pacific." *Foreign Affairs* 39 (October 1960): 56-66.

Kahn, E. J., Jr. *A Reporter in Micronesia*. New York: W.W. Norton & Co., 1966.

Kluge, P. F. "Looking Back." *Micronesian Reporter* (Second Quarter, 1972):17-20.

Liebowitz, Arnold H. "The Applicability of Federal Law to the Commonwealth of Puerto Rico." *Rivista Juridica de la Universidad de Puerto Rico* 37 (1968): 615-675.

Linehan, John A., Jr. *Whither the Marianas: Strategy and Idealism in Conflict.* Montgomery, Alabama: Air University, 1970.

Louis, William Roger. *National Security and International Trusteeship in the Pacific*. Annapolis: United States Naval Institute, 1972.

McCarthy, Eugene J. *The Limits of Power: America's Role in the World*. New York: Holt, Rinehart and Winston, 1967.

Mallery, Otto T. "America Must Translate Trusteeship into Fair Deal for Our Wards in the Pacific." *Saturday Evening Post,* April 16, 1949, p. 12.

Mason, Leonard. "Trusteeship in Micronesia." *Far Eastern Survey* 17 (May 5, 1948):105-108.

Meller, Norman. "Political Change in the Pacific." *Asian Survey* 5 (May 1965):245-254.

Mihaly, Eugene B. "Tremors in the Western Pacific: Micronesian Freedom and U.S. Security." *Foreign Affairs* 52 (July 1974): 839-849.

Mink, Patsy T. "Micronesia: Our Bungled Trust." *Texas International Law Forum* 6 (Winter 1971): 181-207.

Nathan, Robert R., Associates. *Economic Development Plan for Micronesia*. Washington, D.C. : Robert R. Nathan Associates, 1966.

"New Defense Line in Asia?" *U.S. News and World Report*, August 25, 1969, pp. 21-23.

"New Defense Line in the Pacific: Search on for Bases Closer to Home." *U.S. News and World Report,* August 7, 1967, pp. 52-54.

Oberdorfer, Don. "America's Neglected Colonial Paradise." *Saturday Evening Post*, February 29, 1964, pp. 24-34.

O'Connor, Edward C. "Micronesia—America's Frontier in the Far East." *National War College Forum* 9 (Spring 1970) :57-80.

Oliver, Douglas, ed. *Planning Micronesia's Future*. Cambridge: Harvard University Press, 1951.

"Pacific Isles Under U.S.—They're in Bad Shape." *U.S. News and World Report*, November 21, 1966, pp. 84 ff.

Perkins, Whitney T. *Denial of Empire: The United States and Its Pacific Dependencies*. Leyden: A.W. Sythoff, 1962.

Price, Willard. *America's Paradise Lost*. New York: The John Day Company, 1966.

_____. *Japan's Islands of Mystery*. New York: The John Day Company, 1944.

Quigg, Philip W. "Coming of Age in Micronesia." *Foreign Affairs* 47 (April 1969): 493-508.

Reisman, W. Michael. *Puerto Rico and the International Process: New Roles in Association*. Washington, D.C.: American Society for International Law, 1975.

Richard, Dorothy E. *United States Naval Administration of the Trust Territory of the Pacific Islands*. Three volumes. Washington, D.C.: Office of the Chief of Naval Operations, 1957.

Russell, Ruth B. *The United Nations and United States Security Policy*. Washington, D.C.: The Brookings Institution, 1968.

_____ assisted by Jeanette E. Muther. *A History of the United Nations Charter: The Role of the United States, 1940-1945*. Washington, D.C.: The Brookings Institution, 1958.

Sayre, Francis B. "The Advancement of Dependent Peoples." *International Conciliation* 435 (November 1947): 693-699.

_____. "Legal Problems Arising from the United Nations Trusteeship." *American Journal of International Law* 42 (April 1948): 263-299.

Stern, Paula. "Uncivil War Afflicts the Peace Corps: Confronting the Pentagon in Micronesia." *New Republic* 161 (August 23 and 30, 1969): 14-16.

Trumbull, Robert. *Paradise in Trust*. New York: Sloane, 1959.

"Trust Betrayed." *Economist* 225 (November 18, 1967):734.

Tudor, Judy. "Datsuns or Dignity—That's the Choice Facing the U.S. Trust Territory." *Pacific Islands Monthly* 40 (June 1969): 25-26.

_____. "Peace Corps: Fine But Micronesia Needs Aid at the Grass Roots." *Pacific Islands Monthly* 38 (May 1967): 39-40.

Van Cleve, Ruth Gill. *The Office of Territorial Affairs*. New York: Praeger, 1974.

Wainhouse, Davis W. *Remnants of Empire: The United States and the End of Colonialism*. New York: Harper & Row, Publishers, 1964.

Webb, James H. *Micronesia and U.S. Pacific Strategy: A Blueprint for the 1980's*. New York: Praeger, 1974.

Index